FAKE GEEK GIRLS

CRITICAL CULTURAL COMMUNICATION
General Editors: Jonathan Gray, Aswin Punathambekar, Adrienne Shaw
Founding Editors: Sarah Banet-Weiser and Kent A. Ono

Fake Geek Girls

Fandom, Gender, and the
Convergence Culture Industry

Suzanne Scott

NEW YORK UNIVERSITY PRESS
New York

NEW YORK UNIVERSITY PRESS
New York
www.nyupress.org

A portion of chapter 6 was first published as the article *"The Hawkeye Initiative:* Pinning Down Transformative Feminisms in Comic-Book Culture through Superhero Crossplay Fan Art" by Suzanne Scott from *Cinema Journal* 55:1, pp. 150–160. Copyright ©2015 by the University of Texas Press. All rights reserved.

References to Internet websites (URLs) were accurate at the time of writing. Neither the author nor New York University Press is responsible for URLs that may have expired or changed since the manuscript was prepared.

Library of Congress Cataloging-in-Publication Data
Names: Scott, Suzanne, 1979– author.
Title: Fake geek girls : fandom, gender, and the convergence culture industry / Suzanne Scott.
Description: New York : New York University Press, [2019] |
Series: Critical cultural communication | Includes bibliographical references and index.
Identifiers: LCCN 2018026984 | ISBN 9781479838608 (cl : alk. paper) |
ISBN 9781479879571 (pb : alk. paper)
Subjects: LCSH: Fans (Persons) | Women in popular culture. | Sexism in mass media. | Feminism and mass media.
Classification: LCC HM646 .S36 2019 | DDC 305.42—dc23
LC record available at https://lccn.loc.gov/2018026984

New York University Press books are printed on acid-free paper, and their binding materials are chosen for strength and durability. We strive to use environmentally responsible suppliers and materials to the greatest extent possible in publishing our books.

Manufactured in the United States of America

10 9 8 7 6 5 4 3 2 1

Also available as an ebook

For Luke, my favorite fanboy.

CONTENTS

Introduction

Make Fandom Great Again

In a March 2017 interview with *ICv2*, Marvel Comics' senior vice president of sales and marketing, David Gabriel, blamed a slump in October–November comic book sales on the changing tastes of comic book readers. More precisely, Gabriel blamed the sales slump on a perceived *lack* of changing tastes among comic book readers. In a quotation that rapidly spread across digital fan platforms like Twitter and Tumblr, Gabriel bluntly stated, "What we heard [from some comic retailers] was that people didn't want any more diversity. They didn't want female characters out there. That's what we heard, whether we believe that or not. I don't know that that's really true, but that's what we saw in sales."[1] It is significant that Gabriel's comment conflates diversification with the development of female characters, particularly considering that Marvel Comics' diversity initiatives of the past several years have included racially recasting iconic superheroes such as Spider-Man (mixed-race teen Miles Morales, who first donned the webslinger's suit in 2011) and Captain America (with Cap's black friend and fellow superhero Sam Wilson taking up the iconic shield in 2015).

There are two primary takeaways from Gabriel's statement. The first is that the blame for Marvel Comics' sales slump lies with female comic book fans, particularly those who have vocally criticized comic books' lack of creative and representational diversity. This framing reaffirms that Marvel still considers women to be a surplus audience for mainstream superhero comics, and that they presume male readers are unlikely to invest (emotionally or economically) in female-led titles. Placing the blame on female fans for a sales slump precipitated by an array of issues, ranging from oversaturation of the market[2] to Marvel's own unpopular crossover events and the corporate propensity to continuously reboot titles,[3] thus has a subtextual goal: to attempt to quash further calls for diversity through the logics of market rationalization. Second, and equally importantly, Gabriel's statement reaffirms Marvel's commitment to its "meat and potatoes" fanboy base, a code phrase used within the comic book industry to justify abandoning diversity titles and initiatives.[4]

Facing immediate pushback from predominantly female and minority comic book fans, and a wave of think pieces contesting his statistical claim about the comparatively low sales for "diversity" titles, Gabriel quickly walked back his response. Clarifying that Marvel remained committed to its newer female characters, Gabriel suggested that he was merely responding to comic retailers' concerns about the company's perceived "abandonment of the core Marvel heroes."[5] Ironically, and as many fans were quick to point out on social media, Marvel's sales slump was due in part to its own abandonment of one of those core heroes in 2016 with the (re)launch of *Steve Rogers: Captain America #1*, which culminated in 2017's crossover event series *Secret Empire*. The deeply unpopular reveal that Captain America was a Hydra Agent provoked immediate outrage from fans, who objected to a character created by Jewish men to explicitly fight Nazis becoming an agent of Marvel's fictional Third Reich. The character was billed by one blogger as "the hero that bigoted comic book fans deserve,"[6] and other fans were quick to draw parallels between the erosion of Captain America's character and more cancerous forms of prejudice spreading through geek culture and society at large.

The past decade has been marked by growing fan activist efforts surrounding issues of diversity in media production cultures, and pushback from mostly cisgendered, heterosexual (cishet, hereafter), white, male fans who view these efforts as an unwelcome encroachment of "political correctness" and "SJWs" (a pejorative term deployed by antifeminist, racist, homophobic, or transphobic commenters online to disparage "social justice warriors") into geek and fan culture. As the aforementioned controversy surrounding Gabriel's comment makes clear, industrial "diversity" initiatives are often viewed skeptically by marginalized fans as performative or perfunctory, particularly when they are ultimately wielded to justify the industry's commitment to preexisting demographic conceptions of fans as straight, white men. A vicious cycle has accordingly emerged: minority fans offer justified critiques of hegemonic production cultures and media representations, content producers offer (routinely half-hearted) responses to speak back to these concerns, and media industries dismiss minority fans' textual predilections as too niche when these efforts are not immediately successful, thus further empowering a segment of entitled white, straight male fans to dismiss minority fans' concerns and invalidate their claim to "authentic" fan identity.

Unwittingly, both Gabriel's dismissal of diversity initiatives and Marvel's repeated corporate calls for fans to exercise "patience" with their fascist makeover of Captain America perfectly reflect the fan culture war that has evolved over the past decade and its connections to our broader political landscape. Just as "meat and potatoes" evokes a sense of stasis and stability, comfort and conformity, the anxieties underpinning this incident (and, indeed, undergirding misogynist pushback to the mainstreaming of fan culture) are rooted in the fear of change. Digital media platforms may have amplified the voices of minority fans, but as a market segment, fangirls, fans of color, and queer fans are still considered outliers rather than central to popular conceptions of "fan" demographics. This is especially the case with video games and comic books, which are still staunchly considered to be masculine fan preserves, even as audience data increasingly challenge those assumptions. Importantly, these two elements frequently form an insidious feedback loop, as evidenced by the mounting "frequency and intensity" of harassment of female video game players in recent years and "the growing presence of women and girls in gaming not as a novelty but as a regular and increasingly important demographic."[7]

Perceived shifts at the micro level of media textuality and target demographics are thus deeply bound up with macro cultural concerns that conflate legitimate criticisms of systemic and intersectional forms of oppression with a censorial rise of "PC culture," and dramatically overstate the power and privilege of minorities in the process. Our cultural moment is one in which diversity is routinely positioned as a zero-sum game, and whether the topic is comic book superheroes or immigration, pushback is predicated on the same flawed logic: more for someone else will inevitably mean less for me. The "me" in both of these scenarios, whether we are discussing comic book fans or American working-class voters, is normatively codified as white, cishet men. I preface *Fake Geek*

Girls with a discussion of the controversy surrounding Gabriel's comments because this book is centrally concerned with how androcentric conceptions of fan culture and identity have become entrenched despite fan studies' characterization of fandom as a decidedly feminine and potentially feminist space. Marvel Comics' statement, and the centrality of male comic book retailers and fans to their market rationalization, sets the stage for this book's attempt to map the growing industrial and fancultural efforts to marginalize female fans over roughly the past decade (2006–2017). In theorizing the industrial desire to contain and circumvent female fan engagement, this book addresses how the mainstreaming of fan culture has been marked by a backlash from (predominantly white, cishet) male fans, reflecting the growing cultural influence of the alt-right and Men's Rights movements, and refracting the media industry's gendered messaging about which "fans" they value within convergence culture.

Ironically, those initiating the backlash against fangirls or striving to police "authentic" fan identity along gender lines are typically those who have gained the most power and privilege from geek culture's movement from the margins to the mainstream. It is thus, paradoxically and overwhelmingly, white, cishet men who tend to decry the loss of fandom's subcultural authenticity, even as they reap the demographic, industrial, authorial, and representational benefits of this loss. It is vital to acknowledge from the outset that the fanboys who envision geek culture as an inherently masculine preserve represent a small (albeit disproportionately vocal and vitriolic) percentage of all male fans. Likewise, boundary policing within fan cultures is not new, nor an exclusively masculine pursuit, with gatekeeping practices historically functioning as "part of the initiation, the us versus them, the fan versus the nonfan."[8] This book explores the growing tendency to strictly gender these categories as an act of exclusion rather than initiation.

Without question, the terms "fanboy" and fangirl" are problematically essentialist fan identities, constructing too simplistic a binary to adequately reflect the diversity of fannish self-identification or multivalent forms of fan participation. Julie Levin Russo has argued that "fanboy"/"fangirl" is a necessary taxonomy because we have yet to come up with any terminology to replace it,[9] but I would further contend that the "fanboy"/"fangirl" taxonomy remains dominant, resonant, and useful precisely because it is stringently gendered. How fans participate, and whose participation is valued by media industries and fan scholars alike, is commonly determined by these labels. As Russo notes, the impulse to "move beyond" these gendered terms could "lead us away from this attention to power and into a more insidiously 'neutral' map of our diverse fannish and academic pursuits."[10] Rather than "move beyond" the fanboy/fangirl binary, falling prey to the logic of "posts" (postfeminist, postracial, and so on), it is increasingly vital to consider how this binary is produced and performed. Like Russo, I understand that "mobilizing this idiom in relation to the heterogeneity of fan activity risks imprecision and oversimplification" but agree that "it is irreplaceable as an abbreviation for disparities that we have collectively come to recognize as infused with gendered inequality."[11]

As the following chapters will explore, those who incorrectly insist that fan and geek culture has historically been and thus must remain a male-dominated space have had their viewpoint tacitly endorsed time and again by the culture industries in their hailing of a "fan" demographic. Because the growing cultural influence of fans has unquestionably been a byproduct of media convergence, the culture industries' growing promotional dependency on fan labor within digital participatory culture is tempered by nostalgia for a past in which they need not be as attentive to the demands of fans. As I have argued repeatedly elsewhere,[12] the media industry's supposedly collaborationist embrace of fan culture over the past decade has cultivated a structured secondariness for female fans and their preferred modes of engagement, which in turn is used to rationalize fangirls' dismissal and harassment by a small, if voracious, segment of fans. This vicious cycle is at the heart of this book's consideration of the fan culture wars that have developed over the past decade.

While this project centers gender in its discussion of the claim to and contestation over fan identity, fan privilege and nostalgia impact all marginalized groups of fans. It is not my intent to avoid more intersectional work, and I explicitly address this fan-scholarly tendency and its impact on the feminist potentialities of both fandom and fan studies in the book's conclusion. I also wish to be mindful of Rebecca Wanzo's critique of the tendency to frame fans as "oppositional" consumers, thereby "valoriz[ing] people who have claimed otherness for themselves, as opposed to having otherness thrust upon them."[13] It is precisely some fanboys' desire to retain this uniquely privileged claim to "otherness," and the exclusivity it affords, that has resulted in the further "othering" of female fans within contemporary geek culture.

Though any study of bias against fangirls must acknowledge the fact that queer women and women of color are more vulnerable to attacks on or dismissals of their claims to fan identity, my decision to focus on how the mainstreaming of fan culture has impacted women generally was made for several reasons. First, the field of fan studies has from its inception characterized fan culture as a female-dominated and potentially feminist space. This emphasis has been rightly challenged as too limiting as the field itself diversifies and expands alongside the growth of digital fan culture, but gender remains central to the field's enduring investment in exploring the production and circulation of transformative works (e.g., fanfiction, fanvids, fanart) within fan communities. Second, gender has been the most prominent axis of identity in constructions of the "fan" within the cultural imaginary, followed closely by race (specifically, whiteness).[14] Accordingly, gender tends to be most actively utilized to either include or exclude people from fan subject positions, and/or to pathologize fans more generally via the feminization of the fan subject. Last, but certainly not least, while any fan who does not conform to the archetypal "fanboy" demographic has unquestionably felt the impact of both industrial and fan-cultural efforts to codify fan identity over the past decade, women have felt the brunt of these efforts most acutely. It is my hope that this book's survey of androcentric fan culture and hegemonic fan identity writ large will be productive for future considerations of racism, ableism, ageism, sizeism, homophobia, xenophobia, and transphobia within fan communities.

This book examines the gendered tensions surrounding the mainstreaming of geek and fan culture through three interrelated lenses: fan studies' legacy of focusing on female audiences and their practices, the media industries' conceptualization and cultivation of a desirable "fan" demographic that serves their promotional interests, and fans' coordinated performances of fan identity and attempts to deny others' claim to the (sub)cultural category of "fan."[15] Thus, I am more interested in considering how various systems and stakeholders work to shape and validate an androcentric cultural conception of the "media fan" than

in ethnographically exploring the lived experience or creative production of individual fans or particular fan communities of practice. Rely-
ing predominantly on (para)textual and discourse analysis to consider
how contemporary fan identities are mutually (and, often, narrowly)
constructed by media industries, content creators, journalists, and fans
themselves, this book begins unpacking the proliferation of misogyny
within contemporary geek culture. To do this, we must situate the development of these conditions over the past decade within convergence
culture.

Confronting the Convergence Culture Industry

Tracing the profound industrial, technological, and cultural shifts that
accompanied media convergence in the early and mid-2000s, the 2006
publication of Henry Jenkins's *Convergence Culture: Where Old and New
Media Collide* was received by many scholars as a spiritual successor
to his foundational fa;¹ studies work from 1992, *Textual Poachers: Television Fans and Participatory Culture*. And, indeed, fans featured heavily
into Jenkins's *Convergence Culture* narrative, as the audience segment
that had most actively moved "from the invisible margins of popular
culture and into the center of current thinking about media production
and consumption"[16] during this period's development of digital tools
and platforms to support participatory culture. Because convergence is
simultaneously "a top-down corporate-driven process and a bottom-
up consumer-driven process,"[17] Jenkins was quick to note that media
producers "responded to these newly empowered consumers in contradictory ways, sometimes encouraging change, sometimes resisting
what they see as renegade behavior."[18] What remains unspoken in much
of Jenkins's account is how deeply gendered conceptions of "renegade"
fan behavior are, and how frequently they are aligned with the transformative impulses of female fans. However economically motivated, or
conditional, or even well-meaning the media industry's embrace of fan
culture may have been, what has emerged in convergence culture's wake
is a gendered politics of participation that is designed to privilege male
fans and their preferred modes of participation.

Convergence Culture masterfully traced how industrial shifts, as well
as the development of digital technologies and the resultant threat to

analog content and advertising models, necessitated the media industries' move from a prohibitionist to a more collaborationist stance towards fandom and participatory culture. Jenkins himself acknowledged that these "empowered" or "elite" consumers, those who "exert a disproportionate influence on media culture in part because advertisers and media producers are so eager to attract and hold their attention," are also "disproportionally white, male, middle class, and college educated."[19] This emphasis on the reciprocal relationship between what kinds of fans or fan practices are "empowered" within convergence culture and how cultural conceptions of the "fan" are, in turn, wedded to desirable industry demographics and modes of engagement is at the center of this book's exploration of gender bias within contemporary geek culture. Just as Jenkins called for a focus on the "cultural protocols and practices"[20] of participatory culture, this book explores the fan-cultural gatekeeping protocols and the media industry's gender-biased practices that have emerged out of the conditions described in *Convergence Culture*.

We obviously cannot equate all fan labor on digital platforms with exploited labor, or assume that fans are not deeply cognizant of the economic and promotional motivations precipitating the media industry's conditional embrace of fan culture. Fans are, after all, incredibly skilled at evading and critiquing systems of capital and hegemonic culture, even as they play within the walled gardens of commercial media texts that do not always reflect their identities and values, or traverse platforms designed to curtail and commoditize the participation they purport to facilitate. It is tempting to extol the conditions of convergence for forcing media industries to revalue fans and cultivate more dialogic relationships between media creators and consumers. However, we need to remain critical of claims that media production has been democratized, or that legacy systems of cultural production do not continue to wield disproportionate power.

In order to begin exploring the after-effects of convergence culture and the gender-biased byproducts of these newly forged "collaborationist" ties between media producers and consumers in the digital age, this book focuses on the impact of the *convergence culture industry* on female fans. This portmanteau, my terminological play on Adorno and Horkheimer's infamous 1944 missive, "The Culture Industry: Enlightenment as Mass Deception," might seem cynical at best, and wholly inappropriate for a book about media fan culture at worst. After all, the first wave of fan studies in the late 1980s and early 1990s, like much of the feminist media studies of the 1980s and subculture studies of the 1960s and 1970s before it, was designed to directly speak back to the Frankfurt School's hypodermic conception of media consumers as cultural dupes. In particular, Adorno and Horkheimer's conception of mass media audiences as mindless consumers of industry-sponsored ideology, incapable of distinguishing between fiction and reality, has come to function as a scholarly straw man within the field of fan studies. As Matt Hills succinctly summarized in his 2002 book *Fan Cultures*, cultural theorists and fan scholars routinely depict Adorno and his Frankfurt School compatriots "as elitists, as pessimists, and as 'unsophisticated' thinkers intent on demonising mass culture and denying any power or agency to its audiences."[21] It remains essential that scholars foreground fan agency in their accounts of contemporary industrial efforts to contain or co-opt fan culture. At the risk of replicating the more polemical properties of their conception of "the culture industry," however, I believe it is equally essential to revisit and revise Adorno and Horkheimer's concerns to address the convergence culture industry's gendered valuation of fan engagement.

Though written nearly sixty years apart, Adorno and Horkheimer's and Jenkins's texts grappled with similar seismic shifts in media culture, tracing the potential cultural impact of how emergent technologies were shaping industrial practices in the late 1930s and the early 2000s, respectively. While we obviously cannot neatly equate the Hollywood studio system output critiqued by Adorno and Horkheimer with the vast array of participatory digital media tools and platforms Jenkins championed, both works are at their core concerned with a moment of heretofore unprecedented *access* to media. For Adorno and Horkheimer, this access was to art itself through various forms of mass communication and entertainment (e.g., film, radio, etc.). Jenkins focused on access to the means of cultural production, through a growing array of user-friendly tools and technologies to produce, remix, and share media and network knowledge (photo and video editing software, wikis, etc.). Despite being similarly concerned with a historical moment of change for media industries and its impact on media consumers, these two deeply influential media studies texts are diametrically opposed in tone. Adorno and

Horkheimer decried the media industry's tendency to "perpetuate the appearance of competition and choice,"[22] while Jenkins fixed his attention on the "democratic potentials" of media convergence while remaining mindful of "the various barriers that block the realization of those possibilities, and look[ing] for ways to route around them."[23]

One of the primary reasons fan scholars tend to dismiss "The Culture Industry" out of hand, or sidestep it entirely in their consideration of fan/industry relations, is that Adorno and Horkheimer's homogeneous vision of the easily swayed mass media audience is antithetical to Jenkins's foundational conception of fans as "textual poachers"[24] and *Convergence Culture*'s subsequent framing of fans as "the most active segment of the media audience, one that refuses to simply accept what they are given, but rather insists on the right to become full participants."[25] I am in no way claiming, as Adorno and Horkheimer did of the culture industry, that the convergence culture industry succeeds in stamping out the audience individuality, or unilaterally accomplishes its goal to "intentionally integrate its consumers from above."[26] Texts remain polysemic, and media audiences and fans continue to subvert claims of "passive" consumption via their analytical interaction with media objects and their own transformative textual production (e.g., fanfiction, fanart, fanvids, etc.). The convergence culture industry, like the culture industry before it, may *desire* a more docile or commoditizable vision of fan engagement, but that does not prohibit fans from routinely resisting or circumventing these efforts.

Just as Adorno and Horkheimer emphasized the impacts of industrial and representational standardization on mass audiences, I am utilizing the term "the convergence culture industry" as an analytic to interrogate how industrial efforts to standardize the cultural category of "fan" have exacerbated longstanding gendered tensions within fan culture. Because fannish "authenticity" can be either biologically or demographically delineated (with women being less naturally capable of corporeally conforming to the stereotypical depictions of male, adolescent geeks, nerds, and fans) or gendered in terms of preferred forms of participation (e.g., collecting fan ephemera being coded as a historically "masculine" pursuit), what emerges is something of a zero-sum game for women who wish to traverse outside the boundaries of transformative or female-dominated fan communities into "mainstream" fan culture.

Female fans are subtly and structurally squeezed out of the prevailing conception of the "fan" within the cultural imaginary, either due to their lived identity markers or via the industrial devaluation of historically female-dominated forms of fan participation. When female fans are acknowledged, it is commonly through carefully cordoned off and definitively feminized fan objects (boy bands, YA franchises, romance novels) rather than as an essential and preexisting component of the bourgeoning "fan" and "geek" demographic.

The "fanboy" may ultimately be an abstraction in this construct, but it has nonetheless become a core ideological product and weapon of the convergence culture industry. Fans have always been highly commoditized and commodity-driven consumers, but the convergence culture industry's standardization and attempted massification of fans as a niche audience, coupled with the attempted "fanification" of mass audiences to adapt to participatory culture, has created conditions in which male fans and historically masculinized fan practices are privileged. Adorno and Horkheimer's term ultimately sought to interrogate the systemic commercial drives of mass media industrialization and track the resultant "commodification, standardization, and massification"[27] of media objects. The convergence culture industry functions similarly, systemically attempting to forward an industrialized vision of fan culture.

If Adorno and Horkheimer viewed the culture industry as cultivating a homogeneous audience and stamping out individualism, then the convergence culture industry attempts to reign in the least passive collective of consumers (fans), and to homogenize fandom itself. The convergence culture industry is equally concerned with discipline and control, but it must operate within the emergent (and decidedly more unwieldy and undisciplined) conditions of participatory digital media culture. Media industries operating within a convergence context need audiences to be active, to behave like "fans," but they would prefer prescribed modes of activity that are promotionally beneficial and not ideologically challenging. The convergence culture industry's systemic support of some fan identities and modes of fan engagement over others in no way forecloses the capacity of fans to subvert these models of prescribed participation. But, importantly, to be noncompliant often results in having one's fannish authenticity called into question. Thus, a key distinction is that fans themselves are now working as the agents of the convergence culture industry, reinforcing these industrial predilections and routinely using them to alternately dismiss and harass female fans.

It is precisely because I am interested in how an androcentric conception of fan culture has become standardized that I am harking back to Adorno and Horkheimer's term, rather than deploying more contemporary and flexible iterations from media industry studies like "the cultural industries"[28] or "the creative industries."[29] The productive plurality of these terms may be inherently more useful for theorizing the complexity of our contemporary mediascape, and they certainly provide much-needed conceptual coverage for the more problematic facets of Adorno and Horkheimer's conception of "the culture industry." I agree that contemporary iterations of the cultural and/or creative industries, and their relationship with audiences, are inherently "*complex, ambivalent,* and *contested*"[30] spaces, and should be theorized accordingly. However, I am centrally invested in tracing how the convergence cultural industry, like the culture industry before it, strives to "hammer into human beings," and fans specifically, a "concept of order,"[31] even if it does not always succeed. This deep investment in maintaining the status quo is a direct response to the growing centrality of fans' place within the creative industries and media fans' increasing unwillingness to accept the culture industries as they are. It is driven simultaneously by industrial nostalgia for analog, less participatory general audiences, and fan-cultural nostalgia for a more exclusive and subcultural conception of fan identity.

In the conclusion of *Convergence Culture*, Jenkins frames himself as a critical utopian, a positioning that echoes fandom's own "balance between fascination and frustration"[32] with media objects. Jenkins makes a distinction between critical utopianism, which stresses empowerment, and critical pessimism, which is founded on the "politics of victimization. One focuses on what we are doing with media, the other on what media is doing to us."[33] It is not my intent to replicate Adorno and Horkheimer's hypodermic views of media power; rather, my goal in exploring the convergence culture industry and its gendered impact on fan culture is to adopt a position of critical ambivalence and to acknowledge that marginalization and victimization do occur. If *Convergence Culture* justifiably focused on what fans were gaining from their shift from the margins to the mainstream, then this book catalogues the gender imbalance that haunts the convergence culture industry's conditional "empower-ment" of consumers.

The chapters that follow take up many of the core concerns laid out in Adorno and Horkheimer's initial essay on the culture industry, as well as Adorno's 1963 addendum, "Culture Industry Reconsidered." In updating these concerns, each chapter of this book is designed to address a specific set of symptoms of the convergence culture industry and explore its gendered ramifications for the mainstreaming of fan culture over the past decade, while remaining attentive to the transformative interventions of fans and fan scholars. Collectively, the chapters that follow suggest that misogyny within contemporary fan culture has flourished in part because the convergence culture industry has rendered fangirls an invisible or undesirable segment of the "fan" market. This is also a book about how fan culture's shift from the margins to the mainstream and the convergence culture industry have impacted fan studies as a subfield of feminist media studies. The fanboy's visibility is, in many cases, a byproduct of his compatibility with the more easily marketable or co-optable modes of fannish participation valued by the convergence culture industry.

Because this has, in turn, been perceived to threaten the feminist and subversive valences of the field, chapter 1 addresses the connection between the marginalization of female fans facilitated by the convergence culture industry and concerns about a potential decentering of female fans within fan studies. Calling for a need to reinvest in the questions of power that shaped the first wave of fan studies, chapter 1 homes in on two of fan studies' structuring dichotomies: the "incorporation vs. resistance" paradigm, and the oft-critiqued divide between "affirmational" and "transformative" gendered modes of fan engagement. These binaries (much like "fanboy" and "fangirl") may be essentialist, but they are also necessary to understanding the convergence culture industry's incorporation of affirmational fan culture, and resistance to this from feminist fan scholars invested in transformative works and fan cultures.

Chapter 2 addresses the shifting journalistic and representational valuation of the fanboy within the convergence culture industry. Much as Adorno suggests that "the culture industry fuses the old and familiar into a new quality,"[34] this chapter suggests that the convergence culture industry has fused longstanding fanboy pathologies with distinct strains of hegemonic masculinity. In the process, it has written women out of the cultural narrative of fans' ascendance as a power demographic, and helped determine who can easily claim (or dismiss others' claim to) fan identities. The (in)visibility politics documented in chapter 2 sets the stage for chapter 3's analysis of the rise of gendered boundary-policing practices and spreadable misogyny within fan culture, and reflects which modes of fan engagement are being celebrated or subsumed (chapter 4), as well as which fans are able to professionalize within the convergence culture industry (chapter 5). Collectively, these chapters consider why certain fan practices (and by extension, certain fans) have been embraced by the convergence culture industry, and how fanboys in turn exercise their status as a prominent "appendage of the machinery."[35]

Chapter 3 examines how "new hegemonic fandom" (to borrow a term from Matt Hills) and hegemonic masculinity intersect and are performed in physical spaces and across social media platforms. Focusing on how intra-fannish policing practices do not merely work to position some fans as "good" or "bad" but work to deny access to the identity of "fan" writ large, chapter 3 homes in on the "idiot nerd girl" meme that emerged in 2011, and contextualizes it within broader "fake geek girl" discourses that grew in volume and scale circa 2012. Surveying just a small sample of the spreadable misogyny circulating within contemporary fan culture, this chapter also actively considers how feminist fans intervene into these efforts to alienate women within geek culture. Moving from the localized efforts to contain fangirls discussed in chapter 3 to more systemic and structural concerns, chapter 4 investigates how media industries' partial and conditional embrace of fan culture and participatory practices subtly colors perceptions of which fans are valued within a post–Web 2.0 media landscape driven by user-generated content. Because the convergence culture industry, like the culture industry before it, "endlessly cheats its consumers out of what it endlessly promises,"[36] this chapter considers both the legal and the ideological "terms and conditions" that govern industrially sanctioned modes of fan participation. This chapter focuses on two key issues. First, it considers how fan labor has been industrially co-opted, contained, and commercialized through a series of test cases. Second, I will address the growing prominence and industrial reliance on enunciative forms of fan production, such as livetweeting and the emergence of fan aftershows like AMC's *Talking Dead*.

This discussion of enunciative fandom will set the stage for chapter 5's discussion of *Talking Dead*'s host, Chris Hardwick. Hardwick, the founder and promotional figurehead of Nerdist Industries, is used to explore how professionalization runs apace differently for fanboys and fangirls, as well as what types of fan identities and practices are most easily assimilated into industrial and promotional contexts. Hardwick, in his presentation as a "striking yet familiar" fanboy, and in his role as a prominent and promoted "moderator" of fan culture, perfectly exemplifies the potentially censorial dimensions of the convergence culture industry, in which "everything is directed at overpowering a consumer conceived as distracted or resistant."[37] This chapter's analysis of the androcentrism of archetypal forms of professionalized fan identity, "fanboy auteurs" and "fantrepreneurs," builds on the prior chapter's engagement with fan labor, addressing how female fans are received and scrutinized differently from their fanboy counterparts when attempting to leverage fan identities and labor into "professional fan" status.

Unlike the prior chapters, which survey the ways in which female fans and their creative practices have been marginalized or contained, chapter 6 contemplates the ways in which geek girls *are* hailed within the convergence culture industry. Analyzing the growing intersections between fan-oriented fashion and cosplay as a fan practice (e.g., constructing costumes inspired by fictional characters and embodying those characters in real-world spaces such as fan conventions), this chapter examines the broader politics of conceptually moving from poaching (as a mode of feminist intervention) to pinning (as a feminine curatorial practice on sites like Pinterest) as a fan practice alongside contemporary industrial efforts to route female fans towards neoliberal modes of consumer engagement. It would be easy to critique these postfeminist moments of fangirl outreach via fashion and beauty culture as yet another effort by the convergence culture industry to "[overpower] a consumer conceived as distracted or resistant."[38] However, an analysis of "everyday" or "casual" cosplay merchandising trends offered by fancentric retailers (Her Universe, Hot Topic, etc.) and trompe l'oeil dress designs that replicate male character costumes suggests a more complex negotiation of gendered fan identity. Building on existing research on fancentric digital retail spaces and literature exploring the subversive potentialities of cross-dressing and drag, I contend that these male character dresses and their connection to "crossplay" (cosplay in which a fan embodies a character of a different sex) afford a space for fannish commentary on women's capacity to fully embody a mainstream/masculinized fan identity.

The conclusion will contemplate the ongoing place of feminism within contemporary fan culture and studies through an interrogation of the conceptual limitations of gender as fan studies' core axis of analysis, while reasserting the political project of first wave fan studies. Just as Adorno interrogated the ways in which the "consensus which [the culture industry] propagates strengthens blind, opaque authority,"[39] the conclusion of this book will interrogate to what extent fan studies' consensus approach to addressing identity primarily through gender, and the field's ties to Western white feminism, potentially undermine its political capacity. The conclusion thus calls for more intersectional approaches in fan studies that actively consider how additional axes of identity beyond gender (race, age, sexuality, ability, etc.) shape fan identities and cultural conceptions of the fan within the convergence culture industry.

Collectively, these chapters call attention to efforts to standardize fandom and fan identity over the past decade, even as fan culture expands and diversifies at an exponential rate. The convergence culture industry's desire for a universal (and, thus, a comprehensible and eventually manageable) conception of the fan echoes the culture industry, in which "individuals are tolerated only as far as their wholehearted identity with the universal is beyond question."[40] Fan scholars Kristina Busse and Mel Stanfill have both remarked on how identity impacts contemporary conceptions of the "fan," acknowledging that though fandom continues to carry social stigmas that impact men and women alike, the stigmas themselves are gendered (fans are "feminized")[41] and raced (fans represent an "insufficient whiteness" because they are seen as lacking self-control).[42] Though male geeks and fans might be culturally conceived as failing to behave "in a way consistent with constructed-as-white normative, middle-class, heterosexual masculinity,"[43] Stanfill contends that white, heterosexual fanboys' capacity to be recuperated into that category (and claim the privilege that accompanies it) is central. This also helps entrench a standardized, universal conception of fan culture that welcomes women as long as they are willing to be "just one of the guys" (e.g., to not call attention to their individualized, identity-based responses to media objects).

MFGA: When Popularity Breeds Populism

My desire to revisit Adorno and Horkheimer's formulation of the culture industry is also motivated by the fact that our current sociopolitical moment was presaged by the growing strains of bigotry and nativism within fan and geek culture over the past decade. It is important to remember that Adorno and Horkheimer, as Jews who fled Nazi Germany in the 1930s, had witnessed the media's propagandistic potential first-hand. This historical and personal context is key to understanding Adorno and Horkheimer's conception of the culture industry and their concerns about its influence. In following the myriad and mounting instances of bias against female fans and performances of male privilege within fan culture over the past decade, it is easy to see how the "myth of nerd oppression" that "let every slightly socially awkward white boy who likes sci-fi explain away his privilege and lay his *resentment* at the feet of the nearest women and people of color"[44] is part and parcel of the growing sociopolitical influence of the alt-right and men's rights movements. Similarly to the ways in which Trump's infamous campaign slogan resonated with his supporters, those fans at the forefront of the campaign to "make fandom great again" by actively targeting marginalized fans paradoxically do so by claiming a marginalized status themselves. Anyone paying attention to fan culture over the past decade is deeply familiar with the cognitive dissonance that marks so many emergent right-wing collectives, the desire to paint oneself as an oppressed group while literally embodying privilege.

The nostalgia of the "again" in this inherently regressive slogan is at the heart of its insidious appeal, evoking a desire to return to a cultural moment when white male supremacy remained (comparatively) unchallenged, civil rights movements had yet to gain traction, and diversity was not something that had to be dealt with. Lamentations about "mainstreaming," and the accordant loss of "authenticity" and subcultural capital are, of course, nothing new, and the "Make Fandom Great Again" ethos underpinning the more overt or violent efforts to silence female fans or fans of color may be driven by a wide array of motivations. Still, they frequently coalesce around a similar desire to retain a white-male-supremacist conception of fan identity and exemplify a more general pushback to the ever more visible and vocal displays of diversity in fan culture. Thus, while this book is not directly about our contemporary political moment, it does suggest that we can learn a great deal about the interplay between overt misogynistic displays and more covert efforts to alienate women within fan culture, and within culture at large.

I am not the first to make this connection. In the wake of the 2016 presidential election, a wave of think pieces sought to explain the motives of Trump voters and grapple with the growing influence of the alt-right. Because the alt-right movement is so closely associated with white nationalism and its accordant dissemination of racist, antisemitic, and antifeminist ideologies, many journalists and bloggers looked to the GamerGate controversy, and its deep roots within Internet trolling subcultures, for answers. Launched by an August 16, 2014, blog post from the disgruntled ex-boyfriend of game designer Zoe Quinn alleging infidelity with a game journalist in exchange for positive reviews of her indie game *Depression Quest*, GamerGate purportedly began as a set of discussions and demands around ethics in games journalism. The accusations were quickly debunked, but within days of the initial post Quinn had been targeted and threatened on social media and doxxed (her personal information such as phone number and home address published online for the purpose of real-world harassment). Those involved with the "movement" insisted that there was no misogyny underpinning their campaign for ethics in game journalism, but because the "movement" was initiated by painting Quinn as sexually pandering to and preying on game journalists, it quickly devolved into a widespread and vile digital harassment campaign that disproportionately targeted women in game development, as well as feminist gamers, scholars, and critics.

The complexity of GamerGate is perhaps best summarized in a *Deadspin* article by Kyle Wagner entitled "The Future of the Culture Wars Is Here, and It's Gamergate":

> By design, Gamergate is nearly impossible to define. It refers, variously, to a set of incomprehensible Benghazi-type conspiracy theories about game developers and journalists; to a fairly broad group of gamers concerned with corruption in gaming journalism; to a somewhat narrower group

of gamers who believe women should be punished for having sex; and, finally, to a small group of gamers conducting organized campaigns of stalking and harassment against women. This ambiguity is useful, because it turns any discussion of this subject into a debate over semantics. Really, though, Gamergate is exactly what it appears to be: a relatively small and very loud group of video game enthusiasts who claim that their goal is to audit ethics in the gaming-industrial complex and who are instead defined by the campaigns of criminal harassment that some of them have carried out against several women. (Whether the broader Gamergate movement is a willing or inadvertent semi-respectable front here is an interesting but ultimately irrelevant question.)[45]

Wagner's assessment that the "movement" would ultimately be defined by its most vicious and sexist participants was correct. By the time the mainstream news media picked up the story in early September, GamerGate had become synonymous with critiques of the toxic masculinity of "gamer" fan identities.

Articles with titles like "What Gamergate Should Have Taught Us about the 'Alt-Right,'"[46] "GamerGate to Trump: How Video Game Culture Blew Everything Up,"[47] and "Under Trump, Gamergate Can Stop Pretending It Was about Games"[48] all point to the 2014 "movement" as a bellwether for the increasingly brazen behavior of the alt-right. Even the de facto journalistic home of the alt-right, *Breitbart*, acknowledged, "Leftists Think GamerGate Caused Donald Trump: Maybe They're Right," drawing on #Gamergate participant survey data to connect the dots between the "hardcore 'gamer' demographic and the economically disadvantaged voters who propelled [Trump] to victory in the rust belt."[49] Within this context, feminist fans and video game scholars (many of whom were actively targeted by GamerGate "activists") decrying the rise of hegemonic and hypermasculine gamer culture must feel a bit like Cassandra, prophesizing the rising tide of antifeminist, xenophobic, and nationalist sentiments of the alt-right to deaf ears.[50]

While the 2016 presidential campaign and its aftermath exposed deeply entrenched biases against an array of minority groups, this book focuses on the decade leading up to this cultural moment. Specifically, I would suggest that the "war on women" that has intensified within fan and geek culture over the past decade offers an illustrative space to begin garnering an understanding of why Donald Trump's "Make America Great Again" ethos struck a chord with (predominantly white, straight, cisgendered) voters. This "war on fangirls," in which women are routinely derided for critiquing hegemonic media representations or calling for more diversity within the culture industries, or dismissed as "fake geek girls" (thereby foreclosing their access to the identity of fan and attempting to silence them), has accompanied the mainstreaming of geek and fan culture.

We can view GamerGate as a boiling point within geek culture, the culmination of nearly a decade of simmering and subtle messaging that female fans are an encroaching force that needs to be repelled. Likewise, we can view GamerGate as a moment of convergence between growing strains of misogyny within geek culture and the growing influence of the alt-right in culture at large. Not only is there a great deal of demographic overlap between the two "movements," but they share spaces of origin and organization (e.g., platforms like 4chan and Reddit, characterized by the ability to post anonymously), are rooted in similar complaints about "PC culture," and utilize similar strategies of harassment (e.g., organized barrages of sexist and racist slurs on social media, doxxing). GamerGate, and the sustained harassment responding to feminist critic Anita Sarkeesian's "Tropes vs. Women in Video Games" video essay series in 2012 that set the stage for it, are unquestionably the most visible and violent manifestations of the sort of gender bias against female fans that this book surveys. Though these are extreme examples, the underlying sentiments and discursive strategies permeate "fake geek girl" accusations and corresponding efforts to dismiss and degrade female fans. Whether in digital or real-world spaces, female fans are routinely required to defend and authenticate their fannish credentials at best, and at worst subjected to out-and-out harassment.

I am ultimately more interested in cataloguing and contemplating less spectacular examples of how this gender bias in fan and geek culture is established, sustained, and performed by a variety of stakeholders. The political right's "war on women" may manifest most spectacularly in misogynist performances (e.g., Trump's now-infamous "grab her by the pussy" *Access Hollywood* tapes) but is arguably more damaging when slipped quietly into legislative policy (e.g., expanding efforts to block access to abortion). Likewise, this book's consideration of the "war on

The Motion Picture Fan

By La Touche Hancock

He's a spunky little fellow, without a trace of yellow,
He knows his motion picture A. B. C.
He rivals all the sages, and accurately gauges
The films that will be pleasing to a "T".

He's very free with strictures, on inappropriate pictures,
On every mechanism he's *au fait*,
He can talk about the locus, of the fluctuating focus,
And let you know the minute it's O. K.

Should he discourse on shutters, weigh every word he utters,
You'll find he won't make much of a mistake.
His original disclosures, on powder and exposures,
Are anything, believe me, but a fake.

So on ad infinitum, you'll find there's not an item,
On which he will not have his little say,
He's business-like, and handy, in fact, he's quite a dandy,
This hero of the motion picture day!

Figure I.1. An early example of how gendered fan identities are entrenched, from a 1911 issue of the *Motion Picture Story Magazine*. La Touche Hancock, "The Motion Picture Fan," *Motion Picture Story Magazine* 1.5 (June 2011): 93, https://archive.org.

fangirls" that has developed over the past decade focuses on the more subtle, yet ultimately more pervasive and pernicious efforts to alienate women from geek culture and fannish identities. This is accordingly not a book about what actual fans have done and continue to do, but a consideration of the myriad, subtle ways in which fan entitlement is bred. Thus, my core concern is to explore how the convergence culture industry has modeled and sanctioned a narrow, frequently gendered, vision of fan identity and participation over the past decade and how the resultant entrenching and exacerbation of fanboy privilege has, in turn, promulgated misogynist boundary-policing practices within fan culture.

Is it as simple as suggesting that none of this is new, and what has shifted is not only the visibility of fan culture but also the visibility of misogyny within fan culture? Perhaps. To contemplate the default masculinization of fan identities, we might reach back into the annals of the earliest movie fan magazines. In just its third month of publication, in April 1911, *Motion Picture Story Magazine* featured a poem by La Touche Hancock entitled "The Motion Picture Fan" (figure I.1].[51] This "hero of the motion picture day" is presented as the archetypal affirmational male fan, celebrated for his attention to technological detail ("Should he discourse on shutters / weigh every word he utters") and his professionalism ("he's businesslike and handy"). This "dandy" cinephile "without a trace of yellow" certainly resonates with the paternalistic and often pervasive instances of "fansplaining" within contemporary geek culture. After all, as the poem goes, "So on ad infinitum, you'll find there's not an item, / On which he will not have his little say." Alternately, we might date fandom's "War on Women" to the 1920s, and the underrepresentation of female fans in the letters columns of science fiction magazines like *Amazing Stories*. Had those early fan spaces been networked and tagable, we might be more mindful of the long history of fan privilege.

Though I contend that this contemporary "war on fangirls" is a product of the convergence culture industry, made visible though the memetic flow of content across social media platforms, even these limited historical examples suggest that this war is also deeply rooted in analog media biases. These biases range from what Charlotte Brunsdon has called "the historical connotative femininity of mass culture"[52] to the generic "pink ghetto" described by Janice Radway.[53] As both media fandom and fan studies are most conceptually tied to television, we must acknowledge that historically the notion of the "passive" spectator, the "'other' people helpless before the television set are implicitly feminine."[54] Likewise, we might consider the boom in fancentric superhero, science fiction, and fantasy media properties through Derek Johnson's claim that contemporary media franchising models work to revalue "feminized" serial narrative forms through masculinized industrial and economic logics in order to maintain the connection between masculinity and cultural legitimacy.[55]

Fandom's war on women thus draws on media industries' historical devaluation of female audiences and longstanding conceptions of space (real or virtual) as mapping and maintaining gendered structures of power. Adorno contends that "what parades as progress in the culture industry, as the incessant new which it offers up, remains the disguise for an eternal sameness."[56] I would make a similar case for the convergence culture industry, which disguises its eternal desire for an audience it can easily monetize and control through its limited and deeply conditional embrace of fan culture. There are other, decidedly more hopeful narratives this book might have told about how these same industrial, technological, and cultural conditions have helped foster fan activism. Though the growing power of fans within our contemporary mediascape may well be a mark of progress, it also frequently resists a progressive vision of fan culture. The multivalent forms of nostalgia that this book explores—industrial nostalgia for analog audiences and minimal economic imperatives to engage participatory fan cultures, fannish nostalgia for subcultural exclusivity, fan-scholarly nostalgia for an equally exclusive (albeit decidedly more progressive) focus on female fan communities and transformative practices—collectively emerge from the convergence culture industry's efforts to standardize an androcentric vision of fan culture.

1

A Fangirl's Place Is in the Resistance

Feminism and Fan Studies

On January 21, 2017, an estimated four million people took to the streets to participate in the Women's March on Washington and in various sister marches across the United States and around the globe. Responding to both the divisive election of Donald Trump as the forty-fifth president of the United States and the growing political and cultural influence of the alt-right, the Women's March featured an array of protest signs that wielded pop-culture iconography to offer political commentary. Like many fans still mourning the untimely death of actress Carrie Fisher, I composed a protest sign rooted in both my own identity as a lifelong *Star Wars* fan and the tradition of transformative criticism within female fan communities. Invoking Fisher's most iconic role, Princess Leia, and bearing the slogan "A Woman's Place Is in the Resistance," the poster appropriated the nostalgically sexist refrain that is routinely used to silence any woman who dares express an opinion on the Internet: "A woman's place is in the kitchen." A pink-tinged version of this Princess Leia poster created by graphic designer Hayley Gilmore was widely disseminated on social media and displayed at the Women's March alongside handmade iterations like my own, with the "Resistance" symbiotically referencing *Star Wars*' fictional Rebel Alliance and calls to "Resist" Trump's political agenda and rising antifeminist sentiment.

Commenting in *Wired* on Hayley's design and the ubiquity of Leia protest posters at the Women's March, Angela Watercutter made a point of acknowledging both Fisher's and the character's feminist legacy, citing the place of prominence of female protagonists in the most recent entries of the *Star Wars* film franchise as clear marks of progress.[1] Missing from this celebratory narrative was any mention of fan backlash to the *Star Wars* franchise's evolving (if still not sufficiently multifaceted) commitment to representational diversity, ranging from outcry that "having two *Star Wars* movies in a row with female protagonists is taking things too far, and is a clear sign of political correctness taking over Hollywood"[2] to a fan edit of *Star Wars: Episode VIII—The Last Jedi* (2017) labeled "The Chauvinist Cut" that attempted to excise female characters from the film. Nor does this narrative of progress account for the thinly veiled sexism in some critical responses to these female protagonists. For example, Todd McCarthy complained in his review for the *Hollywood Reporter* that *Rogue One: A Star Wars Story* (2016) lacked "a strong and vigorous male lead (such as Han Solo or John Boyega's Finn in 'The Force Awakens'),"[3] erasing the significance and centrality of the franchise's first female protagonist, Rey, to *The Force Awakens'* artistic and commercial success. Thus, just as fandom is often characterized by the interplay between fascination and frustration with media objects, Leia protest posters at the Women's March were polysemic: they expressed solidarity with a female-led resistance movement and mourned the passing of a popular feminist icon, but they also bore the marks of fannish frustration with both a media object and surrounding (fan) culture that has historically privileged and empowered white men at all levels of its production, textuality, and consumption.

I preface this chapter's exploration of the evolving place of feminism within fan studies with an anecdote of how a fictional feminist icon was mobilized as an expression of real-world feminist anxiety and resistance for a number of reasons. The first is to emphasize that fandom and feminist politics have long been intertwined, with the "resistance" of female fans often placed at the center of scholarly accounts of what makes fandom a distinct mode of media consumption. The brief list of broader fannish, critical, and industrial biases obscured in this narrative of the Princess Leia poster's place of prominence at the Women's March brings us to another key point: namely, that any discussion of the feminist capacity of fan culture or scholarship requires that we grapple with industrial efforts to contain and circumvent female fan engagement. To do this, we must recognize that the same transformative and critical qualities that make female fan communities distinctive for researchers also render them disruptive and undesirable for media producers. A related third point is that it is the feminist dimensions of fan culture (however problematically assumed or inferred) that have frequently rendered female fans en masse as "threatening" to the status quo, and have provoked fanboys' desire to police the boundaries of "authentic" fan identity along gender lines. Finally, just as many cultural critics justly accused the Women's March of being an exclusionary exercise in white feminism (performatively obfuscating the fact that a majority of white women voted for Donald Trump), it is essential that we cast a similar critical eye on the intersectional failings of feminist work within fan studies. I take up this issue in more detail in the book's conclusion, but it bears stating clearly at the outset that any call to tactically reinvest in fan studies' feminist roots requires that we confront the field's propensity to focus on white, straight, Western female fans.

This chapter unpacks the long, and occasionally fraught, relationship between feminism and fan studies, and contemplates why gender remains the primary axis of fan identity engaged by scholars. Fan studies has experienced rapid growth and diversification over the past decade alongside fan culture, and has similarly confronted anxieties around how this perceived "mainstreaming" would impact the discipline's original emphases on pleasure and power. "Mainstreaming" has long been a dirty word within subcultural communities, evoking crass commercialization of grassroots community practices and a loss of authenticity, all of which are encapsulated in the ultimate critique of "selling out." To sell out is to become popular, and to have that success provoke resentment within the subcultural communities that used to be able to claim ownership over a cultural object. Mainstreaming is also importantly marked by diversification, and it is in this tension that we can begin to interrogate the interrelated, yet ultimately divergent, anxieties around the mainstreaming of fan culture and fan studies.

Below, I will briefly survey fan studies' feminist roots, before moving on to two of the field's structuring dichotomies: the framing of fans' relationship to media industries, producers, and texts through the incorporation/resistance paradigm, and the delineation between "affirmational" and "transformative" modes of fan engagement. These oft-deployed theoretical binaries, while not sufficiently flexible, remain significant in large part because they allow us to interrogate the centrality of gendered fan cultures and industrial power to the field. Next, I will consider how the specter of a postfeminist fan studies haunts debates over the scope of "fan" identities and the future of the field. To conclude, I will address a common critique of first wave fan studies, described as

the "Fandom Is Beautiful" phase, in order to call for a renewed investment of the feminist valences of the field in this cultural moment of
growing antifeminist sentiment and escalating performances of toxic
masculinity within fan culture.

Shipping Feminism and Fan Studies

Media fan studies emerged in the late 1980s and early 1990s and was
informed by multiple strains of media studies, including television
studies, subculture studies, feminist media studies, and queer theory.
Focused predominantly on female fans and the texts produced and circulated within the communities they formed, fan studies immediately
differentiated itself from the male-dominated studies of music subcultures that had emerged out of the Birmingham School in the 1970s, and
prior cultural studies work focused on class and race. By homing in on
female media fans and their negotiated reading practices, first wave
fan scholars built on existing ethnographic work focused on derided
"feminine" genres such as romance and soap opera.[4] Contemporaneous
work by queer theorists like Alexander Doty also foundationally shaped
early fan studies' theorizations of the textual production and consumption of slash fanfiction, fanart, and fanvids by predominantly straight
female fans. The place of prominence of slash (a term that encompasses
an array of homoerotic reception and production practices exploring
the emotional and physical relationships between characters of the same
sex that are canonically platonic) within fan culture offers compelling
evidence of Doty's claim that "basically heterocentrist texts can contain
queer elements, and basically heterosexual, straight-identifying people
can experience queer moments."[5] Though work on this topic within
fan studies has evolved to engage queer audiences more explicitly, early
work on slash tended to characterize its creators and consumers as
mainly "heterosexual, cisgender, white, middle class American Women,"
an assumption that "led to skewed conclusions about fan motivations for
participating in certain types of transformative fanworks,"[6] and perhaps
unintentionally had a chilling effect on more robust considerations of
intersectional fan identities.

From the field's inception, though, fannish pleasures and feminist
politics were conceptually intertwined. Constance Penley was one of

the earliest fan scholars to suggest that, even though many female fans might not openly embrace the label of "feminist," their reading and writing practices offered "an indirect (and sometimes not so indirect) commentary on issues usually seen as feminist, such as women's lack of social and economic equality, their having to manage a double-duty work and domestic life, and their being held to much greater standards of physical beauty than men."[7] Penley speculated that female fans' reticence to "speak from a feminist position," despite their declarations of left-leaning politics, might be due in part to much of second wave feminism's "moralistically anti-pornography" stance[8] and the centrality of erotica to female fan culture. Class was also positioned as a factor, with feminist identities being aligned with middle-class professional status, which many of Penley's interview subjects did not identify with.[9] Penley makes it clear that female fans' "affiliation is to fandom," rather than feminist politics, but her emphasis on the "feminist *sentiments*"[10] voiced by fans and undergirding fans' transformative textual production helped shape the field's frequent equation of "fandom" and "feminism."

In reality, much like Penley's interview subjects, scholarly work describing fandom as a politically charged, progressive, and female-driven space has its own tendency to avoid the dreaded "F-word," and rarely situates fans within the feminist movement's various waves, factions, or discontents. There are, of course, notable exceptions, such as Louisa Stein's 2015 book *Millennial Fandom*, which makes an explicit connection between "third wave" (circa 2000 onwards) fan studies "locating fandom within the fabric of the everyday" and third wave feminism's "unsettling of divides between the personal and the political."[11] Even when one accounts for multiple feminisms, it is impossible to paint fan culture as a universally "feminist" space, but it is precisely this politicized conception of the "fan" that initially made fan culture an appealing topic of study. What makes Penley's early work especially significant is that it explicitly locates fan culture and fan studies within feminist media studies, while acknowledging that fans themselves might not embrace that label or consciously embody its politics. Applying Michel de Certeau's notion of "Brownian movements," or tactical interventions of the powerless into various systems of power,[12] Penley chose to view this tension between "the feminist concerns of the fans and their unwillingness to be seen as feminists" as an opportunity to move beyond conceptions of "authentic" feminist thought,[13] and to interrogate trends within feminist media studies, as well as feminist research ethics.[14]

Other influential fan studies essays from the 1980s were essential to centering themes of gendered pleasure and power within the field, linking female fan culture with a rejection of patriarchal and binaristic conceptions of gender that are damaging to men and women alike. Joanna Russ's "Pornography by Women for Women, with Love" and Patricia Frazer Lamb and Diane L. Veith's "Romantic Myth, Transcendence, and *Star Trek* Zines," for instance, both established concepts that continue to resonate within contemporary fan studies: fan texts being conceptualized as a "labor of love,"[15] presumption of a female writership and readership for fanfiction,[16] discussions of how thinly drawn female television characters lead to the "coding" of male characters as "female" in slash stories,[17] and so on. Importantly, both of these essays frame slash fanfiction as reflecting the "desire for true equality with men and reciprocity in their intimate relationships,"[18] affording "a situation in which questions about who is the man and who is the woman, who's active and who's passive, even who's who, *cannot even be asked.*"[19] The communal cultural production of female fans was thus theorized as an inherently feminist "project of working against the patriarchal grain and imagining a utopian, truly equal world."[20]

The year 1992 presented a watershed moment for the nascent field, marked by the publication of Camille Bacon-Smith's *Enterprising Women: Television Fandom and the Creation of Popular Myth*, Henry Jenkins's *Textual Poachers: Television Fans and Participatory Culture*, and Lisa A. Lewis's edited collection, *The Adoring Audience: Fan Culture and Popular Media*. Lewis's anthology devoted an entire section to essays exploring the intersection of "Fandom and Gender," and female fan communities and practices dominated both Jenkins's and Bacon-Smith's conception of fan culture as a distinct (and distinctly gendered) mode of media consumption. Bacon-Smith grappled most actively with sexism within science fiction fan culture, citing the 1960s as the period in which women became visible within science fiction fan communities. Bacon-Smith was mindful to interrogate claims from male interview subjects and prior academic work suggesting that "before *Star Trek*, the only women who attended meetings and conventions were girlfriends of fans, or women looking for men,"[21] arguing that this "outdated opinion" cast a shadow on the treatment of female fans through the 1980s.

It is impossible not to be struck by the resonances between the moment Bacon-Smith describes in *Enterprising Women* and the contemporary efforts to thwart women's claims to fan identity within the convergence culture industry. A woman entering fan culture or fannish spaces is still routinely "considered fair game, sexually, unless she [can] prove her intelligence, in which case she [can] receive an uneasy acceptance as a 'guy.'"[22] Female fans within the convergence culture industry are fighting a similar battle as their 1960s counterparts who "dared to breach the stronghold," those who "demanded (and continue to demand from a hostile minority) an equal place in fan activities."[23] The fact that fan culture has expanded so dramatically, but women continue to be framed as an invasive and unwelcome presence, is disheartening.

Just as small subsets of fans have responded defensively to the mainstreaming of fan culture, fan scholars have had to confront their own set of disciplinary "growing pains." In particular, scholars invested in preserving and expanding on the core concerns and subjects of study from the first wave of fan studies (and I would include myself in these ranks) have periodically expressed concern that female fans and foundational conceptions of fandom as a feminist space might be obscured or diluted. The fact that many scholars touting "produsers"[24] in digital media ecologies failed to sufficiently acknowledge the influence that fangirls' textual practices have had on the purportedly "new" modes of participation that convergence culture facilitates has only exacerbated these tensions. We clearly cannot neatly equate the contemporary spike in scholars engaging with fandom and participatory culture with a "masculinization" of fan studies.[25] Nor can we claim that most contemporary scholarly work on fans openly favors, or even expressly identifies, male fans over female fans. Still, because the convergence culture industry privileges (or at the very least increases the visibility of) masculinized forms of fan engagement and scholarly accounts of that engagement, anxieties surrounding a remarginalization of work on female fans and more politicized forms of fan participation have emerged over the past decade.

A Tale of Two Binaries

Convergence Culture documented a transitional moment for fan culture, but it also marked a moment of transition for the field that Jenkins's work helped establish and continues to shape. As a rare scholarly text that permeated a wide array of academic subfields as well as media industries, *Convergence Culture* helped cultivate fan studies into a far more topically diverse and interdisciplinary field, but also triggered anxieties (however unrealized) that fan studies would stray too far from its feminist roots (however presumed). This section explores two of fan studies' most enduring and contested theoretical binaries that are frequently invoked to contemplate gendered forms of fan engagement and debate the future of the field: the incorporation/resistance paradigm that dominated the first wave of fan studies, and more contemporary delineations between "affirmational" and "transformative" modes of fan engagement with media objects and production cultures. The convergence culture industry has incorporated fans at unprecedented rates: demographically and representationally (as discussed in chapter 2), as creative laborers (addressed in chapter 4), and as media producers or consultants to better court and moderate relationships with fan audiences (such as the emergence of "fanboy auteurs" and "fantrepreneurs" discussed in chapter 5). Resistance also occurs on multiple fronts, ranging from fans' continued counterhegemonic readings of media texts to their textual poaching and transformative production. There are also more passive forms of tactical resistance, such as fans' adoption of arcane tagging practices and locked communities, that attempt to obscure fan practices from the industry's view.

Finally, we must interrogate fan studies' perceived incorporation into the convergence culture industry, and what is motivating scholarly resistance to that potential incorporation. As the incorporation/resistance paradigm has adapted to engage with the shifting industrial valuation of fan culture, new categorizations like affirmational/transformative have emerged to characterize which fans and fan practices are more easily incorporated, and which fans are deemed resistant by the convergence culture industry. Both of these structuring binaries, or modes of categorizing industry/fan relations, are at their core about the standardization of "authentic" ways of doing fandom or fan studies. If the convergence culture industry seeks to standardize media fandom, wedding incorporation with authentication, then certain fan scholars are anxious to do the opposite, authenticating a conception of resistant fans as the field's standard. Because gender is central to these categories, as well as fan scholars' proclivity to retain or complicate or move beyond them, they present a primary site of resistance to the convergence culture industry's own deeply gendered conception of the "fan."

Incorporation/Resistance

The first wave of fan scholarship drew on Michel de Certeau's *The Practice of Everyday Life* to consider how fans (and minority audiences in particular) were "making do" with what the media industry was providing. Scholars applying de Certeau's discussion of strategies and tactics and poaching[26] to the power dynamic between media producers and consumers positioned fans as waging a tactical resistance, creating "interpretive communities that in their subcultural cohesion evaded the preferred and intended meanings of the 'power bloc' [. . .] represented by popular media."[27] This characterization of fans as "resistant" readers was central to salvaging fans and fandom as a viable subject of academic study, first "removing the taint of consumption and consumerism" and then "revaluing fan activities by stressing that fans are consumers who are also (unofficial) producers."[28] As the primary subjects of the first wave of fan studies, fangirls in particular were presented as "resistant," not just "making do" but actively speaking back to the patriarchal and heteronormative values of mass media texts.

Scholars have since critiqued early fan studies' "dominant discourse of resistance" as overly simplistic, since "neither mass-mediated fan texts nor fans' readings of such texts can easily be identified as hegemonic or subversive."[29] This dialectical division between "hegemonic" and "subversive" fandom is commonly referred to as the incorporation/resistance paradigm.[30] Fan studies has, on the whole, replicated this dichotomously valued and gendered view of incorporation and resistance, endorsing the latter through a celebration of the transformative textual production of female fans. Because the incorporation/resistance paradigm is intimately connected to the construction of fans as a "socially stigmatized group who fail to conform to dominant, hegemonic ideals of 'detached,' normative"[31] models of consumption, it might initially appear that this structuring binary has no place within contemporary fan studies. After all, the convergence culture industry has to some extent "normalized" fannish consumption practices, rendering participatory consumption not just expected but desirable. The growing body of work on digital fan labor, however, speaks powerfully to a continued need to engage industrial incorporation, particularly as the modes of fan engagement that have been more easily assimilated and celebrated are those that conform to the convergence culture industry's own hegemonic conception of fan culture.

The convergence culture industry has exacerbated anxieties that fans' textual production will be incorporated by the industry and sold back to them, with many scholars echoing Fiske's concerns from 1991 that this might function

> as a form of containment—a permitted and controlled gesture of dissent that acts as a safety valve and thus strengthens the dominant social order by demonstrating its ability to cope with dissenters or protesters by allowing them enough freedom to keep them relatively content, but not enough to threaten the stability of the system against which they are protesting.[32]

Responding to growing concerns about the exploitation of fan labor, Jenkins argued in 2007 that, while scholars should not blindly celebrate "a process that commodifies fan cultural production and sells it back to us with a considerable markup [. . .] these same trends can also be understood in terms of making companies more responsive to their most committed consumers, as extending the influence that fans exert over the media they love."[33] While I do not disagree with Jenkins in theory, in practice it is difficult to elide the fact that gender biases forcefully shape which forms of fan participation can be commodified, which fans are valorized as "committed consumers," and how the mutual reinforcement of these two factors ultimately shapes which fans are capable, through their incorporation, of exerting (limited) influence over media culture. If fangirls are positioned as a "resistant" consumer collective, it is often not by choice.

This is a primary reason why many self-identified feminist fan scholars, myself included, are reticent to frame the incorporation/resistance paradigm as a relic of fan studies' past, especially as "incorporation" refers to increasingly alluring and subtle forms of "fan outreach" within the convergence culture industry. In combating and inverting the prevailing notion that "consumption is feminine and bad, production is masculine and good,"[34] the first wave of fan studies has been justly criticized for "going to the other extreme of celebrating the freedom and autonomy of the viewer"[35] in its attempts to portray female fans as successfully evading, or resisting, the culture industry. Matt Hills has rightly complained that scholarly descriptions of fannish "resistance" to the "Culture Industry" inevitably produce "one-dimensional and thin depictions of cultural heroes and villains, but [. . .] equally one-dimensional representations of cultural power, rather than perceiving 'resistance' as happening internally, within both 'the Industry' and 'fan communities,' and even 'in' the academy in a variety of ways."[36] I agree that we need more nuanced models of cultural power, but what is somewhat obscured in Hills's call is how fans' lived experience of these power dynamics, as well as their tendencies towards "resistant" behavior, is shaped by their real-world identities.

What I find generative about the convergence culture industry as an analytic is that it allows us to address the complexities of industrial, technological, and cultural shifts, acknowledging the systemic influence of industry without foreclosing fannish agency. I am not the first to grapple with these conditions and their impact on the incorporation/resistance paradigm. For example, Paul Booth has proffered the term "convergent incorporation" to articulate the merging of "industry-specific discourses of immersive 'hailing' with the interactive and polysemic practices of individual viewers."[37] Booth's term nicely captures the push and pull of contemporary forms of incorporation, but it does not adequately consider which types of fans are hailed, or how creating "a 'safe zone' of fannish enthusiasm" that "sequesters fandom into a particular arena" might be more or less safe for particular fans. In other words, the convergence culture industry may similarly sequester some fans, but it also actively excommunicates others.

The convergence culture industry addresses identity in a more targeted way than the dual concepts of the culture industry and convergence culture, which have historically avoided a sustained conversation about how gender shapes these cultural conditions. Given the culture industry's enduring issues with gender inequality,[38] and Adorno and Horkheimer's own "'feminine,' eunuch-like" characterization of audiences taken in by its products,[39] we cannot afford to erase gender from the conversation. Similarly, Catherine Driscoll and Melissa Gregg have addressed the disturbing tendency to sideline gender in much of the work on media convergence, correctly noting that contemporary constructions of "participatory culture" have a tendency to equate "participation" with "participation in an industrially determined mediascape."[40] This conceptual collapse of industrial incorporation and fannish "participation," when coupled with the surgical removal of gender from these conversations, dangerously obscures the fact that "the diversity of consumers is an obstruction" within this model.[41] This point is of particular importance because the argument against the incorporation/resistance paradigm can code as a postfeminist call to move away from a valorization of female fans generally, rather than a need to better account for the complex valences of contemporary fan culture specifically. It is precisely because of these tensions that scholars quickly embraced the gendered designations of "affirmational" and "transformative" modes of fan engagement, but were also quick to critique their terminological limitations.

Affirmational/Transformative

Many fan scholars have dismissed the incorporation/resistance paradigm as too rigid, especially as the industry's prohibitionist crackdowns on fan production have given way to collaborationist courtship of fan communities and practices. Within these evolving conditions of the convergence culture industry, a new paradigm emerged to demarcate between fandom's own "prohibitionist" and "collaborationist" views of media industry, texts, and creators. In a June 2009 LiveJournal and Dreamwidth post titled "Affirmational Fandom vs. Transformational Fandom," obsession_inc defined what they perceive to be the two predominant modes of fan participation. Obsession_inc defines "affirmational" modes of fan participation as those that reaffirm the source material or debate elements of the text while staying firmly within the established "rules" of the fictional universe.[42] Obsession_inc rightly contends that this is clearly the "most awesome type of fandom for the source creator to hang out with, because the creator holds the magic trump card of Because I'm The Only One Who Really Knows, That's Why, and that is accepted as a legitimate thing."[43] It is imperative that we do not devalue affirmational modes of fan participation, which might include discursively debating fan theories or collecting/curating fan objects, but it is worth noting that fan legitimation and industrial incorporation are conceptually linked in this model.

If the convergence culture industry strives to craft a standardized vision of fan culture that nostalgically attempts to revive the predigital imaginary of a docile and financially dependable audience base, then this vision is one that inevitably privileges affirmational modes of fan participation. Obsession_inc refers to fans that tend towards this affirmational mode as "*sanctioned* fans" and claims that "the majority of fans that trend strongly toward affirmational fannish activities are male."[44] Though there are obviously exceptions, obsession_inc's gendered generalization resonates with Jenkins's early applications of reader-response theory to suggest that gendered reading strategies play a role in female fans' propensity for transformative textual production, with men tending to "read for authorial meaning" and defer to the author's authority, focusing on mastering information and solving any narrative puzzles the text might present.[45] Female fans, conversely, approached the text more dialogically, immersing themselves in the fictional world in order to contribute to it, "focusing less on the extratextual process of its writing than on the relationships and events."[46] Rhiannon Bury has noted that Jenkins's discussion of gendered reading strategies "stops short of explaining *why* boys and girls would be offered different narratives in the first place"[47] or of examining the industrial conditions that shape why female fan culture must learn to "make do" with mainstream media objects. For the purposes of this argument, what is of central importance is that affirmational fans are "sanctioned" by the convergence culture industry because they are willing to enter into a relationship with both the text and its producers that is ultimately more monologic than dialogic, facilitating the fan's industrial incorporation as a promotional agent.

Conversely, obsession_inc frames "transformational" fandom as "all about laying hands upon the source and twisting it to the fans' own purposes," neatly aligning with the resistant and textually productive tendencies of female fans celebrated in the first wave of fan studies. Because transformational fandom centrally "values fanon over canon, appropriation over documentation, and multiple interpretations over hierarchical authority," these fans are accordingly considered to be "nonsanctioned fans" by the industry. The "transformative" designation is not an invention of obsession_inc's, but has been widely adopted in fan communities as both a descriptive term and a legal defense to discourage the classification of fan texts as "derivative" works and to protect them under fair use doctrine. The Organization for Transformative Works (OTW), a nonprofit organization created by fans in 2007 to preserve and legally protect transformative forms of fan production such as fanfiction, fanvids, and fanart, defines "transformative work" as work that takes "something extant and turns it into something with a new purpose, sensibility, or mode of expression." Aligning fans' transformative works with the legal definition of transformative use, or something that "adds something new, with a further purpose or different character altering the [source text] with new expression, meaning or message" offers the OTW a legally defensible position. This protectionist mission is also explicitly gendered, stating that the OTW "grew out of a practice of transformative fanwork historically rooted in a primarily female culture" and that "we also specifically value that history of women's involvement, and the practices of fandom shaped by women's work."[48]

Affirmational and transformational fandom, like the incorporation/resistance paradigm before it, must be viewed as a continuum. Indeed, when obsession_inc's terminology began to be deployed by fan scholars in conference presentations and publications as shorthand for addressing gendered modes of fan engagement, many critiqued the terms' polarizing view of fan participation. It is true that there is an array of fan practices, from crafting prop replicas[49] to creating GIFs, that "represent a liminal space *between* fans' appreciation of the text, and their appropriation (and transformation) of the text."[50] Sam Ford subsequently proposed "accretion fandom" as an alternative to "affirmational" to describe instances when "the complexity and intensity of fan activity comes not from producing discrete fan texts but from the deep, everyday practices of unpacking meaning and debating issues surrounding the flow of new source material."[51] It is easy to understand why many scholars are uncomfortable with these gender-demarcated categories and desire to move beyond totalizing or essentialist conceptions of fan participation. It is not my goal to endorse a monolithically gendered view of fannish participation, especially as most fans vacillate between these two poles. As a female fan, my own participation within fan communities and culture has skewed "affirmational" or "transformative" depending on a wide array of shifting conditions, from my relationship to a given media text or form to the affordances and limitations of my own leisure time or disposable income at various points in my life. I have composed and consumed fanfiction and collected comics and toys, livetweeted and debated theories with fellow fans, bought fan merchandise, pored over fan wikis, and cosplayed.

What I find productive about this binary is its emphasis on how sanctioned and nonsanctioned modes of engagement are gendered, and how this "sanctioning" is replicated and reinforced within fan communities. These categories quite literally *affirm*, albeit in sweeping terms, which fans and fan practices have been embraced by the convergence culture industry, and allow us to address industrial and intra-fannish attempts to discursively discipline impulses to *transform* intellectual property or fan culture itself. Consider, for example, the fact that transformative fans and their practices are disproportionally and publicly shamed in both mainstream media representations and promotional paratexts such as creator or cast interviews.[52] Here, and in an array of similar incidents, fannish "resistance" to hegemonic media representations, clear messaging about the limitations of fan cultural incorporation, and the devaluation of transformative fan production all converge through the discursive disciplining of female fans. Moreover, moments like these can be viewed as tacitly endorsing fans who skew more affirmational, a fact that is often used as intra-fannish leverage to dismiss women within fan culture more generally.

Rather than abandoning the affirmational/transformative dichotomy, we need to more thoroughly consider its resonances with the incorporation/resistance paradigm. Because the convergence culture industry is centrally concerned with standardization, it is more productive to approach the delineation of "affirmational" and "transformative" fandom as experiential categories rather than discrete or stable fannish identities. Instead of approaching the categorization of "affirmational" and "transformative" fan engagement as an extension of Jenkins's early work on gendered reading strategies, and how this in turn leads to differing modes of textual engagement and production, it is more useful to consider how the convergence culture industry has endeavored to brand fandom as an affirmational and/or male space *in spite of* the growing visibility of transformative (or even explicitly activist) forms of fan engagement.

Because even the most transformative fans are also voracious consumers, any effort to retain fan studies' branding as a subfield of feminist media studies must also be mindful of "the rising visibility of safely affirmational feminism" within this cultural moment.[53] In addressing the symbiotic boom in both "popular feminism" and "popular misogyny," Sarah Banet-Weiser is similarly concerned with the impact of mainstreaming within this cultural moment, and how popular feminism "eclipses, in the name of individual cases of abuse, the structural critique academic feminists have been making for years."[54] While intra-fannish responses to the "mainstreaming" of fan culture frequently manifest in efforts to alienate marginalized fans and entrench perceptions of geek culture as a white, male space, feminist fan scholars pushing back on the mainstreaming of fan studies often do so out of concern that these forces will succeed. Thus, while both forms of pushback are nostalgic for a potentially lost past, frequently misrepresenting or oversimplifying that past in the process, it must be recognized that fan-scholarly backlash to the mainstreaming of fan studies is differently motivated. In forwarding what some might consider an "exclusionary" vision of fan studies, these scholars strive to protect those fans who have become most vulnerable within the convergence culture industry, precisely because they do not demographically or productively conform to a standardized conception of fandom.

Branding Fandom and the Specter of Postfeminist Fan Studies

Contra Penley's early accounts of female fans reluctant to brand themselves as "feminists" in spite of their vocal support of affiliated causes, many contemporary fans do not hesitate to embrace the term and embody its project through an array of fan activist work. We could accordingly make an argument that the feminist dimensions of fan culture have never been more vibrant, but they have simultaneously been disproportionately under threat by antifeminist sentiment, both intra-fannishly and on a broader cultural scale. These cultural conditions have unquestionably contributed to some feminist fan scholars feeling similarly under threat. Despite their centrality within the field of fan studies, women being written out of the history of fan culture has been a point of concern that has only been exacerbated by the convergence culture industry's championing of the fanboy, and these stakes are far higher than the issue of who can easily occupy the label of fan. Connecting claims to fan identity with similarly androcentric conceptions of technological mastery, Stein suggests that "the same gendered discourses that may overall shape how women perceive their own relationship with technology also shape what fan histories get told, recorded, and listened to."[55] Similar critiques have been made by female fan scholars concerning the erasure of fangirl-centric digital production practices, like vidding (or fan-produced video edits composed to music), within cultural and scholarly narratives surrounding the rise of remix culture.[56]

In 2007 and again in 2009, Henry Jenkins gathered groups of academics on his blog to address these disconnects, first via a series of "Gender and Fan Culture Debates," and second through conversations exploring the continued use of the term "aca-fan" to describe the hybrid identity of many fan scholars. The Gender and Fan Culture Debates explicitly responded to growing concerns about the erosion of fan studies' feminist roots, that convergence culture was making fan culture "more mainstream and acceptable, but also more commodified and privileging fanboy over fangirl practices." The perception for some participants was that fan studies had followed suit and "splintered along gendered lines, with prominent male academics emphasizing fanboy & industrial practices, leaving many female academics on the margin."[57] While these debates reflected less a case of gendered infighting than the "growing pains" of a subfield at a moment of profound transition, many of the debates reflected that calls to move beyond gender as a core critical axis in our considerations of fans and fandom were premature, not to mention problematic.[58]

The Gender and Fan Culture Debates reflected anxieties that fan studies might be sublimated into the convergence culture industry, or begin to center its standardized conception of the media fan, excluding the common critical domains of female fans and fan scholars. The aca-fan debates similarly evoked long-simmering tensions about the scope of the field, raising concerns about the exclusionary potential of "aca-fandom" as a concept, and how this methodological approach might place too much emphasis on scholars' personal tastes, inevitably limiting the field of study. Because "aca-fandom" as a scholarly identity or method was situated within traditions of women's studies, LGBT studies, and ethnic studies and conceptually linked to subjective turns in cultural analysis in which marginalized scholars brought their own identities and experiences to bear on the communities they studied, many conceptualize the term as "inherently feminist."[59]

Perhaps unsurprisingly, responses in the debates tended to break along gendered lines, with men deriding aca-fandom as a scholarly stance[60] or questioning the ongoing need for the term,[61] and women staging defenses of its connection to broader identity politics and affective modes of writing.[62] My own conception of the term "aca-fan" echoes Louisa Stein's, namely, that it is "a broad and robust term, capable of containing multiple definitions, but all of which speak to an awareness of a blurring of subjectivities and roles, where fannish affect and insight inform academic perspectives and goals and vice versa."[63] Positioning the term as feminist is thus more concerned with foregrounding the personal dimensions of both feminist and queer media studies that have shaped the field, and more generally acknowledging that subjective scholarly work often remains controversial or devalued. Objectivity/ subjectivity obviously presents its own problematically gendered binary, and provides one rationale for why female scholars (many of whom expressly dislike the term) will still defend "aca-fandom" conceptually, as it affords a vital space to articulate and analyze lived identity politics.

Both sets of debates were overwhelmingly collegial and constructive affairs, with the vast majority of participants adopting a centrist position. Still, they function as an archival reminder of a gendered rift in fan studies of this period that was born out of the convergence culture industry's gendered revaluation of fans. Reflecting on both sets of debates in an article celebrating fan studies as an "undisciplined discipline," Sam Ford stresses that the strengths of the field lie in its flexibility and interdisciplinarity.[64] Indeed, Ford's own work on wrestling and soap operas fandoms productively defies many of the binaristic logics surveyed in this chapter. Thus the core challenge in formulating fan studies as a distinct field is similar to the one fans themselves face: namely, how to maintain a cohesive sense of community while remaining flexible to new ideas and approaches. Ford is correct in asserting that these debates moved the field forward in important ways, inspiring collaborations and productive dialogues about how the field is conceived by various constituents, but his account does not sufficiently address the anxieties that inspired these debates and continue to persist in spite of them.

These debates surrounding the scope of the field, and the definition of "fan" more generally, were revived in a 2014 *Cinema Journal* roundtable addressing Henry Jenkins, Sam Ford, and Joshua Green's 2013 book *Spreadable Media*. Of all the roundtable's participants, Kristina Busse argued most forcefully that *Spreadable Media*'s somewhat loose conceptualization of "fans" as "the commercializable audiences, who happily seem to collaborate in their own exploitation," might precipitate the field's "focus away from the marginal media fan, who was mostly commercially nonviable, often resistant, and uncooperative [. . .] in spite of capitalist alternatives and not because they didn't exist."[65] According to Busse, what is "excluded and marginalized in *Spreadable Media*, then, are the very founders of the concept of fan, the unruly and aggressively anticommercial, the queered and sexually explicit, the anticapitalist and anticopyright."[66] Though it is not wholly fair to level this critique at *Spreadable Media*, given its scope and content, I am deeply sympathetic to one of Busse's core points, namely, that discursively, "like 'queer,' 'fan' also has much to gain from becoming more inclusive, but even more to lose from becoming all-inclusive."[67]

Other participants like Melissa A. Click and Sharon A. Ross pushed back, with Paul Booth suggesting that *Spreadable Media* might alternately be viewed as a democratic exercise, focusing on "a particular type of fan audience that tends to go underrepresented in fan literature—the mainstream fan, or the fan who doesn't want to subvert the status quo."[68] As Jenkins rightly noted in response, at the heart of all of these debates surrounding the future of the field was "the terminological confusion that has always surrounded the term *fan*."[69] Much as the convergence culture industry is invested in branding an androcentric conception of fan culture, we can similarly view these growing fan-scholarly debates as concerned with the affordances and limitations of the centrality of gender and feminism to fan studies' brand.

When fan scholars over the past decade express perfectly valid concerns about fan studies taking a hierarchical approach delineating particular forms of fan engagement as more/less worthy of study, but do not consider the broader systems of structural inequity that have made female and/or transformative fan scholars grow increasingly defensive about maintaining their place within that hierarchy, we arrive at the reason why many fan scholars continue to invest in polarizing fan studies frameworks. This is not a case of clear "camps" (e.g., those advocating for the expansion of the field do not wish to do so at the expense of feminist or politically engaged work on fan identity and power, and vice versa), but instead a more general expression of concern that moving towards an increasingly casual or generalizable conception of the "media fan" might evolve into a more insidious "postidentity" turn in the field.

It is vital to acknowledge that perception is not reality, and there is still ample work being done on female fans, identity politics, and power that offers a powerful rebuttal to this claim. However, just as some feminist scholars have suggested that rhetorics of "choice" are repurposed within postfeminism to reinforce conservatism and a return to traditional gender roles,[70] there are palpable anxieties within some corners of fan studies that the growing scope of the field might function similarly, "choosing" to center more industrially valued (and, thus, inherently more conservative or capitalist) modes of fan participation going forward. Tensions surrounding the perceived "pastness" of feminism to the expanding field, coupled with more celebratory views of fan consumption as a site of "empowerment," all neatly resonate with the core critiques of postfeminist culture.[71]

Fan studies' historic emphasis on female-dominated fan communities as politically charged and potentially feminist spaces, like feminism under postfeminist culture, are thus not so much rejected as supplanted by their own success. As a result, feminist fan scholars who critique these shifts within and expansion of the field in any way, not unlike feminists within the postfeminist model, can be easily aligned with feminist stereotypes and dismissed as "killjoys" or "man haters" (at both the academic and the fannish level). Similarly to the ways in which postfeminism perpetually "raises the premium on youthfulness, installing an image of feminism as 'old' (and by extension moribund),"[72] proponents of first wave fan studies' conceptions of the "fan" are similarly painted as clinging to the past rather than embracing a more polyvalent future of the field. In reality, much as postfeminism problematically links liberation to neoliberalism and aspirational consumption,[73] fan-scholarly concerns are frequently rooted in the notion that to emphasize more "mainstream" forms of fannish participation is to inevitably end up championing these models of consumer citizenship.

In *The Aftermath of Feminism*, Angela McRobbie offers a play on Stuart Hall's work on articulation to consider how the institutional prog-ress of feminism has been slowly eroded over the past several decades and replaced with postfeminism.[74] If Hall's work on articulation em-phasized forging connections between various social justice movements, then McRobbie's core concern with disarticulation is that it "functions to foreclose on the possibility or likelihood of various expansive inter-sections and inter-generational feminist transitions."[75] This, ultimately, both defuses the power of feminism and limits its scope in terms of which women it speaks to by maintaining divisions across various axes of identity (race, age, class, sexuality, ability, and so on). My own con-cern for fan studies' relationship to feminism is similar, namely, that the field's exponential growth could function as a moment of disarticulation within a field that desperately needs to forge the sort of connections that Hall describes.

Fan-scholarly uneasiness about the potential "disarticulation" of fan studies and feminist media studies reveals the complex negotia-tions within a field at a moment of transition. None of the scholars pushing for a more expansive conception of fandom or fan studies, or calling for more work on affirmational fan practices, frame this as a "backlash" against feminist or transformative fan studies. It is often the case, though, that they are negotiating a somewhat different set of relationships among culture, politics, and feminism than those ad-vocating for a continued emphasis on the resistant work of minority fan cultures and communities. The concerns surrounding a potentially "postfeminist" fan studies are thus less about the growing attention paid to male fans and practices that have been heretofore undertheorized in the field, and more about the erasure of gender and fan studies' feminist roots within contemporary accounts of the field. To argue for a need to continue to study gender within fan culture obviously does not limit that study to female fans. Indeed, if anything, we need to be investing in con-versations about how contemporary instantiations of toxic masculinity originate within geek and fan culture.

Fandom Is ~~Beautiful~~ Toxic

It is difficult not to see the irony in feminist or transformative-focused fan scholars expressing concerns about the growing inclusivity of the field's conception of the "media fan," when those same scholars would undoubtedly decry the sexist impulse of some fanboys to protect their conception of fan culture as a white, straight, male preserve. Both groups are motivated by similar nostalgic desires to retain what they feel is special about fan culture, expressing anxieties about the identity's and/or the field's history being erased by an influx of new members. Where this comparison breaks down is in the realization that the protectionist impulses of feminist fan scholars are motivated in part by the rising anti-feminist sentiment within geek and fan culture itself. Much like efforts to invent a so-called alt-left as a foil/attempted distraction from the growing political sway of the "alt-right," or contemporary false equivalences that neo-Nazi and antifa (or antifascist) protesters are "morally indistinguishable,"[76] which obfuscate the underlying ideological intent of each collective, the protectionist means might appear similar, but the ends are diametrically opposed in their political projects. Marginalizing new additions to fan studies or fan culture is not the answer in either case, but at this moment fan studies cannot afford to adopt a postfeminist stance, not only because its intersectional work has only recently begun in earnest but also because fandom has become a hotbed for increasingly intersectional forms of toxic masculinity.

By framing fans, and female fans in particular, as resistant readers and textual poachers, fandom was broadly conceptualized by early fan scholars as a "vehicle for marginalized subcultural groups [...] to pry open space for their cultural concerns within dominant representations."[77] When they dubbed the first wave of fan studies as the "Fandom Is Beautiful" phase,[78] Jonathan Gray, Cornel Sandvoss, and C. Lee Harrington correctly, if somewhat dismissively, hit on a core failing of the field's early politicization of fan production and culture. It is easy to justify this "fandom is beautiful" ethos of first wave fan scholarship as a necessary intervention, as it worked to revalue preexisting fan pathologies and positively differentiated fans from more general conceptions of the "audience." It is equally easy to critique first wave fan scholars' politicized vision of "resistant" and "subversive" fan culture as not sufficiently nuanced, or to claim that early conceptions of fan culture as a feminist space were overdetermined, given fans' frequent reluctance to self-identify as such. However, as the chapters that follow will make clear, it is precisely because of the convergence culture industry's gendered depatholigization and affirmation of *certain* fans and *certain* fan practices that we must reinvest in and reimagine fan studies' commitment to studying female audiences and feminist modes of fannish resistance.

On the surface this seems unnecessary, especially considering that work on gender and fan culture, as well as questions of identity and power, continue to occupy a place of prominence within the field. However, when examining this cultural moment in which fan privilege is industrially produced and fannishly performed, we can trace an interesting parallel history between the cultural ascendance of the fan and anxieties about the "mainstreaming" of fan studies over the past decade. To see the specter of postfeminism within fan studies, we need only look at a recent roundtable of white men discussing the future of comics studies identifying "representation of" studies as one of the problems "endemic to a young field,"[79] dismissing scholars doing work on identity in a medium in desperate need of academic analyses of representation in relation to fan culture. Work on contemporary digital fan cultures or fannish "user-generated content" in which gender is either decentered or elided exacerbates the anxiety that female fans will be erased from both the culture and the field they helped establish.

In a 2014 rebuttal to Gray, Sandvoss, and Harrington's characterization of first wave fan studies titled "Fuck Yeah, Fandom Is Beautiful," Francesca Coppa notes,

> Do not get me wrong: I am not actually trying to argue that fandom is some sort of utopia. As my colleague Rebecca Tushnet wryly notes [. . .], "Fandom is made of people, and people are sometimes awful to each other." [. . .] But fandom *is* made of people with all their imperfections as well as their strengths, and for every flame war or rivalry there are corresponding acts of friendship and generosity, not to mention opportunities for collective action.[80]

As with "incorporation/resistance" and "affirmational/transformative," painting contemporary fan culture as beautiful or toxic presents a false dichotomy and fails to sufficiently explore the degree to which these characterizations work reciprocally.

To Coppa's point, an abundance of truly "beautiful" instances of collective action have mobilized in response to the growing strains of toxicity in contemporary fan culture. As evidenced by the anecdote that opened this chapter, as well as numerous other examples provided throughout this book, fan activism has never been more prolific or connected to broader sociopolitical movements.[81] But we also should not overlook the degree to which fan activists have been provoked by shifting sociocultural conditions and attacks on a wide array of minority groups when we debate the scope and future of the field.

The fact that the term "fan" has grown increasingly interchangeable with the designations of "geek" and "nerd" to symbolize a set of popular character archetypes and audience segments certainly support Henry Jenkins's 2007 claim that the term "fan" has, somewhat paradoxically, become so elastic, so pervasive, that it is in danger of being erased or rendered devoid of meaning.[82] But rather than considering the possibility, as Jenkins does, that "fandom has no future,"[83] I would instead argue that its future is currently being determined, and that who is determining it is of great significance. Roberta Pearson argues that "[f]an studies began as an act of reclamation and celebration; reclamation from the geeky image constructed by the media [...] and celebration of fannish resistance to capitalist incorporation."[84] The fact that more generalizable, and thus more insidiously gender-neutral, accounts of digital fan culture tend to privilege affirmational and industrially sanctioned (e.g., historically masculinized) modes of fan participation has only exacerbated this. It is precisely the slippage between (or conflation of) studies of transformative fan works, positive valuations of fans as resistant readers, and feminist fan studies that leads to these anxieties. When any of these elements are decentered, there is an implicit danger of decentering women from the conception and study of fan culture.

Arguing for a reinvestment in and reimagining of fandom as a feminist space does not mean we should paint a utopian vision of fan culture as inherently progressive. Work within contemporary fan studies often falls prey to the assumption that because feminism is culturally embedded in the field, or "equality" has been conditionally achieved in fans' movement from the margins to the mainstream within the convergence culture industry, the work of feminist fan studies is done. There is no one way of doing fan studies, just as there is no one way of doing fandom, and it is certainly not my intent to be prescriptive. I merely wish to reassert the significance of media fan studies' political project, particularly at this cultural moment of transition and potential rebranding for the field.

In witnessing how the convergence culture industry brands authentic modes of fan engagement, and some fans weaponize this branding to police the authenticity of other fans, I am reminded of Sarah Banet-Weiser's argument that a hallmark of our contemporary brand culture is that authenticity itself is branded. So, it is not the mainstreaming or commoditization of geek culture that concerns me, but rather the convergence culture industry's branding of fandom as an innately masculine space. As Banet-Weiser notes,

> Because a brand's value extends beyond a tangible product, the process of branding—if successful—is different from commodification: it is a cultural phenomenon more than an economic strategy. [. . .] Commodification is a marketing strategy, a monetization of different spheres of life, a transformation of social and cultural life into something that can be bought and sold. In contrast, the process of branding impacts the way we understand who we are, how we organize ourselves in the world, what stories we tell about ourselves.[85]

The branding of fan identity by the convergence culture industry, the vision of fan culture being bought and sold, is one that more often than not reentrenches male privilege and remarginalizes female fans. This story being told, that fan culture is a masculine preserve, or that women are welcome as long as they are willing to conform, to become "just one of the (fan)boys," is powerful. It has lodged itself in the corners of the fan-cultural consciousness, particularly within historically male-dominated media forms such as video games and comic books. With that said, it is important to remember that fans and scholars are storytellers as well. We are, for better and for worse, brand ambassadors. We are responsible for the stories we tell about fan culture, and we need to be attentive to whom we are telling them to (whether to media industries, fans, each other, or some combination thereof).

This chapter has told one story about the mainstreaming of fan studies over the past decade, and its perceived impact on the feminist roots of the field. But, if fandom has taught me anything, it is that there is always room for counternarratives, multiplicity, competing visions, and radical transformations. Anxieties about retaining the feminist valences of the field are unquestionably fed by the convergence culture industry's subtle erasure of women from their desired "fan demographic," the rise of antifeminist sentiment on a broader sociopolitical scale, and increasingly bolder and more prolific misogynistic pushback against women within fan culture. The following chapters tell these intimately connected stories, ones that leave little conceptual room for female (much less feminist) fans.

2

"Get a life, will you people?!"

The Revenge of the Fanboy

In 1986, *Saturday Night Live* aired a sketch in which guest host William Shatner, when confronted by a cadre of enthusiastic Trekkies at a fan convention, notoriously told *Star Trek* fans to "Get a Life!" For Henry Jenkins, who deployed Shatner's punchline as the title of *Textual Poachers'* first chapter, the "Get a Life!" sketch served as a concentrated expression of the mainstream media's efforts to pathologize and, ultimately, contain fans via stereotypical representations. The "Get a Life!" sketch has since become a form of scholarly shorthand, with fan scholars drawing on the sketch to discuss issues ranging from the evolution of fan representations to debates around professionalization and fan labor and analyses of which modes of spectatorship have been normalized within convergence culture.[1] The sketch continues to function as the primary signifier of the sorts of pathologized fan representations that fan studies has historically attempted to recuperate, and that the current fancentric media landscape has purportedly moved past.

The title of this chapter quotes Shatner's unabridged message to fans in order to suggest that the portion of the iconic punchline that has been surgically removed in these prior analyses, the "you people" Shatner urges to "get a life," is ultimately more important to an analysis of how fan identities are shaped and standardized by the convergence culture industry. Journalists, marketing departments, industry executives, and media producers all contribute to the construction of a narrowly defined, and often rigidly gendered, vision of fan identity. Unsurprisingly, the industrial embrace of the fanboy as both a power demographic and a character archetype over the past decade reinforces Hollywood's ongoing allegiance to sixteen- to thirty-four-year-old straight, white, cisgender men as their default target audience. This commitment works to demographically and representationally recuperate the fanboy into hegemonic masculinity, obscuring and further marginalizing fangirls, queer fans, and fans of color in the process.

This chapter narrativizes the shifting cultural capital of fanboys within the convergence culture industry, and contends that privilege exists even in the most pathologized of fan representations. In analyzing the discursive and representational (re)construction of the fan between 2005 and 2018, we can better observe how a delimited and distinctly gendered construction of "you people," of fans, has evolved alongside the convergence culture industry's demographic and representational recuperation of the fanboy. Shifting our focus to the construction of fans as a collective "you people" allows us to simultaneously acknowledge the fan pathologies that remain embedded in contemporary descriptions and representations of the fan, as well as consider which fans are made visible or marginalized in these moments. These (in)visibility politics set the stage for chapter 3's consideration of gendered boundary-policing practices and the rise of spreadable misogyny within fan culture, as well as reflecting which modes of fan engagement are supported and which fans are able to professionalize within the convergence culture industry (addressed in chapters 4 and 5). What follows, then, is an examination of the subtle dance between fan visibility and pathologization that has evolved over the past decade. As the fan purportedly rises to power and is revalued by media industries, the discursive and representational delimiting of "you people" helps determine who can easily claim (and thereby dismiss others' claim to) fan identities.

Princess Nakeds and Dr. Girlfriends

Despite frequent references to the *SNL* "Get a Life!" sketch, there has been surprisingly little scholarly engagement with the gendered presentation of fandom within the sketch itself. The sketch notably features only two female characters, and neither of them is depicted as a fan/ Trekker attending the convention, a category that is exclusively occupied by trivia-obsessed, *Trek* t-shirt–clad, white men in their teens, twenties, and thirties. Women, by contrast, are presented within the sketch as featured guests of the con, visibly uncomfortable and out of place, objects to be ogled or defined exclusively through their relationship to men. First, the sketch introduces a "lovely" actress who was crushed into a cube in the first ten minutes of a *Star Trek* episode, a concise commentary on the show's infamous "Red Shirt" plotting (a trope in which expendable characters destined to die were identifiable by their red Starfleet uniforms) and its frequent sidelining of female characters.[2] Next, the sketch introduces the ex-wife of James "Scotty" Doohan, hawking her memoir *Beam Me out of Here*. The book's title appears to mutually reference her attitude towards her marriage and the fan convention space, as she shifts uncomfortably and smiles wanly, quickly vacating the stage without speaking.

Without question, the fanboy protagonists of the *SNL* sketch present an exhaustive catalogue of negative fan stereotypes and situate the fan as Other: the audience is prompted to laugh at them as "social misfits" or "brainless consumers," who "are feminized and/or desexualized through their intimate engagement with mass culture."[3] Jenkins acknowledged that these stereotypes function differently for male and female fans, and that while male fans may be characterized as "de-gendered, asexual, or impotent, the eroticized fan is almost always female."[4] Importantly, then, fan stereotypes are always already gendered, and fan pathologies are always already feminized, through either the taint of femininity attached to the fanboy's "failed" masculinity or the excessive feminine affect assigned to fangirls. Fanboys, thus, have the flexibility not only to alternately claim and distance themselves from these social stigmas but also to deploy the term "fanboy" as an "assertion of authenticity."[5] As Melissa A. Click has suggested, "[F]anboys have greater visibility in popular culture because their interests and activities have become an unspoken standard. Fangirls' interests and strategies, which do not register when positioned against fanboys', are ignored—or worse, ridiculed."[6] It would be easy to read the squirming of the female characters in the *SNL* sketch as simply another layer of performed discomfort with the "obsessed fan" as a cultural archetype. However, the sketch's erasure of female fans and, by extension, their erasure from the popular conception of "you people," is far more insidious.[7] Thus, not only does the gendered nature of the term "fanboy" prohibit particular fans from "authenticating" their fan identities, but the convergence culture industry's efforts to standardize fan engagement to benefit corporate interests disproportionately favors fanboys.

Because the bulk of this chapter focuses on how the fanboy has been demographically reclaimed and industrially incorporated by the

Figure 2.1. Sidebar image parodying fan stereotypes from an *Entertainment Weekly* special issue on San Diego Comic-Con 2008. Marc Bernardin, "Faces in the Crowd," *Entertainment Weekly*, July 25, 2008, 35.

convergence culture industry, it is illuminating to examine a contemporary incarnation of the "Get a Life" sketch to consider how female fans continue to be strategically sidelined within these reclamation narratives. This satirical sidebar from a July 2008 issue of *Entertainment Weekly* devoted to San Diego Comic-Con International (SDCC) attempted to humorously skewer the common "faces in the crowd" at fan conventions (figure 2.1). Though we should not overlook the fact that *Entertainment Weekly* (in this issue and myriad others) routinely celebrates the fan as an emergent industry tastemaker, this sidebar shares some enduring stereotypes with the *SNL* sketch that deserve attention. White straight men, though unquestionably still pathologized, remain unilaterally privileged as the core fan demographic of both the convention space and the media properties marketed within it. Female fans and convention attendees, meanwhile, can apparently be divided into two camps: "Princess Nakeds" and "Dr. Girlfriends."

Admittedly, all of the SDCC attendee archetypes outlined above perpetuate crude stereotypes about fans generally, and mock male and female fans equally. What makes these two "fangirl" representations particularly pernicious is not the fact that they trade in old pathologies but that they offer no real point of identification for female fans. Even if we assume that the term "Princess Naked" is a reference to the disproportionate number of "Slave Leias" that populate fan conventions (as the accompanying caricature would suggest), the description divorces the archetype from cosplay as a fan practice by pointedly including LARPing (or live-action role playing) as a distinct category. Wearing her costume of "strategically placed electrical tape," the "Princess Naked" under this definition is not attempting to embody Princess Leia, or any character in particular. Rather, "Princess Naked" offers herself up as an always already sexualized object for the fanboy gaze, affirming that fangirls are frequently reduced to "an erotic spectacle for mundane male spectators."[8] Not unlike the *SNL* sketch's *Star Trek* actress crushed into a cube ten minutes into the episode, or the scantily clad models or "booth babes" that are hired to draw attention from attendees at fan conventions, the description of "Princess Naked" promises sexualized spectacle, and ultimately contains women within fannish spaces via a presumed straight male gaze.

The "Dr. Girlfriend"[9] archetype is arguably far more troubling. *Entertainment Weekly*'s description of "Dr. Girlfriends" as unwilling attendees, tagging along after their boyfriends or husbands (the "real" attendees), coupled with a caricature of a horrified-looking woman being forced to carry poster tubes and merchandise, goes beyond simply misrepresenting female fans. The characterization of the "Dr. Girlfriend" implies, in a none-too-subtle "beam me out of here" fashion, that no woman can authentically occupy this fannish space. Ultimately, both the "Princess Naked" and the "Dr. Girlfriend" archetypes are rooted in a heterosexist view of female fan identity, the former hypersexualized and the latter heteronormatively coupled. Female fans, in both cases, are constructed through and safely contained by their male cohort's gaze and companionship.

New Hegemonic Fandom and Hegemonic Masculinity

Though the inclusion or exclusion from the fannish category of "you people" is perhaps more significant than the tonality of specific representations of fans, it is vital to acknowledge that even the most celebratory contemporary depictions of fans continue to trade in old fan pathologies and stereotypes. Fanboys may be disproportionately depicted in entertainment media and celebrated by the popular press over the past decade, but by extension they are also disproportionately stereotyped. Still, it is essential to address hegemonic constructions of fans and fandom (by either the popular press, the media industry, academics, or fans themselves) alongside the gendered power imbalances they emerge from and perpetuate. Matt Hills has described this paradox as "new hegemonic fandom," which works to define "the limits to 'correct'—or hegemonic—media consumption *both positively* where 'everyone has to be a fan of something,' and *negatively*, where 'everyone knows' fans are obsessive."[10] The following sections examining the discursive and representational revenge of the fanboy substantiate Hills's core claim that "fan identities may be becoming contradictorily normative *at the same time as remaining pathologised*."[11] This may be the case, but this process of normalization and pathologization is also distinctly gendered, suggesting a need to consider how this "new hegemonic fandom" is accessed and/or experienced differently by fanboys and fangirls. The convergence culture industry's exclusionary conception of "you people," its own distinct conception of "new hegemonic fandom," has been achieved by nestling emergent conceptions of the empowered "fan" firmly within the comforts of hegemonic masculinity.

As the fan's cultural capital grows, these dividing lines are increasingly drawn intra-fannishly and along gender lines rather than primarily through the object of fandom, and its place within hierarchies of taste and class (e.g., rock groupies are "fans," while opera lovers are "aficionados").[12] Joli Jensen's 1992 essay "Fandom as Pathology: The Consequences of Characterization" remains a resonant work on dominant fan stereotypes, but the facet of her argument that has been somewhat obscured within contemporary fan studies is that pathologized representations of fans ultimately "tell us more about what we want to believe about modern society, and our connection to it"[13] than they do about the fan's (potentially obsessive or excessive) relationship to the fan object. If the fan pathologies Jensen was documenting in the early 1990s reflected broader critiques of modernity's "alienation, atomization, vulnerability, and irrationality,"[14] then the convergence culture industry's conflicted relationship to the fan reflects the anxieties surrounding a post–Web 2.0 mediascape and the gap between its "rhetoric of happy

collaboration" and fans' "actual experiences working with companies."[15]
If the modernity critique documented by Jensen is "nostalgic and
romantic" for a time before the supposed "decline of community and the
increasing power of the mass media,"[16] contemporary fan pathologies
are marked by nostalgia for a predigital fan culture that was less capable
of organizing and exerting power over the mass media.

Hills subsequently suggests that industrial and intra-fan representations have moved from "fandom as pathology" to "fandom as pedagogy," in which fan identities are modeled "as passionate yet polite, as
unruly yet organized into teams, as a 'mass' collective that is valued by
media personnel yet symbolically subordinated"[17] to media producers
and stars. "Fandom as pedagogy" thus still serves a regulatory function,
but is characterized by positive rather than negative reinforcement.
What Hills does not address in depth are the ways in which pathological
representations or the valorization of particular types of fans might be
used as part of this "instruction." Just as Jensen claims modernity was
perceived as bringing "technological progress but social, cultural, and
moral decay,"[18] the convergence culture industry is perceived as technological progress that has decayed the boundaries between fans and
audiences, and the boundaries between industry and fandom. Fandom
may be presented more pedagogically than pathologically, but these
discursive and representational depictions of the "fan" still function to
delimit which fans and fan practices are acceptable within the convergence culture industry.

Over two decades after Jensen's essay was written, the issue is no
longer that "there is very little literature that explores fandom as a
normal, everyday cultural or social phenomenon."[19] On the contrary,
contemporary work on media fandom must acknowledge that "fan audiences are wooed and championed by culture industries, at least as long
as their activities do not divert from principles of capitalist exchange
and recognize industries' legal ownership of the object of fandom."[20]
The massive caveat that these scholars present is deeply gendered, and
is a vital refrain that both underpins the analysis of journalistic depictions and media representations of fans in the next section and echoes
through the subsequent chapters of this book. Because representation
plays a key role in determining which segments of fan culture become
more visible and, theoretically, less stigmatized, I will briefly engage

representational trends in the depiction of fanboys and fangirls in media texts before moving on to consider the gendered revaluation of the fan within the popular press.

Fan Representations

Media representations have long functioned as a primary site in which to reflect on the cultural positioning of the fan at various moments in history, and depictions of fans within the convergence culture industry affirm that the "mainstreaming of the geek runs apace differently for fanboys and fangirls."[21] Media representations of fans continue to serve a disciplinary function by narratively constructing "'acceptable' fan activity [. . .] by building critiques of unruly fans into the text,"[22] but they also increasingly work to valorize and validate the types of fan identities that the convergence culture industry is keen to standardize. Perhaps unsurprisingly, those fans who continue to be the most diegetically disciplined, or who are refused representation as fans entirely, are women. Rather than rehashing the abundance of scholarly work on fan representations,[23] I would like to focus briefly on several representational trends before turning my attention to the ways in which fan demographics have moved from being situated as "empowered" to being characterized as "entitled" within the convergence culture industry.

Alongside journalists' construction of the fanboy as demographic tastemaker, the convergence culture industry's "rebranding cool onto a traditionally nerdy persona"[24] was seen across media platforms over the past decade. Though many of the old pathologies persisted, this spike in fanboy characters has afforded a broader representational range of fannish identities. The fanboy has been routinely refashioned as a romantic hero or an (often reluctant) action hero or superhero, and these representational trends have unquestionably aided the fanboy's recuperation into hegemonic masculinity. At the very least, they affirm Lori Kendall's claim that the representations of nerds (and fanboys by extension) tend to simultaneously challenge and reinforce hegemonic masculinity, as the archetype's liminality "includes aspects of both hypermasculinity (intellect, rejection of sartorial display, lack of 'feminine' social and relational skills) and feminization (lack of sports ability, small body size, lack of sexual relationships with women)."[25] Shifts in fanboy characterization during this period typically fall into one of two broad "unexpected hero" categories that are mutually designed to exploit the fanboy archetype's emotional and physical liminality: the first revalues the fanboy as romantic hero, either as the affable/unexpected lead of a romantic comedy or the romantic foil within sitcoms and teen dramas.[26] The reformulation of the fanboy as a romantic hero often indulges in pejorative depictions even as he is presented as a desirable romantic partner, constructing his liminality as an integral part of his romantic appeal. Though these narratives frequently function as romantic coming-of-age stories in which the fanboy's eventual willingness to abandon the objects of his youth/fandom is rewarded with heterosexual coupling, the fanboy's affective relationship with geeky media properties is also presented as an intrinsic part of his charm. In all of these cases, the character's fannish obsessions are aligned with an affectionate disposition and intense devotion (both towards the objects of his fandom and the object of his affection), even as it is presented as an obstacle to heteronormative coupling that must be overcome.

A second notable representational trend is the reconfiguration of the fanboy as an unlikely action hero or superhero. This character archetype frequently plays on the nerd's liminal positioning between man and machine,[27] which has only grown more prominent since the 1980s as computer usage has become an integral component of our daily work and play. Here, the fanboy's potentially "failed" masculinity is buttressed by his (apparently biologically determined) prowess with video games, computers, and digital technologies. Alternately, these representations self-reflexively deploy the fanboy's knowledge of geek culture, not merely endorsing but openly situating affirmational fandom as his primary strength or superpower.[28] The differences in both volume and tone between fanboy and fangirl characters during this period are important, not just in their ability to reinforce or dismantle pathologized portraits of fans but as a cultural barometer of the relative power of each within the convergence culture industry.

Just as fangirls have been obscured as a segment of the "fanboy" demographic, representations of fangirls within popular media texts have been comparatively scarce, reflecting that no matter "how much the status of the nerd has changed in recent decades, being a nerd is a social identity that shuts out many girls."[29] In order to consider how women continue to be representationally denied fan identities within the convergence culture industry, it seems fitting to briefly examine the most popular and iconic media text within this representational trend, the CBS sitcom *The Big Bang Theory* (2007–present). Sitcoms have historically and generically generated humor from cultural stereotypes,[30] and *The Big Bang Theory* is no exception with regard to its representation of fans and nerds. The four male protagonists, experimental physicist Leonard (Johnny Galecki), theoretical physicist Sheldon (Jim Parsons), aerospace engineer Howard (Simon Helberg), and astrophysicist Raj (Kunal Nayyar), are all presented as unabashed fanboys, and jokes and plotlines routinely revolve around the group's collective obsession with comic books, video games, and science fiction/fantasy media properties. As fans, they are predominantly presented as affirmational fans, avid consumers and collectors rather than producers of their own fan texts (with the exception of Sheldon's little-watched informational web series "Fun with Flags").

The Big Bang Theory is not notable for breaking down or meaningfully challenging pathologized representations of fans. On the contrary, it routinely mines these enduring stereotypes for laughs. Rather, its significance is grounded in the fact that it populates its entire cast of characters with character archetypes that would conventionally be relegated to supporting comic relief, and for its dual address that allows the audience to simultaneously laugh at the shows' nerdy protagonists and laugh with them . . . provided the audience is conversant enough in scientific jargon and fannish references to get the joke. While *The Big Bang Theory* for the most part offers a lovingly comedic depiction of affirmational male fans and their practices, the plotlines of the show's female characters (Sheldon and Leonard's attractive blonde neighbor, Penny [Kaley Cuoco], and the later additions of microbiologist Bernadette Rostenkowski [Melissa Rauch] and neurobiologist Amy Farrah Fowler [Dr. Mayim Bialik] as love interests in season 3) routinely focus on their inability or unwillingness to understand the appeal of comic books, video games, cult movies, and the fan culture surrounding them. One of the series' most recurring and also most revealing jokes features the women (or any female character, for that matter) walking into the local comic book shop repeatedly depicted in the series, only to be confronted with the male gaze of the store's universally white, male inhabitants, who stand slack-jawed in their presence as the laugh track howls. Though the depictions of male comic book shop customers unquestionably conform to the basest of fanboy stereotypes (bespectacled, gangly, or overweight, and so on), the women are clearly portrayed as out of place not because of their mutual lack of interest in comics but rather simply because they are women. Penny, in particular, is consistently presented as being perplexed by the fannish references the show spouts, and is accordingly positioned to provide a point of identification for a mass audience more inclined to laugh at, rather than with, the male characters' discussions of fannish minutiae.

The introduction of two female characters with careers in STEM (science, technology, engineering, and math) is significant, both because the growing presence of these female characters offered a more gender-balanced cast and because it potentially mitigated early (and wholly justifiable) critiques about *The Big Bang Theory*'s latent misogyny. However, even episodes that are narratively designed to expose such gender bias, such as "The Contractual Obligation Implementation" (season 6, episode 19), in which the male protagonists are tasked by the university they work for to speak to a class of young women about careers in STEM, present a conflicted message. After failing to relate to the young women or drum up any interest in pursuing STEM fields, the men place a phone call to Amy and Bernadette, who can speak directly to being female scientists. Though this scene powerfully comments on white male privilege generally, and the geek culture gaffe of inviting only men to speak on a "women in comics" panel specifically,[31] it is undercut by the visual gag of Amy and Bernadette offering advice on STEM careers while dressed in full princess regalia at Disneyland. As Amy laments the need for more female scientists, and the fact that "from a young age, we girls are encouraged to care more about how we look than about the power of our minds," she carefully applies her lipstick and admires her reflection to the riotous laugh track.

Even with the current fixation on fanboys as a popular character archetype, women tend to be cast time and again as "Princess Nakeds" and "Dr. Girlfriends" (albeit with actual doctorates in this case), "either cast as objects of nerd desire or, if they are depicted as fans, often derided as obsessive, silly, and loveless."[32] One need not look further than the show's earliest promotional image of Leonard and Sheldon standing beside an equation-packed blackboard, staring furtively at Penny, who has apparently rubbed a portion of the board off with her breasts and hips, to see which imagined "geek" audience was initially being targeted by this "Smart is the new sexy" ad campaign. Astutely noting that *The Big Bang Theory* must be understood as a mass show masquerading as a niche show, and not the reverse, Heather Hendershot questioned why CBS "pretended to target a geek demographic, when it was really looking for lads all along."[33] Though Hendershot exposes who this recent wave of "nerd-friendly" programming is really targeting, persistently short-changing fangirl viewers or pointedly ignoring them, she fails to fully recognize how interchangeable these "geek" and "lad" demographics have become within the convergence culture industry. *The Big Bang Theory*, not unlike the convergence culture industry it emerged from, thus can be viewed as attempting to navigate its tenuous relationship to fan culture, alternately celebrating and mocking it but always privileging affirmational over transformative fan practices and demarcating fan culture as a decidedly masculine preserve. Even at their most pathologized, fanboy representations still exert their privilege.

A survey of the limited array of fangirl characters in mainstream media reveals that these representations tend to frame the character's fannish affect as a barrier to her "having it all," professionally or personally.[34] This is perhaps a variant of the deeply heteronormative reassessment of fanboys as romantic heroes, but in the fangirl's case this affect is less a part of her appeal than endemic to her inability to couple or procreate. Alternately, these representations mock and attempt to contain the fangirl's perceived emotional "excess," falling back on the most pervasive of fan pathologies in the process. In these constructions, the fangirl is presented as unwilling or unable to distinguish between fantasy and reality, to her social and/or romantic detriment.[35] Becky Rosen (Emily Perkins), of the CW series *Supernatural* (2005–present), is perhaps the most noteworthy and controversial fangirl character of this period, and has disproportionately been the focus of scholarly work on gendered fan representations.[36]

Although she only appears in a handful of episodes of the cult series, the degree of scrutiny that Becky has received, from both fans and fan scholars alike, reflects the burden of representation she carries as well as the unique cultural stakes for fangirl characters in this cultural moment.

This burden of representation is exacerbated by the fact that *Supernatural* has a fraught history of developing character proxies to represent the show's (actual and desired) fan base and of designing self-reflexive episodes to comment on fans and fandom, which in turn reveal a great deal about the gendered valuation of fans within the convergence culture industry. Composed as loving "winks" to knowing fans, they nonetheless function predominantly as an effort to representationally shame certain types of fans and celebrate others. Addressing one of these episodes, in which Becky lures the show's male protagonists to a fan convention for a book series based on their real-life demon-hunting exploits, Catherine Tosenberger puts it best and most bluntly:

> Many [*Supernatural*] fans found it telling that in the episode where fans get to be heroes, it is only the male fans who do so—in utter defiance of the fact that the majority of fans who attend *Supernatural* conventions are women. Becky, the [slash]-writing fangirl, is still presented as deviant and excessive—and, unlike the male fans, Becky is never allowed to be heroic. She is rewarded not with humanization and valorization of her fannishness, but instead with [a writer proxy character's] sexual attentions. Her access to heroism is confined to sex with a heroic man. The message of [the episode "The Real Ghostbusters"] appears to be: fanboys, keep on keeping on—you are dorky but lovable. Female fans, you are creepy, but you might be willing to fuck us real writers, so you aren't *totally* unacceptable.[37]

This may seem overly critical, but it powerfully speaks to the burden of representation that accompanies the comparatively limited array of "fangirl" characters circulating within the convergence culture industry. In either case, whereas the fanboy's incorporation into hegemonic masculinity (however partial or conditional) is routinely framed as empowering or bestowing privilege to a historically "oppressed" archetype, fangirls continue to be defined by/through their relationship to men. Considering the degree to which first wave fan scholars strove to recuperate pathologized representations of fans, it is vital to revive discussions of the continued significance of these representations as fan culture is mainstreamed, particularly as it pertains to the convergence culture industry's purported "empowerment" of fans, and which fans are potentially disavowed in the process.

Building a Power Demographic

As the above analysis makes clear, fanboys may not have fully shed the social stigmas that plagued them long before (and well after) William Shatner publicly told them to "Get a Life." However, the convergence culture industry's revaluation of fanboys certainly affords them a greater degree of power and visibility than their female counterparts. Between 2005 and 2017, the popular press guided and promoted the recuperation of the fan through innumerable articles that both celebrated and attempted to unpack this demographic "revenge of the nerds." When one surveys how discursive representations of the fan within the popular press evolved over this period, three distinct "waves" emerge. Articles composed between 2005 and 2007 tend to focus on the ascent and empowerment of fanboys as demographic tastemakers. Between 2008 and 2014, articles began to grapple with the "mainstreaming" of geek culture and the impact of the fanboy's emergent cultural capital. This is also, importantly, the period in which women are first "discovered" (or acknowledged, however tenuously) as a part of this demographic. The timing is not coincidental, and more often than not explicitly or implicitly conflates the mainstreaming of geek culture with the supposed "invasion" of female fans rather than treating them as a preexisting fan demographic. Articles after 2014 express growing concern about increasingly "entitled" or "toxic" fan communities.

In September 2005, *Time* magazine published an article predicting that "The Geek Shall Inherit the Earth." Noting that the "economic hegemony of the geek in the 1990s, when high tech and the Internet were driving the economy, has somehow been converted into a cultural hegemony," the article cited an array of pop culture evidence that what was once considered "hopelessly geeky—video games, fantasy novels, science fiction, superheroes—has now, somehow, become cool."[38] A wave of articles followed in a similar vein and, whether he was classified as a "nerd," "geek," or "fanboy" (cultural constructions with discrete etymological origins whose terminological borders have been increasingly muddied by journalists over the past decade), by 2007 the fanboy had been solidified as "one of the most powerful taste-makers in Hollywood."[39] *Entertainment Weekly*'s year-end issue proclaimed that 2007 was "The Year the Geek Was King" and *Time*'s 2005 prediction came to full journalistic fruition: "Let there be no doubt: in 2007, from Shia LeBouf in *Transformers* to the sellout crowds at San Diego Comic-Con, the geeks inherited the earth."[40]

Despite all the hype, there was little that was "new" about this new power demographic, only a confirmation of the industry's enduring investment in young men. The discursive construction of a distinct "fanboy demographic" was also deployed to rationalize various Hollywood production trends, from hyperserialized and densely mythologized cult television programs to the onslaught of cinematic and televisual adaptations of superhero comic books. Fangirls were notably not counted among the geeks inheriting the earth, with *Time* likening the industry's recent "discovery" of the fanboy as "a prime demographic to be marketed to" to the "way it discovered teenage girls after *Titanic*."[41] This 2007 article, tellingly titled "Boys Who Like Toys," parenthetically acknowledged that "there are some fangirls," but exclusively addressed fanboys as a desirable demographic, and discussed the influence of "fanboy deities" like *Ain't It Cool News* blogger Harry Knowles and writer/director Kevin Smith.

As the articles of this first wave speculated about the financial viability of the so-called fanboy effect, they failed to acknowledge the fangirls who were central to that demographic's box office and ratings success stories. For example, after it was revealed that women comprised 48 percent of the opening weekend audience for *The Dark Knight* (2008), and thus accounted for nearly half of the superhero film's record-breaking box-office returns, the articles that emerged did not recognize that fangirls were always already part of the fanboy demographic. Rather, they framed *The Dark Knight*'s large female audience as an anomaly and attempted to decipher the film's appeal for women. The film's executive producer, Thomas Tull, cited the "female appeal" of stars Christian Bale and Heath Ledger.[42] Some journalists simply wrote off the large female audience as a manifestation of "rubberneck curiosity" to see Ledger's posthumous appearance as the Joker.[43] The notion that fangirls had long circulated around the Batman franchise was never broached as a potential explanation for the film's success. This gendered genre stratification endures, perpetuating the longstanding and fallacious belief that girls simply are not interested in science fiction, fantasy, and superheroes. When fangirls are invoked as a potential market force, it is almost exclusively through properties that exist squarely within the generic "pink ghetto"[44] of romance melodrama and romantic comedy.

In 2008, "fanboy" was officially canonized in the Merriam-Webster dictionary as "a boy who is an enthusiastic devotee (as of comics or movies)." This depathologized definition speaks to both the growing cultural capital of the fanboy and a normalization of fan identities more generally. In yet another case of women being written out of the history of the ascendance of fan power within the convergence culture industry, there was no corresponding dictionary entry for "fangirl." The year 2008 also signaled a discursive shift, in which journalists began to debate the implications of the fanboy's growing cultural influence and demographic might. In an article for *Wired* magazine detailing the commodification of nerd culture and the male geek's rise to power, Scott Brown arrived at a common conclusion: "We're not attacking the Death Star. We *are* the Death Star."[45] Brown's comment succinctly (and geekily) cuts to the heart of the conflicted space the fanboy has come to occupy within the convergence culture industry, demographically empowered while still depicted as a bastion of "failed" masculinity, outsiders struggling with their newfound "insider" status.

How these dichotomous conceptions of the fanboy and the new hegemonic (masculinity of) fandom it generates work to foster misogyny and gendered boundary-policing practices within fan culture will be addressed in more detail in the following chapter. For now, it is significant to note that articles of this period routinely narrativized the mainstreaming (or mourned the death) of "authentic" fan identities and the growing presence of women within geek culture in parallel. Thus, while the titles of many of these articles present an aura of inclusion, such as "We're All Nerds Now,"[46] they continued to depict a starkly gendered conception of fan culture. A 2009 *Esquire* article, "Beyond Comic-Con: The Rise of the Modern Geek in All of Us," offers a textbook example: moving from a "we're all geeks now" disclaimer to a legitimization of fan culture through its connection to "quality" texts such as *Breaking Bad* and *Mad Men*, before eventually arriving at the inevitable (and inevitably stereotypical) conclusion, namely, that the mainstreaming of geek culture will "also bring that long-missing component that old-school, hard-line geeks probably never thought they'd encounter in their bailiwick: women."[47] Perhaps unsurprisingly, because the vast majority of the articles surveyed from this period were written by men, women are typically either written out of the history of fan culture or characterized/sexualized as interlopers.

Some articles of this period more generally conflate access to fan and geek culture with an inherent loss of subcultural capital. In 2010, comedian and celebrity fanboy Patton Oswalt composed a manifesto of sorts for *Wired* magazine, titled "Wake Up, Geek Culture: Time to Die," complete with images of Oswalt staggering through a postapocalyptic landscape, his survivalist backpack stuffed with old Monty Python action figures and Atari cartridges. Lamenting the mainstreaming of geek culture, in which "everyone considers themselves otaku [fannish] about something,"[48] Oswalt contended that digital culture has made fandom, and the cult objects it circulates around, ubiquitous and immediately available, resulting in a generation of "weak" fans.[49] Some journalists within this period began to question the longevity of the fanboy's influence, pondering why media industries would cater to the "vocal minority" of fanboys, particularly when they could be counted on to economically support geek media properties regardless of their critiques.[50]

More, however, fixed their attention on female fans as those rendering geek culture "weak," citing the invasion of properties like *Twilight* and *Glee* (both marked by adolescent female fan bases) as key signifiers of "How the Nerds Lost Comic-Con."[51] A 2017 *Vanity Fair* article claiming that fans have finally "won the war for Comic-Con" shows just how powerfully entrenched this narrative has become, suggesting that "since *Twilight* invaded in 2008, the San Diego Comic-Con fandom has been exploited and overrun by the slick, glossy marketing machines of studios."[52] Never mind that *Twilight* was distributed by Summit Entertainment, which at the time was an independent production company. Never mind that SDCC had become a promotional behemoth catering to corporate interests well before 2008. Articles such as this one, however unwittingly, do not simply reify but validate the gendered genre bias of the fanboys who openly protested the presence of *Twilight* fangirls at SDCC 2009, holding posters with slogans such as "Twilight ruined comic-con" and "Vampires don't sparkle, they burn."[53] Given that these articles are marked by snide comments that the attendees who "wait in line forever to see the bigger exclusives like *The Walking Dead* [. . .] aren't going to, say, a panel discussing gender, masculinity, and femininity,"[54] the "real" and "die-hard" fans described in all of these articles are male by default.

Articles that actively attempted to celebrate female fans more often than not supported this default androcentric construction of fan identity. Responding to the pervasive view that women need to be lured (or dragged, in the case of "Dr. Girlfriend") to SDCC, the *Los Angeles Times* published "The Girls' Guide to Comic-Con 2009,"[55] featuring a collection of blurbs from online journalists. Claiming that SDCC was "not just for nerdy guys anymore" but rather a "smorgasbord for female fandemonium," the article was supposedly focused on how SDCC is "doing right" by its female attendees, but the way it defined "doing right" was, at best, bound up in regressive gender norms and, at worst, perpetuated pathologized portraits of fangirls. Of the countless male celebrities the article cited as incentives for women to attend SDCC 2009, the regressive and condescending discourse surrounding *Prince of Persia*'s Jake Gyllenhaal ("Women will be rushing the stage, offering to do [his] laundry on those washboard abs") and Benicio Del Toro (promoting his turn as *The Wolfman*, a man who "can sympathize with your monthly curse") were particularly vile, and failed to acknowledge that fanboys engage in similar star worship at SDCC.

Though the titles of these articles covering fangirls as their own distinct demographic were unquestionably celebratory, they also tended to position women as an unexpected, rather than preexisting, fan demographic, emphasizing novelty or anthropological discovery, such as "Introducing the New Face of Fandom: Women."[56] They also almost wholly focused on the surprising financial success of female-driven media properties like *Sex and the City* (2008) or *Bridesmaids* (2011), rather than female fans' ongoing contribution to superhero blockbuster box-office totals or cult television ratings. Articles such as 2014's "The Rise of Fangirls at Comic-Con"[57] unwittingly expose the cognitive dissonance inherent in much of this reporting: male interviewees insisted that, until recently, "men vastly outnumbered women" in fan culture spaces like conventions, while female interviewees pushed back on the "boys' club" logics of these comments, arguing, "It's not that [women are] suddenly here. It's that they're suddenly more visible."[58]

Some outlets did make a concerted effort to speak back to depictions of fan culture as an overwhelmingly male preserve and to explain female-dominated fan practices. In a 2012 multipage spread, *Entertainment Weekly* invited its more general fannish readership to "Meet the Shippers," the "increasingly influential subset of TV fandom fixated on romantic relationships (hence the name 'shippers'), or the potential for romance, between characters."[59] *Entertainment Weekly* situated these female fans as "a minority voice—but an important one," given their outspoken engagement with media objects and creators. Some of the showrunners interviewed for the piece framed the attention as flattering, but others framed female shippers as "'the dim nasties'—who resent [showrunners] for doing [their] job: sustaining the very chemistry that hooks shippers."[60] Though the article certainly pokes fun at "the wacky, weird world of shipping,"[61] it is a fairly unprecedented example of female fannish reading practices being historicized, theorized, and taken seriously by a mainstream media outlet.

The convergence culture industry's investment in the fanboy demographic has yet to show any signs of waning, despite the growing acknowledgment of female fans. One noteworthy piece of evidence that the industry has long-term plans to keep investing in the fanboy demographic was the Walt Disney Company's acquisition of Marvel Entertainment Inc. for $4 billion in August 2009. Disney was openly banking on Spider-Man and Iron Man to develop the company's next generation of fanboy consumers and counterbalance the success of Disney princesses and fairies with young women,[62] and an *Adweek* analysis noted that Disney's acquisition of Marvel could result in more female comic book movie fans, as "Disney is an expert at attracting young women to titles they may not normally be interested in."[63] This quotation is telling, in large part because it frames fangirls exclusively as a "surplus audience" who "might provide supplementary income" but are otherwise "considered irrelevant" (or, worse yet, are seen as a "nuisance" if "these 'undesired' segments overwhelm the core demographic").[64] While Disney's ever-expanding Marvel Cinematic Universe has made some explicit overtures to its massive female fan base, such as the short-lived ABC series *Agent Carter* (2015–2016), female fans have begun to actively demand representational gender parity in superhero franchise slates, most notably through the June 2015 organization of flashmobs at Disney stores and #wewantwidow hashtag activism on social media to demand a stand-alone film for Black Widow.[65] However, if *Wonder Woman*'s lengthy tenure in development hell is any indication, a greater battle still looms to bring superheroine characters to the screen, to say nothing of the underlying industrial paucity of women crafting these fancentric franchises.

From Empowerment to Entitlement

Articles grappling with the ramifications of the fan's newfound privilege began emerging as early as 2008, and by 2015, sparked by numerous incidents in which fan "activism" and "criticism" manifested in virulent social media attacks or organized harassment campaigns, they noticeably shifted in tone. As one journalist noted in response to fan efforts to shut down movie review aggregator *Rotten Tomatoes* in the wake of negative reviews of *Suicide Squad*, "modern-day fans have a tendency to form a threatening swarm and override the comments section with their angry buzzing."[66] By 2014, the discursive and demographic revenge of the fanboy came full circle, with a *New Statesman* manifesto on the issue of "Nerd Entitlement." As author Laurie Penny noted,

> Two generations of boys who grew up at the lower end of the violent hierarchy of toxic masculinity [. . .] have reached adulthood and found the polarity reversed. Suddenly they're the ones with the power and the social status. [. . .] But shy, nerdy women have to try to pull themselves out of that same horror into a world that hates, fears and resents them because they are women.[67]

Though this was not the first attempt to raise awareness about the misogynistic byproducts of the fanboy's newfound privilege, it instigated a new wave of similar think pieces about the feedback loop between strains of sexism within geek culture and this emergent "fan entitlement."[68] The narrowly conceived discursive and representational constructions of "you people" documented in this chapter has both entrenched the power and privilege of male fans and exacerbated their sense of ownership over fan identities and culture. The following chapter explores some of the effects of these intersections among fanboy privilege, toxic masculinity, and gendered boundary-policing practices within contemporary fan culture through the threat of the "fake geek girl." In order to parse how minority fans are paradoxically disempowered and positioned as "entitled" within this cycle by those who are legitimately empowered by the convergence culture industry, I want to close with a discussion about a series of 2016 blog posts on the topic of "fan entitlement."

On May 30, 2016, a *Birth.Movies.Death.* blog post by Devin Faraci titled "Fandom Is Broken" gained traction on social media and immediately provoked an array of response posts. Faraci's thesis began with a simple, and yet incredibly loaded and definitively gendered, question: "What if Annie Wilkes had the internet?"[69] Faraci's primary critique was that social media's creation of an "ever thinner" wall separating creators and fans, and fans' audacious desires to "try to shape [content]" through their criticisms, has produced "some kind of a chamber of screams, where [fans] can and do voice their immediate and often personal displeasure directly and horribly." Many of Faraci's examples of entitled and aggressive fans were male, but because he invoked the deranged fan-girl protagonist of Stephen King's *Misery* from the outset, his critique of fan entitlement was inextricably linked to feminized fan "excess." What was even more disturbing was Faraci's conflation of fan activist efforts for more representational diversity (like *Frozen* fandom's #GiveElsaA-Girlfriend campaign) with creator death threats and the "uglier parts of fandom—the entitlement, the demands, the frankly poor understanding of how drama and storytelling work." This deeply problematic equation of toxic fan practices and broader social justice efforts within fandom persists in 2018, with articles featuring titles like "Internet Fandom Is Running Hollywood" claiming that creative tendencies towards "fan service" have made fan collectives "become more demanding, more critical, and, most of all, more entitled."[70] When articles like these deploy their narrative that "[f]ans control it all. The inmates are running the asylum," they both dramatically overstate the producorial power of fans within the convergence culture industry and dangerously collapse all forms of fannish criticism into one undifferentiated mass that does not adequately consider where these criticisms might be stemming from.

Somewhat ironically, Faraci suggests that the ultimate culprit for this ascendant "ugliness" is the fact that our corporatized, fan franchise-oriented mediascape "has led fans—already having a hard time understanding the idea of an artist's vision—to assume almost total ownership of the stuff they love." As the chapters that follow will suggest, if any demographic has been given a sense of ownership over contemporary fancentric media properties, it is young, white, straight men. And yet, though Faraci is careful to not affix identity markers to the "entitled fans" at the crux of his argument, the bulk of his piece is spent critiquing the practices most associated with fangirls and fans of color in order to defend those who need the least defending: overwhelmingly white, straight, male media producers. Considering the resonances between misogyny in geek culture and our current political moment, it seems pertinent to note that several months after writing the "Fandom Is Broken" post, and in the wake of Donald Trump's now-infamous "grab them by the pussy" comment on *Access Hollywood*, Faraci resigned as the editor-in-chief of *Birth.Movies.Death.* amid similar sexual assault allegations that he apologized for and did not deny.[71] In light of these accusations, Faraci's equation of forms of fan "entitlement" that manifests in the harassment of minority fans, actors, and content producers with the longstanding fan traditions of queering characters and related campaigns to diversify media content is doubly concerning. In his nostalgic lamentation of the good old days, in which the fourth wall was firmly in place and fans knew their place, Faraci perhaps unwittingly aligns himself with the those who would "Make Fandom Great Again" primarily by silencing those voices they have historically not been taught to value. By implicitly aligning fan entitlement with pejorative dismissals of the unreasonable demands of "SJWs," Faraci only exacerbates the sense of entitlement held by some male fans that is ultimately more damaging to fan culture.

Keeping this in mind, we might also consider another high-profile instance of "toxic" and "entitled" fandom, the *Rick and Morty* (2013–present) McDonald's Szechuan Sauce debacle of 2017, to consider how the tendency to flatten an array of "toxic" or "entitled" fan behaviors disproportionately impacts minority fans and creators. After a joke in the season 3 premiere about Rick's deep affection for the dipping sauce, which had originally been produced as a cross-promotion for Disney's *Mulan* (1998) and subsequently discontinued, fans of the show flooded McDonald's social media accounts demanding its return. Not one to pass up the opportunity for a PR stunt, McDonald's agreed to stock the sauce in limited locations for one day only, October 7, 2017. Without belaboring the details, McDonald's radically underestimated demand and distributed only twenty packets. After being turned away empty-handed, *Rick and Morty* fans took their anger out on McDonald's corporate phone lines and social media accounts, as well as in person at various stores, ultimately prompting a more widespread relaunch of the sauce in February 2018. The incident was repeatedly held up by journalists and bloggers as a prime example of how *Rick and Morty* fandom (and fan culture more generally) has grown "entitled" and "toxic,"[72] but it also virally overshadowed and distracted from other, far more insidious instances of toxic masculinity that were taking place simultaneously within the *Rick and Morty* fandom. Specifically, the addition of four women to the heretofore all-male writing staff for season 3 (thereby creating a gender-balanced writers' room) was met with a sustained campaign of harassment by some fanboys.[73]

Two of the myriad responses to Faraci's piece, Charles Pulliam-Moore's "Fandom Isn't 'Broken'—It's Just Not Only for White Dudes Anymore" and Aja Romano's "About Our 'Broken' Fan Culture," neatly encapsulate the responses of marginalized fan collectives to Faraci's claims and their frustration with the broader fan-cultural moment it emerged from. Pulliam-Moore dismisses fandom's "newfound brokenness" as a fundamental misunderstanding by a white, male fan of "what fandom is like on the internet and women, people of color, and queer-identified people."[74] Indeed, the only "new" element in play, according to Pulliam-Moore, is that "the pointed anger is being directed at white men."[75] Contra Pulliam-Moore's claim, fans expressing their frustration with television showrunners (who statistically have been and continue to be white men) is nothing new. What is nascent is pushback against a cultural construction of the industrially "valued" fans, and the clear sense of entitlement *they* carry. In some sense, Pulliam-Moore's comment seems aimed more at Faraci and other fanboys who work to silence or dismiss fans and fan practices that do not mirror their own than at the white, male content creators Faraci was perceived to be defending. Even the title of Pulliam-Moore's piece is telling: though the article acknowledges that fandom has always been a diverse space, the power of the fallacious claim that fandom is "only for white dudes," the distinctly raced and gendered construction of fans, is still present.

Romano, like Pulliam-Moore, engages the problematic "false comparisons between different corners of the fandom political spectrum" at the heart of Faraci's article, correctly noting that "the loudness of what Faraci calls a 'chamber of screams' is, in the case of fans who have had to fight for representation, at least proportionate to the level of yelling members of marginalized groups have had to do throughout history in order to be heard to begin with."[76] Exhaustively documenting years of Faraci's "cavalierly and unilaterally dismissive" tweets and blog posts aimed primarily at transformative fanworks (and, thus, she pointedly notes, aimed squarely at fangirls), Romano powerfully contends that "Faraci is threatened by the whole concept of fan ownership—and he explicitly seems to be most troubled by female fan ownership."[77] In exposing the paradoxically proprietary nature of contemporary fan culture, in which Faraci can simultaneously decry fan entitlement while advocating for "other fans to want the same things from texts that he wants himself—the ultimate mark of fan entitlement," Romano fails to address how think pieces like Faraci's are the culmination of a decade of fanboys being told that their way *is* the way, that they *are* the class of fans the industry is invested in appeasing. Romano closes her response by suggesting that it is "[n]o wonder Devin Faraci finds this new trend of fan empowerment terrifying: his own voice has never been more inconsequential."[78] The following chapter forcefully counters Romano's claim, suggesting that the white fanboy's voice not only still holds a considerable amount of power but is also routinely being deployed to further marginalize and silence female fans. If fandom is broken due to a growing sense of fan entitlement, it is not the relationship between fans and creators that is an issue, as Faraci suggests, but rather the relationship between fans and other fans.

It is not a coincidence that rising concerns about fan entitlement emerged in tandem with the 2016 presidential election and subsequently provoked a wave of calls to "Make Fandom Fun Again." Like many of the think pieces that interchangeably discuss activism by marginalized fan communities and examples of white toxic masculinity within contemporary fan culture as examples of "entitled" fans, with no consideration as to which of these fans benefit from the privilege of their real-world identities or their status within the convergence culture industry, the call to "Make Fandom Fun Again" is a perspective born out of privilege. Echoing the anxieties about postfeminism documented in chapter 1, in which feminist fan scholars might be painted as "feminist killjoys" for not taking a more expansive view of the field, this directive to "Make Fandom Fun Again" quickly and conveniently labels anyone who critiques sexism, racism, xenophobia, or homophobia within the community a "fandom killjoy." Sara Ahmed has suggested that the feminist killjoy is a figure who "kills joy because of what she claims exists," namely, structural inequalities,[79] and fandom killjoys are likewise those who dare to acknowledge all that is "un-fun" about fandom for people of color, women, and queer people. As Zina Hutton notes, because these conversations intimate that "the main thing that makes fandom 'un-fun' is other people being critical of it in any way," even the most warranted or tame critiques from marginalized fans can result in being told, in essence, that "you're not fun. . . . And you apparently don't deserve to have any fun in fandom as a result."[80] It is this vicious cycle we turn to in the next chapter, opening up the conversation about who fandom is more or less fun for that "Make Fandom Fun Again" arguments explicitly attempt to derail. Just as it is unsurprising that "those who do not come up against walls experience those who talk about walls as wall makers,"[81] it is unsurprising that those attempting to build walls and police the perimeters of "authentic" fan culture are the same fans who sit at the center of the convergence culture industry's narrative about the fan's demographic empowerment. Accordingly, we now move from the feminist fangirl killjoy as a scapegoat for the behaviors of legitimately "entitled" and privileged fan identities to consider another gendered construct of the convergence culture industry designed to shore up fanboy privilege: the fake geek girl.

3

Interrogating the Fake Geek Girl

The Spreadable Misogyny of Contemporary Fan Culture

Building on the prior chapter's discussion of how fans have been discursively and representationally incorporated into hegemonic masculinity, this chapter delves into the way the convergence culture industry's androcentric construction of the fan is internalized and manifests in gendered boundary-policing practices within fan culture. The subsequent chapter will address the convergence culture industry's systemic bias against fangirls' preferred modes of engagement, which functions as its own form of gendered boundary policing. This chapter takes a more holistic approach, focusing on how inter- and intra-fannish policing practices do not merely work to position some fans as "good" or "bad" but also work to deny access to the identity of "fan" writ large. By homing in on the "idiot nerd girl" meme that emerged in 2011, and situating this meme within broader "fake geek girl" discourses that grew in volume and scale in 2012, I have two primary goals. First, I would like to consider how longstanding gender biases within digital geek culture have cultivated an understanding of fan culture as a masculine sphere in which women are always already "interlopers." While there is a growing body of scholarly work on digital technologies and toxic masculinity, these works are too rarely deployed by fan scholars in an effort to historicize and theorize contemporary fan gatekeeping practices. A second, related goal is to begin theorizing what I am calling "spreadable misogyny" within geek culture, and female fans' transformative responses to it.

When one examines a subcultural straw (wo)man like the "fake geek girl," there is too often an ahistorical tendency to treat these categories as emergent, rather than sufficiently acknowledging how deeply embedded gendered gatekeeping practices have always been within fan culture. Indeed, the past five years have produced an abundance of think pieces attempting to do just that, ranging from efforts to dispel the pernicious label of "fakeness"[1] to those suggesting that Wolverine of the *X-Men* comics is the fictional face of toxic masculinity within contemporary nerd culture.[2] It would likewise be easy to claim that spreadable misogyny is a byproduct of the rise of social media, or to fall back on old and equally damaging stereotypes about the fanboy's frustrated, failed masculinity. Much as convergence culture emerged from a distinct and historically grounded intersection of technological, industrial, and cultural conditions, I would suggest that the growing visibility of gendered gatekeeping and spreadable misogyny within fan culture similarly emerges out of the intersection of the growth of toxic technocultures and the industrial privileging of a white, straight, cisgendered male conception of the fan. Over the past decade, the convergence culture industry's (limited and conditional) embrace of fan culture has cultivated a sense of entitlement among a particular subset of fans who were already feeling conflicted about the perceived mainstreaming of fan culture. These gendered gatekeeping practices and their proponents present a microcosmic glimpse into the contemporary "war on women," drawing on the logics of historical men's rights movements that formed in response to second wave feminism.

Toxic Masculinity and Digital Culture

Any discussion of gendered gatekeeping practices within contemporary fan culture must be situated within broader analyses of toxic technocultures. Indeed, it often feels as though very little has changed since the early days of Internet forums and MUDs (Multi-User Dungeons) documented in Lori Kendall's 2002 book *Hanging Out in the Virtual Pub: Masculinities and Relationships Online*. Kendall's digital ethnography of the online forum BlueSky continues to resonate, both as an early study of the performance of nerd masculinities in digital spaces, and the ways in which the "gendered social context" of these spaces more often than not "casts women as outsiders unless and until they prove themselves able to perform masculinities according to the social norms of the group."[3] The contemporary outcry over "fake geek girls" invading fan culture is rooted in similar cultural logics, requiring women to perform their competency in masculinized modes of fan engagement (textual mastery, collecting, trivia, etc.). Contra early cybertheorists' optimistic proclamations that the Internet would bring about more identity play and parity, Kendall's work makes it clear how digital spaces have, from their inception, been embedded with a gendered sense of who is embraced as an "authentic" participant, and who will need to prove they are not interlopers. Importantly, Kendall claims that once "gendered meanings permeate and inform" interactions within a particular digital space, thereby creating a set of gendered norms of participation that "conform to dominant masculinity standards,"[4] the effect of nondominant groups on those social norms will be minimal regardless of how much their membership increases. This chapter does engage some of the transformative interventions being made by female fans, and my own views on the "effect" of these nondominant groups is slightly more optimistic than Kendall's. Still, it is the foundational and fallacious perception that women have historically been and continue to be a "nondominant group" within geek and fan culture that is the larger issue.

Adrienne Massanari's 2015 examination of Reddit as a "toxic technoculture" functions in many ways as a spiritual successor to Kendall's work on BlueSky, and is similarly informed by long-term ethnographic study of, and participant-observation within, a particular digital community. Massanari's analysis, much like Kendall's, is born out of concern for the "ongoing backlash against women and their use of technology and participation in public life."[5] Where Massanari's work is especially productive for establishing a theory of spreadable misogyny within fan culture is her study's theoretical grounding in actor-network theory, or "the importance of considering how non-human technological agents (algorithms, scripts, policies) can shape and are shaped by human activity,"[6] as well as her emphasis on platform analysis. I will similarly consider how digital platforms shape fan participation in subsequent chapters, but for the purposes of the analysis that follows, it is Massanari's term "toxic technocultures," and its ongoing "entanglement with geek masculinity,"[7] that I wish to engage.

"Toxic masculinity" has become a common refrain among feminist scholars and cultural critics over the past decade, frequently deployed in conjunction with analyses of the emergent technocultural platforms that structurally cultivate it. In actuality, the term has decidedly analog roots in the Mythopoetic Men's Movement (MMM), which was founded in the 1980s in response to second wave feminism. Around the same time

Kendall was parsing the inherent contradictions in nerdy MUD participants' sexist attitudes and their claim to be "victims of masculinity"[8] in
the early to mid-1990s, male writers within the MMM were utilizing the
term "toxic masculinity" to describe the ways in which men and boys
were responding to a perceived "crisis" in masculinity. "Toxic masculinity" was subsequently deployed by male scholars and organizers within
the MMM to address a variety of sociocultural issues and anxieties ranging from the absence of fathers to "model masculinity" for adolescent
boys[9] to the "toxic hostility toward expressions of genuine masculinity."[10] Shepherd Bliss, one of the founders of the MMM and the man
often credited with coining (or at the very least, popularizing) the term
pointedly framed toxic masculinity as being harmful to both men and
women.[11] Unsurprisingly, however, most of the term's usage during this
period focused on the impact of toxic masculinity on men, rather than
being a way of characterizing how men might communally weaponize
this toxicity to target women.

Interestingly, the same conditions that allowed the fanboy to be incorporated into hegemonic masculinity also created the cultural conditions
for both the growth of toxic masculinity and men's activist movements
like the MMM. If the socioeconomic conditions of the 1980s produced
"an erosion of middle class males' traditional social and economic authority," creating "a pool of bewildered and 'threatened' males, men in
search of the certainties of traditional gender identities,"[12] these same
conditions, and particularly the growing integration of computers into
the dual realms of work and leisure, allowed for the "reconfiguration of
hegemonic masculinity to include aspects of the once subjugated masculine stereotype of the nerd."[13] What fundamentally binds these two
cultural narratives together, and sets the stage for contemporary gender
policing within geek and fan culture, is the "contradictory experiences
of power"[14] these circumstances produced.

Despite frequently embodying the identity markers associated with
hegemonic power (maleness, whiteness, straightness), fanboys have not
only historically been excluded from hegemonic masculinity but have
reclaimed and embraced that exclusion as a core component of their
fan identity. The mainstreaming of geek and fan culture has thus not
only produced contradictory experiences of power for those occupying
liminal masculine identities but has somewhat paradoxically provoked

further exclusion of those who cannot claim similar power, however contradictory. As Kendall concisely argues, this problematic positioning of "the nerd as an oppressed straight white male identity addresses critiques of white straight masculine authority without actually considering the plight of oppressed peoples directly."[15] Rebecca Wanzo, Rukmini Pande, and others have more recently forwarded a similar argument about fan studies' historical failure to engage race in its conception of (predominantly white) fans as culturally "Othered." Fans, geeks, and nerds have long claimed otherness, but never more forcefully than over the past decade as this otherness has been threatened by both the exponential growth of digital fan culture and the (admittedly limited and conditional) embrace of fan culture and the proliferation of cult media properties fans tend to orbit around within the convergence culture industry.

When one examines the growing pockets of toxic masculinity within fan culture, it is important to be mindful of Bliss's insistence that "masculinity is not, by itself, the problem to be fought against, but rather a specific construction of it, a construction shaped by a mold of patriarchy and privilege."[16] However forcefully men involved in the MMM might have *felt* the loss of power, this feeling of potential powerlessness does not eradicate the fact that they had and continue to have greater access to, and the ability to wield, hegemonic power. Fanboys engaged in gendered boundary-policing practices arguably fear the opposite, namely, that the influx of power that has accompanied the mainstreaming of fan culture might be doled out too arbitrarily to those who have not "earned" it. The reality is that their privilege as a consumer base is equally inherited and entrenched, and often remains unacknowledged in discussions of the newly "empowered" fan within the convergence culture industry.

Despite the fact that the MMM aligned itself philosophically with antisexist men's groups in the wake of second wave feminism, it has frequently been read as "an attempt to reaffirm and reinstate male power, and undermine the gains that have been made by feminism,"[17] and accordingly can be viewed as an early incarnation of "men's rights" activism. This is partially due to the desire to delineate between hegemonic and toxic masculinity, and to claim that the latter is not necessarily damaging. Many would justifiably contend that the terms "hegemonic" and "toxic" masculinity are deeply interrelated, if not explicitly interchangeable, or that hegemonic masculinity is ultimately more damaging precisely because of its subtler "common sense" logics. If we are to treat these as distinct, if interrelated, entities, Terry A. Kupers offers a useful definition:

> Toxic masculinity is constructed of those aspects of hegemonic masculinity that foster domination of others and are, thus, socially destructive. Unfortunate male proclivities associated with toxic masculinity include extreme competition and greed, insensitivity to or lack of consideration of the experiences and feelings of others, a strong need to dominate and control others, an incapacity to nurture, a dread of dependency, a readiness to resort to violence, and the stigmatization and subjugation of women, gays, and men who exhibit feminine characteristics.[18]

Though Kupers's research is focused on violence in male prisons, this framing of toxic masculinity as leveraging and exacerbating aspects of hegemonic masculinity is especially useful when contemplating toxic technocultures, which are likewise "enabled by and propagated through sociotechnical networks," leveraging these platforms as "a channel of coordination and harassment."[19] Just as toxic technocultures rely on "an Othering of those perceived as outside the culture,"[20] the gendered boundary-policing practices discussed in this chapter rely on the convergence culture industry's construction of fannish "insiders" and "outsiders." To bring these discussions of toxic masculinity and technocultures into the (fan) cultural framework of post–Web 2.0 participatory culture, the next section builds on Henry Jenkins, Sam Ford, and Joshua Green's concept of "spreadable media" to begin theorizing examples of spreadable misogyny within geek culture. Just as toxic masculinity and technocultures are frequently positioned as "poisoning" potentially neutral or even positive fan identities and platforms, "spreadable misogyny" suggests a need to revisit the viral qualities of spreadable content.

Spreadable Misogyny

When Henry Jenkins, Sam Ford, and Joshua Green's *Spreadable Media* was released in 2013, it was viewed by many as the final entry in Jenkins's "participatory culture trilogy." If 1992's *Textual Poachers* was focused on shifting cultural and scholarly conceptions of fans from passive and/or obsessive consumers to productive and/or politicized cultural critics, and 2006's *Convergence Culture* grappled with the increased visibility of fans and the impact of digital participatory culture, *Spreadable Media* considers a post–Web 2.0 media landscape in which bottom-up circulation is replacing conventional, top-down modes of media distribution. While it would be overly simplistic to create a narrative of linear progression from the fans of *Textual Poachers* operating from "a position of cultural marginality and social weakness"[21] to the empowered users of *Spreadable Media* now "actively shaping media flows,"[22] the authors correctly assert that this more participatory or "spreadable" model increasingly "sees the public not as simply consumers of preconstructed messages but as people who are shaping, sharing, reframing, and remixing media content [. . .] within larger communities and networks."[23] But what of the remixed content's equally constructed messages that are being spread through these communities and networks by users? What happens when fans, instead of reclaiming "feminine interests from the margins of masculine texts"[24] through remixing practices, instead actively utilize spreadable remix culture to reassert the masculinity of those texts and marginalize female fans?

The remainder of this chapter addresses the dark side of the memetic qualities of spreadable media and how they might be appropriated to cultivate spreadable misogyny within geek and fan culture. Jenkins, Ford, and Green's conception of "spreadability" emerges from four intersecting factors: the increased technological capacity to circulate content, the economic structures facilitating or limiting this circulation, the qualities of the text that encourage people to share, and the "social networks that link people through the exchange of meaningful bytes."[25] Spreadable misogyny emerges from similar conditions, fostered not just by the technological capacity to circulate content but also by the capacity to author and circulate it anonymously. The economic structures of media industries also play a role, less in terms of legal restriction/ permission to share content, but more in terms of their tacit endorsement of masculinized modes of fan engagement that cultivate a sense of privilege and "permission" to demarcate whose participation is valued. Gendered genre discourses also play a large role within spreadable misogyny, with particular texts and/or media being framed as more or less desirable or "authentic" geek properties. Finally, and most importantly, spreadable misogyny links people through explicitly exclusionary logics, exchanging bytes that are meaningful in their capacity to marginalize.

As noted in chapter 1, *Spreadable Media* was met with ambivalence (or, in some cases, overt resistance) by some fan scholars. Some of this pushback was due to the fact that, much as with the gendered and limited depictions of newly empowered "fans" documented in the previous chapter, some felt that *Spreadable Media* foregrounded industry-sanctioned forms of fannish participation and audience engagement in its narratives of user agency and empowerment. This directly related to concerns that the concept of spreadability could "never truly break out of the commercial paradigm," with *Spreadable Media* focusing more on neoliberal or industry-sanctioned (e.g. monetizable and/or quantifiable) modes of fan or audience engagement.[26] While I do not wish to dwell on these issues, they unquestionably inform the analysis that follows. If, as Jenkins contends, participatory cultures such as fan culture are "the best mechanism we have for promoting democracy and diversity within our contemporary culture,"[27] then we also need to consider how these same mechanisms might be deployed to hinder the promotion of diversity or reinforce a hegemonic conception of the fan.

To begin answering Jenkins's own call to engage "larger questions about the negative potentials of spreadability,"[28] I pose the term "spreadable misogyny" to add another, admittedly more demoralizing, layer to *Spreadable Media*'s mostly optimistic survey of how spreadability might empower users, or afford collaboration between media fans and industries. This layer, vitally, allows us to still focus on how these qualities might be deployed for good, examining (equally spreadable) responses to spreadable misogyny that draw on fan traditions of poaching and transformative criticism. But first, it is important to consider what might be lost in the conceptual transition from "viral" to "spreadable" media. Jenkins, Ford, and Green position the term "spreadable media" as a tactical move away from the popular usage of "viral media" as a buzzword to describe audience-driven circulation of content. In doing so, the authors seek to actively avoid "the metaphors of 'infection' and 'contamination,' which overestimate the power of media companies and underestimate the agency of audiences."[29] This is understandable, given the overwhelmingly negative connotations of "virality," which evokes images of infection and frames users as "unknowing 'hosts' of the information they carry across their social networks,"[30] rather than as active curators and disseminators of that content.

We can view this emphasis as yet another challenge to the hypodermic views of media power embedded in Horkheimer and Adorno's conceptualization of the culture industry, but in their desire to focus on user agency and move away from a notion in which users are "duped into passing a hidden agenda," the authors do not sufficiently consider the ways in which users might *knowingly* spread memetic content in an effort to ideologically "infect" those who encounter it. I wholeheartedly agree that the term "viral media" problematically downplays user agency, but I believe this analogy becomes useful when we are theorizing moments of spreadable bias within fan and geek culture. Spreadable misogyny is viral in the sense that these messages are designed to attack particular, predominantly marginalized bodies, but more to the point, those fans doing the spreading or "infecting" position themselves as antibodies. Herein lies the paradoxical nature of spreadable misogyny, which strives to virally poison the communal body of fan culture against women, who are themselves presented as a virus that must be quarantined or eradicated.

Benjamin Woo's work on the liminal space that fans, geeks, and nerds occupy between subcultural and mainstream identities can be productively applied here. Woo acknowledges the work done by post-subculture theorists interrogating the continued relevance of the term, but ultimately suggests that examining "how people 'do subculture' through their everyday social practices—practices that actively construct and negotiate the borders between 'subculture' and the 'mainstream,'"[31] is essential. Spreadable misogyny is one, admittedly aggressive, example of "doing fan subculture" that reflects a deep investment in retaining fan and geek culture's subcultural status as it moves inexorably towards the mainstream. Spreadable misogyny concurrently blames marginalized fans for this movement, and actively works to exclude them from it, feminizing the "mainstream" without acknowledging that male fans benefit most actively from mainstreamed fan-cultural identities. Accordingly, these instances pointedly and politically refute Benjamin

Woo's claims that geek culture does not fit neatly within scholarly conceptions of "spectacular subcultures," and that "aggressive tactics to 'win space' [. . .] have been largely absent."[32] Spreadable misogyny is blatantly conceived and deployed as a tactic to win the space of fan culture, or at least definitively determine who is allowed to delimit and patrol its imagined borders by setting up gendered checkpoints. Within this paradigm, women and other marginalized fans are framed as a contagion, responsible for the cancerous spread of fan culture outside of its subcultural spheres, and allows men to position themselves as avenging antibodies, tasked with identifying and neutralizing any entity that is perceived to be "foreign."

To put this another way, spreadable media is most readily embraced by "the people with the least to lose from changing the current system," who are thus most willing to "accept a loss of control"[33] over the circulation of content and the message(s) it conveys. Spreadable misogyny emerges from the same socio-technological conditions and utilizes the same memetic logics, but is performed by those most anxious about perceived changes to the status quo, and as a result desires to control and amplify particular messages to maintain it. Whitney Phillips's work on subcultural trolls and their conflicted relationship to mainstream culture is especially illustrative when we begin to theorize spreadable misogyny within geek and fan culture.[34] Indeed, it would be easy to devote the remainder of this chapter to exploring how the spreadable misogyny of a particular subset of fanboys within geek culture aligns with trolls' performative rejection of emotion and affect,[35] and their mutual reliance on the "adversary method" of argumentation, which "presupposes the superiority of male-gendered traits (rationality, assertiveness, dominance) over female-dominated traits (sentimentality, cooperation, conciliation)."[36] Like trolls, fanboys who engage in spreadable misogyny alternately dismiss overly affective modes of fan engagement and/or label female fans' affect as performative or inauthentic.

Like trolling, spreadable misogyny manifests through a spectrum of behaviors, and it would be irresponsible to assign definitive intent to the creation or circulation of this content. Similarly, it is virtually impossible to verify who, precisely, perpetuates these instances of spreadable misogyny within geek and fan culture. Accordingly, when I assign these actions to fanboys, I take another page out of Phillips's book, speaking not of their biological sex, but rather of the "socially constructed ways in which they present themselves as conventionally masculine."[37] There is another intriguing temporal parallel to draw here, namely, that just as "fake geek girl" discourses were peaking in 2012, trolls were grappling with a similar conflicted relationship with mainstream culture, and pushing back against the notion that "what once had functioned as a highly specialized subcultural marker no longer performed the same subcultural function."[38] In both cases, the irony is that the loudest critics fail to acknowledge that they are "indirectly complicit in propagating"[39] and popularizing these (sub)cultures, or that they continue to exert the most privilege within them.

"Spreadable misogyny" falls perilously short of terminologically encompassing the many, frequently interrelated, forms of "spreadable" racism, homophobia, ageism, xenophobia, ableism, and cis-sexism that are equally byproducts of the toxic masculinity within digital and geek culture. Nor does "spreadable misogyny" sufficiently account for the ways in which this term might privilege concerns about the harassment of white, straight, middle-class women over queer women or women of color. We need not look further than the sustained harassment of actress Leslie Jones timed to her appearance in the all-female reboot of *Ghostbusters* (2016) to realize how this conversation might meaningfully shift when we consider examples of spreadable "misogynoir," which Moya Bailey defines as "the ways that anti-Blackness and misogyny combine to malign Black women in our world."[40] Likewise, while this chapter does examine transformative fan responses to instances of spreadable misogyny pertaining to "fake geek girl" discourses, there is far more work to be done on fan activist campaigns like #buryyourgays and #LGBTfansdeservebetter, which addressed the disconcerting number of queer characters who were summarily killed during the 2015–2016 television season and wielded the underlying principles of spreadable media to more progressive ends.[41] Accordingly, this chapter is overtly positioned as a jumping-off point for further research that engages the varying boundary-policing efforts within contemporary fan culture along additional axes of identity.

I begin with spreadable misogyny in part because it is the most prevalent and visible form of spreadable bias within fan and geek culture. We need not look further than a string of promoted videos from Twitter's

Figure 3.1. Screengrab of Twitter Safety video outlining its "mute" and "block" features. Twitter, "How to Use Mute on Twitter," YouTube Video, 0:28, April 27, 2016, https://youtu.be/4pDvwMiUPdk.

official @Safety account to see that gender is most commonly fore-grounded within contemporary concerns around digital and spreadable harassment. These thirty-second instructional videos, designed to raise awareness around the social media site's "Block," "Mute," and "Report" features, all feature a caricature of a woman with an expression of hor-ror on her face, as she is assaulted by tweets from a grimacing male user (figure 3.1). Before she is buried in this agro avalanche, one of the platform's features (mute, to no longer see a particular user's tweets in your timeline, or block, to restrict a particular account from any interac-tion with yours) is deployed, or a team of helpful Twitter employees and one police officer pop up to promptly address the report of abuse. These videos, which clearly aim to mitigate widespread critiques that Twitter as a platform and the police as an institution have repeatedly failed to intervene in instances of digital harassment, only expose the fantastical nature of these "interventions."

For example, in July 2016, an e-mail response from Twitter's support team to a particularly heinous example of verbal abuse made the rounds on Twitter. A female user reported and submitted a screengrab of a tweet directed at her in which she was asked, "Is your perky butt ready 4 cock" and told "it's time to shove your head in the oven. Will u be the 1st #Holocaust survivor of 2016?" The response from Twitter's support team, after assuring the complainant that the company "takes reports of this nature very seriously," was that they "could not determine a clear violation of the Twitter Rules," despite the fact that the Twitter Rules[42] go on at length about Abusive Behavior that will not be tolerated, including sections on Violent Threats, Harassment, and Hateful Conduct. The e-mail, which notes that Twitter is "unable to accept screenshots" of abusive tweets, ironically concludes by encouraging the user to utilize Twitter's tools to better control what she sees. This echoes the advice that is so often reported as being offered by police when women report pervasive digital harassment and systemic instances of spreadable misogyny: "If you don't like the way you're being treated online, you should log off."[43] This advice is at best absurdly impractical and willfully ignorant of just how reliant contemporary labor and culture are on digital interaction, and at worst is reminiscent of a range of other discursive victim-blaming tactics ("If you don't want to be raped, you shouldn't dress like that."). Related to this book's interest in how the convergence culture industry props up androcentric conceptions of fan culture, this statement also implicitly suggests that this "treatment" is the inevitable byproduct of women entering spaces that are culturally coded as male-dominated, whether that is fan and geek culture specifically, or digital culture broadly.

These safety videos represent female users as damsels in need of saving, but it has been made repeatedly clear that platforms and police are not especially interested in saving them. This overtly gendered depiction of the aggressive male social media user, and the woman helplessly fending off his 140-character barbs, is nevertheless visually striking and conveys that spreadable misogyny has achieved a higher degree of visibility within contemporary digital culture than other forms of spreadable bias. When the tweet accompanying these videos promises "you" more control and protection, that message is directly addressed to (white) women, problematically at the expense of other marginalized communities who experience similar targeted attacks. Though unquestionably many women do feel helpless when they are bombarded with rape or death threats for merely expressing their opinion about a comic book character on the Internet, the analysis that follows also powerfully shows how women within fan and geek culture have taken matters into their own hands, designing similarly spreadable shields to deflect instances of spreadable misogyny and minimize their impact.

The sustained harassment of feminist critic Anita Sarkeesian from 2012 onwards in response to her crowdfunded video criticism series "Tropes vs. Women in Video Games" and incidents like GamerGate are perhaps the most commonly cited examples of the ways in which spreadable misogyny can balloon into full-fledged harassment campaigns via digital platforms. The majority of incidents of spreadable misogyny are not as visible as these two examples, but they can cumulatively be just as dehumanizing. I now turn to a decidedly less violent, but certainly no less damaging, example of spreadable misogyny: the "idiot nerd girl" meme. Indeed, the subtle and satirical nature of this particular instance of spreadable misogyny within fan and geek culture makes it easy to overlook the fact that it operates within the same cultural logics of more pervasive and targeted campaigns of hate speech and harassment. This meme, and the broader "fake geek girl" discourse it propagates, are prime examples of both the virality of spreadable misogyny and the growing strains of toxic masculinity within some segments of fan culture.

The fact that these "strains" represent a small percentage of all male fans, and yet have become such a potentially cancerous force within contemporary geek culture, is all the more reason I am reluctant to abandon words like "viral" and "toxic," however problematic. A critique of the way agency is allocated within these terms cannot be at the expense of a consideration of how these same conditions deny agency to particular groups of fans. It is not an accident that the term "toxic technocultures," with its poisonous implications, has dominated digital scholars' discussion of hypermasculine and misogynist (not to mention frequently racist and xenophobic) spaces like Reddit and 4Chan. Yet, like viruses, these instances of spreadable misogyny often either go untreated or are disseminated by the very technology that enables them to take root. When one account is taken down for abusive behavior (e.g., in the above example, Twitter eventually responded to the user outcry around its lack of response by disabling the offending account), another account is created. This not only makes these "fanboys' rights movements" often appear more pervasive and popular than they truly are (as proponents might be utilizing multiple accounts to "signal boost" their perspective), but it makes this virus incredibly difficult to "treat" through tracking or, in more extreme cases, prosecution.[44] It is at this intersection of toxicity (the willful and malicious spread of poisonous materials) and virality (the capacity to infect a host body and, potentially, a community) that instances of spreadable misogyny like the "idiot nerd girl" meme and "fake geek girl" discourses reside.

Gendered Anti-Fandom

In 2010 and 2011, in the subcultural shadow of the GOP's most recent set of legislative volleys in the "War on Women," the "idiot nerd girl" meme began to spread. This image macro, derived from a 2010 photo of a young woman in black frame glasses with the word "Nerd" written across the palm of her hand, positions the "idiot nerd girl" against a pink background, accompanied by text that marks her affective connection to or knowledge of a particular object of geek culture as either performative or inadequate. This meme, and the proliferation of "fake geek girl" accusations it emerged out of, are symptomatic of a broader trend towards gendered anti-fan practices that either implicitly or explicitly respond to the perceived mainstreaming of geek and fan (sub)culture. Though gendered accounts of anti-fan practices exist, surveying how communities mobilize around a collective disdain for "feminine" texts like Twilight,[45] or work to exclude female fans within male-dominated fan communities surrounding sports[46] or comic books,[47] I propose the need for a more literal translation of the term "anti-fan" to consider the current "War on Women" that the convergence culture industry has often tacitly endorsed.

The literal translation of "anti-fan" I am proposing (fans who direct their animosity not towards a particular media property, celebrity, or genre but rather towards other fans they deem undesirable based on their own fannish self-identification and valuation of fan culture) requires an adaptation of the "atomic model" of textuality proposed by Jonathan Gray.[48] Gray's earliest theorization of anti-fans used this atomic structure to articulate fans' relationship to the text, both in terms of affect (with anti-fans classified as electrons, negatively charged and orbiting around the text and its nucleus of positively charged protons/ fans) and in terms of proximity (with fans occupying the nucleic center, and anti-fans on the periphery with often little more than a paratextual knowledge of the fan object). Though Gray's atomic model is potentially too all-encompassing, rather than abandoning it or replacing it with a taxonomy of anti-fan practices, I find it more productive to reconfigure it to conceptualize fandom on a macro level. The atomic model of contemporary fandom I am proposing would attempt to theorize fans' relationship not to media texts but to media fandom itself.

When we consider how media industries view fans within the convergence culture industry (and, by extension, how fans conceptualize their relationship to fan culture and fannish "authenticity" as it is valued by media industries), textuality still plays a key role. As the analysis of the "idiot nerd girl" meme and "fake geek girl" discourses below suggests, anti-fans (in my use of the term) position themselves as occupying the nucleic space closest to the text, justifying their dismissal of other fans through a perceived lack of knowledge about fan texts and topics. Though they are not "positively charged" in their treatment of other fans, they still function as protons in the sense that these fans tend to be those that the media industry feels most positively about courting as a demographic, and subsequently have come to occupy the nucleic center of cultural conceptions of the "fan" within the convergence culture industry. Fans who are less interested in things like authorial intent, or who skew more "transformative," would be the "electrons" in this model, both because they often respond critically to the text (or prefer the "fanon" of fan-produced media to the "canon" delimited by content creators) and because the convergence culture industry views them as peripheral, potentially "negatively charged" fans.

In Gray's atomic model, non-fans (or casual fans) are positrons, or the positively charged "anti-particle equivalent of electrons" on the outskirts of a text.[49] In my proposed atomic model of contemporary fan culture, the "fake geek girl" or "idiot nerd girl" takes on this role as antimatter, simultaneously an unstable byproduct of the growing "nucleus" of contemporary fandom and a source of potential annihilation for electrons. The positive charge of the positron/fake geek girl is precisely why she poses a threat. Media industries might welcome a growing "mainstream" or "casual" fan demographic, while protons are by design inclined to cast them out. This positronic positioning also helps explain why some female fans (or "electrons") choose to participate in "fake geek girl" boundary-policing practices, as "fake" fangirls threaten the legitimacy of "real" ones more than they do the nucleic center of the convergence culture industry's standardization of fan culture (namely, young men/fanboys). This revised atomic model, importantly, reflects that the "double bind of being too geeky and not geeky enough" that "fake geek girl" discourses produce are virtually impossible to navigate.[50]

Unlike most anti-fan studies, which focus on specific communities of practice, and their relationships to particular media texts, this conception of the "anti-fan" as a fan who actively marginalizes or discredits other fans solely on the basis of identity (gender, race, age, sexuality, nation, size, class, or ability) is situated within a broader set of concerns about the boundary-policing practices that have accompanied fan culture's shift from the margins to the mainstream. This conception of the anti-fan moves beyond textual or paratextual animosity to situate "anti-fandom" as a form of containment, in which the very demographic that has most visibly benefited from the convergence culture industry's embrace of fan culture seeks to marginalize those who were already excluded from its embrace. When this conception of "anti-fandom" is coupled with the anxieties addressed in chapters 1 and 2 that disproportionate attention is being paid to those fans and practices that can be most easily incorporated into preexisting power demographics and promotional logics, it is necessary to revisit and extend Jonathan Gray's initial rationale for the study of anti-fandom. Gray was not disputing the importance of studying fans, but rather was expressing concern about what fan studies "has unnecessarily and unintentionally pushed under, what is missing from its present thrust and what the effects of these omissions have been on the wider discipline of media and cultural studies."[51] Likewise, it is not my intent to dispute the importance of studying the performances and practices of anti-fandom that circulate around a particular text, celebrity, or genre. Rather, I would like to consider what a textual understanding of anti-fandom might unintentionally obscure about the wider cultural context of fandom within the convergence culture industry.

This totalizing conception of "anti-fandom" aligns most closely with Vivi Theodoropoulou's theorization of the anti-fan, which suggests that sports fandom structurally facilitates anti-fandom through the creation of binaries (in the form of team or player rivalries, for example), subsequently creating an anti-fan who "resorts to anti-fandom so as to protect her/his fan object from the threat its 'counterforce' poses."[52] In the case of "fake geek girl" discourses and other modes of gendered boundary policing within fan culture, what anti-fans are attempting to protect is fan culture itself, from those perceived to be interlopers or outsiders. This gender-biased form of "protection," and the exclusionary practices it cultivates, can be viewed as a thinly veiled attempt to reclaim a predigital state of fannish subcultural capital. In nostalgically embracing the sense of exclusivity once associated with occupying a fannish identity, these anti-fan practices paradoxically replicate and reify the feelings of social exclusion that fandom is meant to resolve. Here, the convergence culture industry is simultaneously the precondition and the catalyst for anti-fandom, with fans' growing cultural capital held up as a prime example of the democratizing power of digital culture, even as it exposes and compounds longstanding inequities within that culture. The irony is that this anti-fan backlash against the "mainstreaming" of geek culture is a direct response to the fact that fandom (which has long been conceptualized as an inclusive, even utopian communal sphere) has been made increasingly accessible by the paradigm shifts of convergence culture.

As a byproduct of the convergence culture industry, the "fake geek girl" anti-fan movement may be sustained by the memetic flow of content across social media platforms, but it is rooted in media industries' historical devaluation of female audiences, and longstanding conceptions of space (real or virtual) as mapping and maintaining gendered structures of power. If, as discussed in the prior chapter, new hegemonic fandom is marked by fan identities becoming normalized while remaining pathologized,[53] the convergence culture industry has allowed fanboys to concurrently claim ownership over and police both ends of the pathologized-normative spectrum, ultimately "reinforc[ing] the idea that men get to dictate what is an appropriate level of nerdiness, and that somehow, women are incapable of achieving it."[54] This idea is not exclusively rooted in the anti-fan performances of fanboys, but exists in a more complex matrix in which contemporary journalistic, industrial, and scholarly valuations of the "fan" are shaping the broader cultural conception of the "fan." The erasure of women from this category is also not novel, but rooted in a longer history of obscuring women's participation within subcultural communities.

Sexism and Subculture Studies

Addressing the paucity of female subjects in the subcultural scholarship emerging from the Birmingham School, Angela McRobbie and Jenny Garber's 1977 essay "Girls and Subcultures" is newly resonant in interrogations of the (in)visibility politics for fangirls within the convergence culture industry. Just as McRobbie and Garber suggested that girls within subcultures may have become invisible "because the very term 'sub-culture' has acquired such strong masculine overtones,"[55] my core concern is that fangirls are once more being rendered invisible through androcentric understandings of the "fan." Though media fandom has moved out of the subcultural shadows, McRobbie and Garber's claim that the "popular image of a subculture as encoded and defined by the media is likely to be one which emphasizes the male membership, male 'focal concerns,' and masculine values"[56] has, if anything, become more firmly entrenched as fan culture has become more visible and accessible.

Rather than theorizing girls' marginality within subcultures, it is perhaps more useful, as McRobbie and Garber did, to consider their "structured secondariness."[57] In other words, girls were invisible within postwar subculture studies not only because they were marginalized within subcultural spaces that were predominantly occupied by men and documented by male academics but also because the cultural spaces in which they were central were considered subordinate.[58] Contemporary refrains within fandom's current War on Women, such as "bitch get me a sandwich," or "get back in the kitchen," resuscitate the postwar gendered valuation of public and private spheres McRobbie and Garber were responding to. As the prior chapter suggests, discourses continue to reinscribe the "structured secondariness" of women within the convergence culture industry. My own concerns regarding fangirls' relative invisibility or structured secondariness within the convergence culture industry echo McRobbie and Garber's anxieties that this might create a "self-fulfilling prophecy, a vicious circle"[59] in which women view fan or geek culture as inaccessible or inhospitable.

In unpacking the "complementary if not contradictory" nature of internal fan hierarchies, which gauge both whether one is a "good-enough fan" and whether one is a "good-enough representative to the outside,"[60] Kristina Busse notes that when "fannish rules and norms are broken, fans often come together to criticize the culprit," either through "mocking or outright censure."[61] Busse contends that geek hierarchies are "deeply invested in ideas of normalcy as defined by the outside," and thus thrive on finding another category of fan who is "more unusual, less mainstream," in order to raise one's own status.[62] In the case of the "idiot nerd girl" meme and "fake geek girl" debates, the inverse is true. By identifying geek girls and fangirls as too "normal" or "mainstream" to be "real" fans, male fans belie (or attempt to combat) their own normalcy within the convergence culture industry, positioning themselves as simultaneously the oppressors and the oppressed. The next section explores this paradoxical rationale for the censure of fangirls as "bad" fans through the "idiot nerd girl" meme and the broader "fake geek girl" discourses that surround it.

"Idiot Nerd Girls" and "Fake Geek Girls"

The term "meme" was coined by biologist Richard Dawkins in 1976 to distinguish between genetic characteristics and those that are taught or learned through cultural experience. Patrick Davison adapts Dawkins's definition to classify an Internet meme as "a piece of culture, typically a joke, which gains influence through online transmission,"[63] commonly taking the form of an easy-to-imitate and -disseminate image or video. When coupled with Dawkins's analog conception of the term, Davison's definition suggests that Internet memes both are cultural objects and have the capacity to influence cultural understandings. Limor Shifman's extensive work on memes makes a compelling argument that, though it might appear that "memes are seemingly trivial and mundane artifacts, they actually reflect deep social and cultural structures."[64] It is precisely the meme's capacity to reflect and shape social norms that makes the "idiot nerd girl" a point of concern, as it circulates outside of its originating anti-fan communities into geek culture at large.

The "idiot nerd girl" meme belongs to a subgenre of image macros known as "Advice Animals" that adhere to "a distinct format in which an (often humorous looking) animal is placed in a square with short text at the top and bottom of the square."[65] These three recurring elements of an Advice Animal image macro—the colorful background, the central image of an "animal," and two lines of text (which often echo the conventional joke structure of set-up and punch line)—allow this genre of meme to be both easily identified and easily replicated. Because memes require particular subcultural literacies, both in the way they are "written" and the way they are "read," the simplicity and ubiquity of "Advice Animals" marks them as a comparatively accessible subgenre of image macros to produce and consume, which in turn aids their spreadability. The image or icon at the center of the image macro (be it animal or human) can be positioned as either the giver or receiver of said "advice," but Advice Animals as a memetic subgenre tend to "propagate limited forms of interpretation."[66] The "advice," either given by or directed at the "animal," is blunt, often to the point of being crass, and is determined by the genus of "advice animal" that is used. For example, in addition to the inaugural "advice dog," iterations of the "Advice Animal" meme include "courage wolf," "rich raven," and "socially awkward penguin," each featuring text/ advice relating to their descriptor. The "advice" directed at the "idiot nerd girl" is decidedly judgmental, rather than (humorously) helpful. The message to the "idiot nerd girl," and geek girls by extension, is clear: you will never sufficiently "belong" to geek culture and should be prepared to legitimize your identity as an "authentic" fan when challenged.

This message aligns neatly with what Ryan Milner has called the "masculine participation structure" of many image memes and their surrounding communities of practice, in which "the constructed centrality is male" and accordingly women are routinely constructed as "stupid, irrational, and inconsistent."[67] It is perhaps thus unsurprising that a large percentage of the earliest examples of Advice Animal memes were "explicitly misogynist," with many utilizing rape jokes as their de facto "punchline."[68] As Whitney Phillips bluntly notes, "[T]he origins of this particular species is steeped in violent sexism."[69] Though examples of the "idiot nerd girl" Advice Animal most certainly entrenched a sense of masculine centrality on multiple levels (as the presumed creator and consumer of the meme, and as authentic fans/ geeks/nerds), rarely did they stoop to threats of sexualized violence. Still, the residue of the Advice Animal's sexist origins permeates almost every iteration of the meme.

Figure 3.2. An early example of the "idiot nerd girl" meme. "Idiot Nerd Girl," *Know Your Meme*, 2011, http://knowyourmeme.com.

When the "idiot nerd girl" meme began to spread in 2010 and 2011, gendered tensions sparked by the perceived mainstreaming of fan culture had already been percolating for several years. Historically, a text "spreads particularly far when it depicts a controversy a community cares about at the precise time it is looking for content which might act as a rallying cry,"[70] and we can certainly view the "idiot nerd girl" meme as both a boiling point and a "rallying cry" for anti-fans lamenting the loss of fannish authenticity. The joke structure of the meme performs the slippage among "nerd," "geek," and "fan" identities, with the set-up (or text above the image) generally consisting of the idiot nerd girl enthusiastically expressing her love of a particular object of geek culture, and the punch line (the text below the image) typically exposing or correcting a lack of knowledge (figure 3.2). Almost every example of the meme implicitly critiques the "mainstreaming" of geek culture: idiot nerd girl acquires all of her knowledge of comics from superhero franchise films, has the audacity to self-identify as a gamer despite only playing so-called casual games, and so on.

As Jonathan Gray has noted, anti-fandom is frequently predicated on a media property's "paratextual assemblage,"[71] rather than the text itself. For example, many *Twilight* anti-fans proudly proclaim to have never read the novels or seen the film adaptations, choosing to justify and root their animosity in a peripheral understanding of the text and the paratexts that circle around it (film trailers, news coverage of screaming *Twilight* fangirls, and so on). Fannish authenticity, within the context of the "idiot nerd girl" meme, is conflated with textual mastery. The meme not only critiques, and pointedly genders, those "fans" who only have a paratextual understanding of the text, but it demarcates appropriate fan texts to coalesce around, framing popular texts as paratextual to authentic geek culture. Thus, even if the idiot nerd girl does have a comprehensive knowledge of a fan object, the object itself is deemed unworthy. Ironically, the meme frequently uses examples of mainstreamed geek culture to critique mainstream geek culture. Iterations like "Says 'my precious' in a Gollum voice . . . because she saw it in The Big Bang Theory" visualize the "doublethink" that occurs when fans "do not challenge these socially devalued meanings of fandom, but merely apply them to other fans."[72] Here, this doublethink is a direct product of the convergence culture industry, and is emblematic of image macros' tendency to "simultaneously challenge and contain hegemonic culture."[73] Within the idiot nerd girl meme's gendered brand of doublethink, masculine appreciation of relatively mainstream geek culture fare (e.g., *Back to the Future*, *Halo*) is acceptable, while other mainstream fare (or anything tainted by feminine consumption or mass appeal) is not.

Obviously, it is the "girl" of the "idiot nerd girl" meme that is central, and also a prime example of "gender plus" modes of intra-fannish boundary policing, or "gender plus age or generation."[74] It is unclear whether the idiot nerd girl's idiocy is a byproduct of her gender or age (or some combination thereof), but because the meme has become synonymous with fake geek girl discourses, we must also unpack why "fakeness" is ultimately the more damning category. "Idiot," while unflattering, implies a lack of knowledge, something that theoretically could be attained. The "fake" fangirl, however, implies deceit, infiltration, and performance, rendering it far more pernicious and effective as an anti-fan gatekeeping

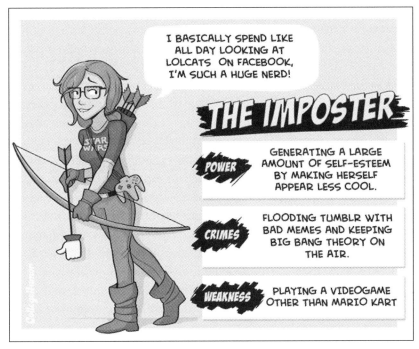

Figure 3.3. *College Humor*'s "Six Supervillains of Nerd Culture" evokes the "fake geek girl" in one of its entries. Caldwell Taylor and Susanna Wolf, "The Six Supervillains of Nerd Culture," *College Humor*, July 12, 2012, http://www.collegehumor.com.

strategy. The "fake geek girl" presents a zero-sum game for female fans, not only because "fakeness" is predicated on the notion that fan affect is quantifiable and must be authenticated but also because within this paradigm, only male fans (or those who align themselves with an affirmational notion of "authentic" fan culture) are empowered to define and delimit what constitutes a "real" fan. Accusations of "fakeness" can always be applied without grounds, and "proving oneself" becomes an ongoing challenge, and one that is ultimately impossible to achieve.

The idiot nerd girl meme, and more comprehensive efforts to identify and shame fake geek girls, have the capacity to cultivate imposter syndrome. This "imposter syndrome" was codified in one of *College Humor*'s trading card–style advertisements featuring the "Six Supervillains of Nerd Culture" (figure 3.3). Though hegemonic masculinity was also mocked through the fanboy supervillain "The Bro," it is notable that the only other depiction of a woman in the ads was not a fan archetype but rather "The Executive," an image of an older woman with grey hair wearing a purple suit, threateningly extending a contract and a pen. It is not unusual for media industry executives, or "The Powers That Be" as they are colloquially referred to within fan culture, to be characterized as "supervillains," as fans routinely direct their animosity towards executives when they feel a franchise has taken a wrong turn. What is notable here is that both the age and the gender of the "Executive" are iconically represented, especially given the paucity of female executives within the media industry. Both "The Imposter," and "The Executive" are explicitly held accountable for the mainstreaming of geek culture, and notably both are positioned as "fake" fans (the former motivated by cultural capital, the latter motivated by economic capital). Whether antifannish forms of spreadable misogyny are subtle and satirical or overt and aggressive, they suggest that male-dominated subcultures are not only "based on a refusal of competencies and dispositions that are culturally coded as feminine; [they] may also work structurally to exclude women from participation."[75]

This is why the "idiot nerd girl" meme's assimilation into, and reflection of, broader "fake geek girl" debates is semiotically significant. Ben Nugent characterizes nerds as "disproportionately male, intellectual in ways that strike people as machinelike, and socially awkward in ways that strike people as machinelike."[76] Geeks, conversely, tend to be characterized by an attachment to a particular brand, subject, or media property. "Geeking out" is inherently social, predicated on an outpouring of affect or enthusiasm, and in this sense, "geek" tends to be more closely aligned with "fan" as a (sub)cultural identity category. We can also see how these categories, at least in stereotypical form, reflect long-standing gender binaries: "nerd" connotes a masculine emphasis on objectivity and intellect, whereas "geek" and "fan" connote feminine excess and emotional attachment. The "idiot nerd" and "fake geek" thus both function as oxymoronic identities, their contradictions explained by their attachment to girlhood. Much in the same way that there is a codified dictionary definition for "fanboy," yet no equivalent entry for "fangirl," there is no equivalent idiot nerd boy or fake geek guy meme. The implication, then, is that girls are an equally oxymoronic fit with the cultural categories of "nerd," "geek," and "fan" writ large.

Remediating Spreadable Misogyny

Jay Edidin[77] was one of the first to reclaim the idiot nerd girl meme (figure 3.4). Using the same memetic spread to reframe the "idiot nerd girl" within broader "fake geek girl" debates, text like "Is new to a fandom . . . gets bullied into leaving because she doesn't know everything yet," "Hasn't read all 900 issues of Batman . . . neither have you," and "Who are you . . . to say she's not" soon began to circulate. As Edidin noted of the reappropriated image,

> I hate the Idiot Nerd Girl meme, but I don't hate Idiot Nerd Girl. [. . .] I like her weary, wry smile, like she knows what the backlash is going to look like and has decided to say her piece all the same. [. . .] I want to ask her what comics she likes and why she likes them, hook her up with

Figure 3.4. One example of how the idiot nerd girl meme was reclaimed as a site of commentary. Esther Zuckerman, "Taking Back a Meme: Idiot Nerd Girl," *Atlantic*, September 10, 2012, https://www.theatlantic.com.

a progressive hackerhive [hacker network], and generally do my part to build an inclusive community where she can be whatever the hell she wants to be.[78]

I want to conclude this chapter by surveying some of the transformative tactics adopted by female fans to document and critique the spreadable misogyny of anti-fan culture broadly, and "fake geek girl" discourses specifically.

These responses frequently come in the form of comics, which is perhaps a nod to the fact that fake geek girl discourses circulate most forcibly within comics fandom and its affiliated spaces, like comic conventions (which now cater to much broader pop culture texts and audiences). Many of these comics parody the paranoia associated with "fake geek girl" debates, such as Jenna Salume's "FGG," which depicts a woman in superheroine garb "stalking" a comic-reading fanboy in a field of tall grass, only to "pounce" (startling him with her skimpy costume and seductive pose) and "devour" (quite literally ripping out his throat and eating him).[79] Others take on the mundane, yet exhausting, experience of having to continually "prove" one's fan credentials to male anti-fans. Sailorswayze's "Am I Right, Ladies" (figure 3.5), which offers a conversational contrast between its two panels, clearly articulates the real-world, lived impact of virtual "fake geek girl" discourses and memes.[80] Sailorswayze's comic suggests that all fannish knowledge, when emanating from a female fan, must be interrogated and explained ("Did you just check Wikipedia?"), or ignored. The provocation, a t-shirt bearing a geek culture icon (the Green Lantern insignia), seems an especially pointed jab at how merchandising trends reflect the gendered hypocrisies of mainstream geek culture, an issue I will return to in chapter 6.

Tactical pushback to fake geek girl discourses came in an array of transformative forms. For example, in July 2013, the Doubleclicks, a geek girl band consisting of sisters Aubrey and Angela Webber, released their song "Nothing to Prove" on YouTube. The song's titular refrain is a clear rebuttal to the growing tide of "fake geek girl" claims, and concludes with the following call to arms:

> You can stop—never say "fake geek" again
> Our club needs no bouncers—all who want in get in

Figure 3.5. This comic by sailorswayze satirizes the ways in which women are consistently tasked to authenticate their fan identities in ways male fans are not. Sailorswayze, "Am I Right, Ladies," *Sailorswayze.tumblr.com*, http://sailorswayze.tumblr.com /post/35678126959/am-i-right-ladies.

But go ahead, if you want, to own that role fully
I ain't got nothing to prove to a bully!

Though the song lyrically and playfully stresses the importance of unity, and the utopian potential of fandom, the music video visually and critically takes on the "idiot nerd girl" meme, and its divisive impact on female fans. The video consists of a series of images of fans (mostly women, but some men, and several notable geek culture icons such as Kelly Sue DeConnick and Wil Wheaton) that were crowdsourced by the band via their Tumblr. The Doubleclicks specified that all submissions be standardized in form (a five- to eight-second video of the fan holding up a legible sign directly under their chin), and requested that content address either "what got you into geekdom," fan experiences (either positive or negative), or "a message you would like to give to the bullies who try to shame women out of the geek community."[81] Though the band claims the video's aesthetic was inspired by the book trailer for *Dear Teen Me*,[82] the formal resonance with the "idiot nerd girl" image macro is striking.

Replacing the standardized image of the "idiot nerd girl" with crowdsourced images of geek girls, and then pointedly selecting a range of ages, sizes, and ethnicities to represent the "geek girl," explicitly challenges the homogenizing impact of "fake geek girl" claims on female fans. Whether or not they would be deemed so by anti-fans, the geek girls featured in the video are not only decidedly real but also reflective of the diversity of fan culture that the meme attempts to obscure and regulate. The text may not be formally divided in the video as it is in the "idiot nerd girl" meme, into clear "set-ups" and "punch lines," but many of the individual signs retain the meme's aesthetic structure (e.g., "That look of surprise when I talk about *Star Trek*? It gets old."). Some of the submissions use two signs (e.g., "I grew out my hair" "So I could dress up as Princess Leia"), making this aesthetic connection to the meme even more explicit.

One of these instances in which two cards are used to critical effect represents the turning point in both the song and the video. After two verses underscored by crowdsourced images of female fans/geeks, smiling and holding up signs detailing how they entered fandom, the

Figure 3.6. One example of the crowdsourced commentary on "fake geek girl" discourses featured in the Doubleclicks' music video for "Nothing to Prove." The Doubleclicks, "Nothing to Prove," YouTube Video, 4:18, July 23, 2013, https://youtu.be /s4Rjy5yW1gQ.

Doubleclicks themselves appear on the screen. As the song's lyrics transition from depicting fandom as a space of acceptance to detailing how "now ignorant haters come to prove me wrong / tell me I'm not nerdy enough to belong," the Doubleclicks drop their sign/claim that "[b]eing a geek girl is really awesome!" to expose another: "except when it isn't." What follows, over the song's titular chorus, is a much more somber array of images (figure 3.6), detailing anti-fan biases around race ("Being Asian and a Geek doesn't mean I have to like anime") and sexuality ("I was told I traded my cleavage for free comics"), in addition to gender ("I love video games . . . but boys tell me I'm not a 'real' gamer"). Considering that the video begins with a relatively utopian construction of fandom as a safe space for all who feel marginalized, and concludes with a rapid-fire montage of other geek girls (again alluding to the scope and diversity of "geek girl" identities), the song's time signature is reminiscent of a waltz, a dance with the "haters" that suggests geek girls are weary of following, and are primed to lead.

Fandom's War on Women

There are generative parallels to be drawn between contemporary geek culture's gatekeeping practices and strategies deployed in the political Right's current "War on Women" in the United States. While we cannot, and should not, equate reproductive rights with, for example, the right for female fans to reproduce uncensored fanfiction through Kindle Worlds, these respective "wars" are mutually preoccupied with policing female bodies and sexuality. Though this chapter has not engaged with convention culture directly, there are myriad examples of how this war is transcending virtual spaces to influence physical ones.[83] Fan conventions are a prime "battleground" in which digital discourses around "authentic" fandom and "fake geek girls" are mobilized and enacted, as the anti-*Twilight* protests at San Diego Comic-Con 2009 suggest. In some cases, these anti-fan performances at conventions are tacitly endorsed, or overtly led, by media producers. Comic writer and artist Tony Harris's 2012 Facebook screed against "CON-HOT" "COSPLAY-Chiks [sic]" is one of the more visible, and vitriolic, examples of this trend. After the disclaimer that he "appreciates a pretty Gal as much as the next Hetero Male," Harris goes on to frame female cosplayers as "more pathetic than the REAL nerds," as they pander for sexual attention and "prey" on virginal fanboys. Concluding with the note that fans who share his perspective "are LEGION," he directed the following message to female cosplayers: "YOU DONT [sic] KNOW SHIT ABOUT COMICS, BEYOND WHATEVER GOOGLE IMAGE SEARCH YOU DID TO GET REF ON THE MOST MAINSTREAM COMIC CHARACTER WITH THE MOST REVEALING COSTUME EVER. [...] Yer [sic] not comics." The impact of these sorts of remarks on female cosplayers resonates with Doreen Massey's assertion that the "gendering of space and place both reflects and has effects back on the ways in which gender is constructed and understood in the societies in which we live."[84] Digital discourse inevitably impacts the treatment of female fans in physical fan spaces, which strip away the (relative) anonymity of the virtual, for better or for worse.

The "War on Women" taking place within contemporary fan culture that this chapter has only begun unpacking is unsettling, and ultimately difficult to conceptualize, because it is so diffuse. Accordingly, I find the militaristic framing of an anti-fan "War on Women" productive, if ultimately insufficient, for many of the reasons outlined in Susan Faludi's *Backlash: The Undeclared War against American Women*. Faludi acknowledges the metaphor's allure but argues that "by imagining the conflict as two battalions neatly arrayed on either side of a line, we miss the entangled nature, the locked embrace, of a 'war' between women and the male culture they inhabit."[85] Faludi suggests that the backlash to the advances of second wave feminism constituted the true war, stating, "When feminism itself becomes the tide, the opposition doesn't simply go along with the reversal: it digs in its heels, brandishes its fists, builds walls and dams. And its resistance creates countercurrents and treacherous undertows."[86] Much as contemporary "men's rights" movements present one visible "opposition" to the perceived "tide" of feminism, anti-fandom as I am defining it here exposes its privilege, even as it claims a victimized status. I would suggest that contemporary anti-fan efforts to police fannish authenticity along gender lines, such as the "idiot nerd girl" meme, are best understood as simultaneously a byproduct of and a backlash against the convergence culture industry, in which fandom itself has become the tide.

My call to theorize the anti-fan's position within an atomic model of fandom itself productively forces us to grapple with the contradictions of the convergence culture industry, which has (conditionally) embraced some segments of fan culture while marginalizing others. Just as anti-fandom is a key space in which to consider how hegemonic values are upheld, Faludi cautions that a backlash is "most powerful when it goes private, when it lodges inside a woman's mind and turns her vision inward [. . .] until she begins to enforce the backlash too—on herself."[87] This is my central concern with the idiot nerd girl meme, and so many other examples of spreadable misogyny that attempt to disenfranchise young women who are attempting to find their place within geek culture. Yet, as the transformative interventions above suggest, backlashes like those Faludi discussed in 1991, which "churn beneath the surface, largely invisible to the public eye,"[88] now play out publicly across social media platforms. McRobbie and Garber concluded their study of girls and subcultures with the suggestion that, instead of trying to understand girls' subcultural presence or absence, perhaps we should recognize that there is "a whole alternative network of responses and activities through which girls negotiate their relationship to subcultures or even make positive moves away from the subcultural option."[89] The current prolif-eration of fangirl-friendly blogs suggests that these alternative networks are not only formed but growing stronger, but their transformative im-pact at the industrial and cultural level has yet to be determined. While they are creating spaces for female geeks and fans to make these "posi-tive moves" away from an increasingly hostile subcultural option, they should not be the only option.

This isolationist approach, a response to gendered anti-fan practices, has the potential to confirm the idea that women do not have a place within "authentic" geek and fan subcultures, rather than acknowledging that they always have been present and remain central to that culture. By focusing on fan identity as a motivator of anti-fan performances and practices, we are able to not only consider how anti-fandom constitutes a gendered form of boundary policing that has been exacerbated by fan culture's shift from the margins to the mainstream within the conver-gence culture industry but also begin to gauge the impact of these per-formances and practices on fan culture broadly. Much as Horkheimer and Adorno expressed concerns that "the attitudes the culture industry calls forth [. . .] are anything but harmless" and can "chime in with currently popular hate campaigns,"[90] the propagandistic valences of spreadable misogyny reflect the ways in which the convergence culture industry, however unwittingly, "chimes in" with the broader sociopoliti-cal War on Women and nativist trends in culture at large. If memes like the idiot nerd girl or fake geek girl accusations more generally func-tion as a form of negative reinforcement, wielded by those who have been centered in the convergence culture industry's conceptualization of the fan to disenfranchise those already on the margins, the subsequent chapter turns its attention to purported moments of positive reinforce-ment of fan participation. However, because these instances of collab-orationist outreach by media industries structurally favor historically masculinized modes of fan engagement, they might be used as further ammunition in the current "War on Fangirls."

4

Terms and Conditions

Co-Opting Fan Labor and Containing Fan Criticism

The prior two chapters have considered the convergence culture industry's androcentric construction of fans as an emergent power demographic and how some male fans, in turn, have utilized that cultural leverage to marginalize women within geek culture or deny their claims to fan identity. This chapter investigates how media industries' partial and conditional embrace of fan practices and participatory culture subtly colors these perceptions of which fans are (in many cases, quite literally) valuable within a post-convergence media landscape. In grappling with these shifting socio-technological conditions, driven by user-generated content and a growing industrial imperative to quantify audience "engagement," the convergence culture industry has more often than not attempted to remediate analog industry/fan relations. The convergence culture industry's assimilative approach offers amnesty to those fans who are willing to submit to the surveillance and subsequent monetization of their fan labor, and continues to systemically crack down on "those fan uses of copyrighted intellectual property that challenge corporate productive and distributional hegemony."[1] Unlike the prior chapter's discussion of spreadable misogyny as an explicitly gendered form of intra-fannish policing, this chapter focuses on the far more subtle and structural, but no less insidious, messages being sent to female fans engaged in transformative or critical textual production.

In order to interrogate both the legal and ideological "terms and conditions" that govern industrially sanctioned modes of fan participation, this chapter focuses on two key issues. The first is how fan labor has been industrially co-opted, contained, and commercialized. The test cases below, examining efforts to monetize transformative fan production, the emergence of "official" fan remixing tools and contests, and fan-centric publishing platforms, are designed to explore how the convergence culture industry conditionally facilitates fan production. Second, I will revisit John Fiske's taxonomic approach to fan production in order to address the growing prominence of and industrial reliance on enunciative forms of fan engagement. In his examination of predigital fan culture, Fiske defines enunciative fan practices as fan talk or style that generates and circulates "certain meanings of the object of fandom within a local community."[2] This discussion of enunciative fandom through an analysis of AMC's fan aftershow *Talking Dead* will set the stage for chapter 5's discussion of those, like *Talking Dead* host Chris Hardwick, who have professionally leveraged their own fan identities to speak on fandom's behalf.

The terms and conditions that govern sanctioned forms of fan participation within the convergence culture industry function as a form of "fanagement," and disproportionally target the transformative works that have been historically produced by female fans. Matt Hills offers the term "fanagement" to describe industrial modes of "responding to, and anticipating, fan criticisms, as well as catering for specific fractions of fandom who might otherwise be at odds with the unfolding brand, and attempting to draw a line under fan resistance to diegetic and production changes."[3] Ironically (or fittingly, depending on your perspective) "fanagement" is performed through the very narrative models that purportedly reflect the fan's growing power and influence within the convergence culture industry. Hills focuses on how transmedia tie-ins and paratexts (e.g., novels, radio plays, comics, and so on) work to disciplinarily shut down fan debates and diminish "fan criticisms of the brand."[4] I am concerned with a related form of fanagement, one that is invested with protecting a branded conception of fan culture and uses similar strategies to corral and contain fan critiques.

Louisa Stein takes a slightly more Althusserian approach in her analysis of efforts to construct and court Millennial fans, contending that a television network "interpellates an ideal viewer who is liminal and yet poised to be mainstream, expert at media and yet potentially malleable for advertisers, willing to go the extra mile in terms of textual investment and yet happy to play within the officially demarcated lines."[5] This notion of the interpellated fan thereby "combines all the positive fan qualities such as sustained viewer interest and commercial viability while engaging fannishly in ways preferred and controlled by the studios."[6] The test cases below reflect the convergence culture industry's emergent and gendered approaches to "fanagement," exploring which fans are being hailed by media industries and which fan practices have either the industrial capacity or the fannish desire to be interpellated.

Fan Labor

From the first wave of fan studies onwards, scholars have frequently situated fandom as a space of "constant struggle between fans and the industry, in which the industry attempts to incorporate the tastes of the fans, and the fans to 'excorporate' the products of the industry."[7] This "struggle" within analog fan culture was primarily one of legal/industrial versus affective/fannish claims to "ownership" of media texts, in which fans "perceive themselves as rescuing the show from its producers."[8] As "The First Rule of Fandom" (much like the first rule of *Fight Club*) became increasingly difficult to maintain in the digital age, and fans and industry alike were forced to deal with the dissolution of the "Fourth Wall,"[9] this "struggle" has increasingly taken place over the incorporation of fan *labor*. Issues surrounding affective and legal ownership persist, but they have been rendered increasingly complex by fans' increased access to the means of cultural production, as well as the industry's growing economic reliance on fan "engagement" as a metric.[10]

In *Convergence Culture*, Henry Jenkins broke the media industry's response to "fan productivity [going] public"[11] in the digital age into two camps: prohibitionists and collaborationists. Prohibitionists, primarily "old media" such as the film and television industries, initially attempted to "regulate and criminalize many forms of fan participation that once fell below their radar"[12] and subsequently have grown too visible and valuable to be ignored, and too voluminous to be comprehensively censured. This regulatory approach to fan participation and production, typically marked by cease and desist letters on the grounds of copyright infringement, is indeed on the wane. However, the lingering threat of legal censure remains one of the central reasons why some fans are hesitant to move away from strictly noncommercial modes of fan production and distribution. As old media companies, and in particular the television industry, have adopted more collaborationist approaches over the past decade, they have also revalued fans as promotional laborers and "grassroots intermediaries."[13] At first glance, this would appear to be a tentative industrial endorsement of fandom, a step towards acknowledging the creative viability of fans' transformative textual production and the important role fan labor plays in the promotion and success of media properties. To what degree the convergence culture industry's collaborationist turn is motivated by a desire to colonize and control fandom (or, at the very least, endorse and standardize a version of fandom that can be most effectively capitalized on) is unclear. What is clear is that fan and digital media scholars routinely fail to interrogate how this new collaborationist approach to fandom has traded legal censure for creative censure.

Because digital media have created a growing imperative to mobilize and monetize fan participation, media corporations have been forced to shift away from their historically prohibitionist responses to fan production. The contemporary moment is a far cry from the late 1990s and early 2000s, in which media industries commonly "adopted a scorched-earth policy towards their consumers,"[14] but prohibitionists and collaborationists ultimately remain ensconced on the same "side," with consumers and fans on the other, "asserting a right to participate in the culture, on their own terms, when and where they wish."[15] I am sympathetic to Jenkins's desire to celebrate the media industry's move towards more collaborationist policies, regardless of the market forces motivating this change of heart, and my intention here is not to unilaterally dismiss the media industry's collaborationist turn as a calculated, covert move to co-opt fandom for profit. I have argued elsewhere[16] that the industrial adoption of a more collaborationist approach to fandom may be the lesser of two evils, but it is equally concerned with ideological control.

A central concern regarding the emergence of these "official" or "authorized" industry collaborations with fan culture is that "certain groups of fans can become legit if and only if they follow certain ideas, don't become too rebellious, too pornographic, don't read too much against the grain."[17] In short, fandom's collaboration with the industry is equated with "legitimacy," but this legitimacy is only granted when fandom affirmationally agrees to play by the convergence culture industry's rules. These "certain groups" that are strategically excluded from sanctioned fan culture appear to reference the female creators and consumers of slash fanfiction, fanart, and fanvids, but they more generally encompass female fans, their reading practices, and their gradual exclusion as "legitimate fans" in the convergence culture industry's emerging collaborationist model. This ultimately exclusionary gesture of inclusivity results in what Roberta Pearson identifies as one of the central paradoxes of convergence culture, namely, "that the very digital media that have been hailed as blurring lines between producers and consumers and creating a more participatory culture instead reinforce cultural hierarchies."[18]

Though collaborationist industry approaches endorse fannish, participatory consumption generally, they do so through a hierarchical fragmentation of existing fan communities and fan practices in an attempt to construct an authorized, cohesive, "official" fandom. The convergence culture industry's creation of "official" fan enclaves unsurprisingly privileges affirmational modes of consumption, promotion, and singular (frequently hegemonic or heterosexist) textual interpretations that neatly align with an intended/authorial reading of the text. Fans' transformative works have little place in this model, and when they are solicited it is through a tightly regulated framework of contest rules and terms of use, as the test cases below explore in more depth.

Despite being focused predominantly on nineteenth-century literature, Joanna Russ's 1983 book *How to Suppress Women's Writing* remains an invaluable critical catalogue of the ways in which the creative work of women has historically been (and continues to be) dismissed, ignored, derided, or credited to male influence or the author's inherently "masculine" traits. Much as Russ notes that "it's important to realize that the absence of formal prohibitions against committing art does not preclude the presence of powerful, informal ones,"[19] I would suggest that the convergence culture industry's collaborationist turn has disproportionately placed informal prohibitions on those modes of fan production historically aligned with female fan communities. Offering a transformative play on Russ's work in their essay "How to Suppress Women's Remix," fan scholars Francesca Coppa and Rebecca Tushnet levy a similar argument, stating that even within our robust contemporary remix culture, digital distribution platforms remain "structurally inhospitable" to historically female-centric forms of fan remix like vidding.[20] This hostility can range from the overly stringent enforcement of anti-piracy policies like the Digital Millennium Copyright Act (DMCA) to the development of tools like YouTube's Content ID screening system (which flags videos prior to upload for the inclusion of any copyrighted materials), neither of which adequately account for fair uses of copyrighted materials by fans in their production of transformative works. Somewhat ironically, if Russ was concerned about the systemic efforts to erase the creative contributions of women, Coppa and Tushnet suggest that many female fan producers have responded to the inhospitable nature of digital platforms and anxieties surrounding fanworks' growing visibility to industry by going further underground, password-protecting transformative fanworks, or pulling them from the Internet entirely.[21] If "remix is threatened by both visibility and invisibility,"[22] then the remainder of this chapter is focused predominantly on which modes of fan production are rendered more or less visible by the convergence culture industry's conditional embrace of fan culture.

Whenever we discuss the "interpellated fan" hailed by contemporary media industries, or their efforts in "fanagement," what we are in fact discussing are exercises in tokenism. Drawing on the work of psychologist Judith Long Laws, Russ contends that tokenism is a core political rationale for why female writers have been historically ignored, derided, and discredited. Laws suggests that tokenism is "found wherever a dominant group is under pressure to share privilege, power, or other desirable commodities with a group that is excluded," but in reality what is being sold is "a promise of mobility that is severely restricted. [. . .] [T]he Token does not become assimilated into the dominant group, but is destined for permanent marginality."[23] The convergence culture industry, like its namesake, functions similarly, promising greater participation but only "fus[ing] the old and familiar into a new quality."[24] It is important to remember that the media industry is an *industry*, and thus its primary objective will always be the protection and continued monetization of its intellectual property. However, I would contend that the convergence culture industry's tokenist approach to fan culture, the deeply selective "terms and conditions" it has placed on fan practices and labor, destines female fans to occupy a permanently marginalized place within this evolving "collaborationist" relationship.

Containing, Co-Opting, and Commercializing Transformative Fan Practices

The transformative textual production of fans has long been considered a form of "women's work" on a number of levels. The most literal interpretation is that the communal forms of fannish textual production commonly studied by fan scholars (e.g., fanfiction, fanvids, etc.) have been overwhelmingly produced by women. A second, and equally important, connection that links fan production and "women's work" is that both are unpaid labor, more commonly framed as "labors of love." In both cases, the laborer is positioned as performing a sort of "care work," born out of affection for a person or a media object, and thus is not considered or valued as "labor" in the conventional understanding of the term. Just as many feminist media scholars have critiqued this gendered double standard, Francesca Coppa frames its fan equivalent best, and most bluntly:

> Fandom is a subculture well on its way to becoming culture, and while that has many benefits, it also raises the risk of re-marginalizing the groups that the subculture once represented. [. . .] I worry about women becoming, yet again, a minority voice in a mixed gender fannish culture in which the makers of Chad Vader get a movie deal and the makers of the K/S vid Closer flee the internet when their vids go viral.[25] The media—especially the genre media which has been the center of so much fannish activity—has typically courted a male demographic, despite (or perhaps because of) their female-dominated audiences. And female fans have typically made lemonade from these lemons; it's no accident that so much "remix" culture happens in the context of minority communities: women, blacks, and the disabled. But in the end, my lovingly crafted fanwork is not your marketing team's "user-generated content."[26]

Coppa's coda is significant, as it perfectly encapsulates the cognitive dissonance that occurs when fan practices or "labors of love" are assimilated as promotional paratexts and must conform to industry logics.

The convergence culture industry's "collaborationist turn" has resulted in a growing body of work on the exploitation of fan labor. In particular, Tiziana Terranova's work presaged the concerns of many contemporary fan scholars about the convergence culture industry's conflation of participation and free labor within digital culture, resulting in "productive activities that are pleasurably embraced and at the same time often shamelessly exploited."[27] Mark Andrejevic similarly expressed concerns about the growing industrial reliance on audience labor and interrogated the continued use of Jenkins's once-empowering description of fans as "textual poachers," observing that "the 'poachers' are helping to work the field for its owners"[28] with more and more frequency within convergence culture. The fan labor hailed and interpellated by the convergence culture industry unquestionably falls into this category, but it is vital to caution against summarily dismissing industry/fan relations as "exploitative." Discoures surrounding fan exploitation too readily strip fans of agency, invariably invoking regressive understandings of fans as "cultural dupes"[29] that harken back to Horkheimer and Adorno's depiction of audiences within the culture industry. The convergence culture industry is far subtler in its appeals to fan labor, in large part because of the unique technocultural and industrial contexts it operates in.

When media industries attempt to co-opt fan texts that have historically circulated within a gift or a "digi-gratis" economy,[30] the result is the emergence of what I have dubbed a "regifting economy," with all the negative social connotations attached to that term.[31] If, as Lewis Hyde has argued in his anthropological study of gift economies, "[T]he cardinal difference between gift and commodity exchange [is] that a gift establishes a feelingbond between two people,"[32] then "we cannot really become bound to those who give us false gifts."[33] Regifting economies that emerge when media industries co-opt, contain, or commercialize fan production for their own purposes present similarly "false gifts" to fan culture, and ultimately strive to "regift a narrowly defined and contained version of fandom to a general audience," swapping "grassroots fandom's organically generated output and fluid exchange of fan works for the regulation and resale of fan works through contests and the elusive promise of credibility."[34] In addition to unpacking the legal "terms and conditions" governing instances in which media industries solicit fan production, the test cases below collectively suggest that industrial regifting economies may seek to commodify, but ultimately contain, historically feminized modes of fan engagement.

Corporatized Fanfiction Platforms and Kindle Worlds

Fanlib, a short-lived fanfiction site that sought to monetize fan production in exchange for prizes and proximity to media creators, has become
an exemplary "bad object" for fan scholars discussing the industrial
co-optation of fan labor, and an urban legend among fans anxious about
industrial encroachment into transformative fan production cultures.
Founded in 2007 in partnership with a variety of media companies, from
Simon & Schuster to Showtime, Fanlib has been overwhelmingly viewed
as a crass, failed attempt by "(male) venture capitalists to profit financially from (female-generated) fan fiction."[35] While Fanlib appeared on
its surface to be endorsing and facilitating fans' transformative tendencies, in reality the site forced fans to give up all rights to their work, and
in exchange offered no legal protection if media companies chose to
come after fans for copyright infringement. The site provoked immediate pushback from preexisting fanfiction communities, and within a
year it had been purchased by Disney and shuttered.

Fanlib's fatal flaw, according to fan scholar Karen Hellekson, was
"misreading 'community' as 'commodity.'"[36] It also appeared to fundamentally misread both its prospective user base and the appeal of
industrial proximity for fanfiction authors and readers, evidenced by
this Internet advertisement for Fanlib that was subsequently hacked by
an anonymous fangirl (figure 4.1). The first two images, which constituted the original ad for the site, are not only rooted in longstanding
pathologies concerning the fanboy's "failed masculinity"; they blatantly
misgender the vast majority of the site's potential users, namely, female
writers and readers of fanfiction. The "lib" in Fanlib was not a reference to the site's primary function as a digital repository, or fanfiction
"library," but was rather a play on the fill-in-the-blank narrative functionality of Madlibs, the story template game in which players provide
particular words to customize a preexisting story, often with nonsensi-
cal results. This ad promises a decidedly different, and far more ironic,
interpretation: liberation. This promise of fannish empowerment, of a
fanfiction archive on industrially sanctioned steroids, was immediately
undermined by Fanlib's draconian approach to ownership and legal cul-
pability. As the transformative addition to the ad makes clear, fanfiction
by fangirls has been historically uninterested in garnering industrial

Figure 4.1. Ad for the for-profit fanfiction site Fanlib (*left and middle panels*), with a transformative addition by an anonymous female fan. "Life with Livejournal," *Life without Fanlib*, May 23, 2007, https://life-wo-fanlib.dreamwidth.org.

legitimacy at the expense of "censorship, ownership, or bullshit," reveling in the transformative genre's "pleasures of unpublishability," unhindered by the constraints of the media texts it uses for inspiration and embedded within the literacies of a particular fan collective.[37]

In lieu of further litigating the failure of Fanlib,[38] or what it potentially represented about the convergence culture industry's initial illiteracy with regard to the appeals of fannish gift economies, it is more instructive to consider a slightly less controversial and more contemporary for-profit fanfiction publishing effort: Amazon's Kindle Worlds. Framed as a natural extension of Amazon's popularity as a self-publishing platform, Kindle Worlds launched in 2013 as "a place for you to publish fan fiction inspired by [. . .] featured Worlds, engage an audience of readers, and earn royalties."[39] It was precisely because of this conclusive promise to route a percentage of the profits from each sale back to fanfiction authors (reportedly 35 percent for stories over ten thousand words, or 20 percent for shorter works of fiction)[40] that Kindle Worlds was met with more ambivalence than its predecessors. Meaningful "terms and conditions" that govern fannish creativity still exist, both via the small number of licensed storyworlds fans are allowed to write within and through content guidelines specific to each media property. Some of these terms and conditions are fairly arcane and do not meaningfully hinder fans' creativity. For example, if you plan to compose *G.I. Joe* fanfiction for Kindle Worlds, the content guidelines specify that "[t]he character, Snake Eyes, shall never be depicted or described as a fan of the [American baseball team] the New York Yankees," due to the fact that Hasbro is headquartered in Boston.[41]

In most cases, however, the Kindle Worlds content guidelines place restrictive terms and conditions on the forms of fanfiction that have historically circulated within female fan communities, and were central to their classification as feminist cultural products. It is common to see content guidelines like this set for the CW series *Gossip Girl* (2007–2012), where approximately 25 percent of the guidelines aim to restrict particular forms of romantic or sexual content (figure 4.2). These restrictions surrounding erotic content almost unilaterally appear as the first

kindle worlds

Gossip Girl Content Guidelines

1. Pornography: We don't accept pornography or offensive depictions of graphic sexual acts.
2. Offensive Content: We don't accept offensive content, including but not limited to racial slurs, excessively graphic or violent material, or excessive use of foul language.
3. Illegal and Infringing Content: We take violations of laws and proprietary rights very seriously. It is the authors' responsibility to ensure that their content doesn't violate laws or copyright, trademark, privacy, publicity, or other rights.
4. Poor Customer Experience: We don't accept books that provide a poor customer experience. Examples include poorly formatted books and books with misleading titles, cover art, or product descriptions. We reserve the right to determine whether content provides a poor customer experience.
5. Excessive Use of Brands: We don't accept the excessive use of brand names or the inclusion of brand names for paid advertising or promotion.
6. Crossover: No crossovers from other Worlds are permitted, meaning your work may not include elements of any copyright-protected book, movie, or other property outside of the elements of this World.
7. No erotica, including frequent, prominent, or graphic descriptions of sexual acts.
8. Your Work may not be a novelization of a Gossip Girl television series episode.

Figure 4.2. A typical set of content guidelines for Amazon's Kindle Worlds. "Gossip Girl Content Guidelines," *Amazon*, https://images-na.ssl-images-amazon.com.

(and theoretically most important) rule, and are reiterated towards the end of each set of "World" guidelines. The distinctions between "pornography" and "erotica" are purposefully muddy, and what qualifies as an "offensive" depiction of sex remains pointedly flexible and subjective. Here, without actively labeling homoerotic content as "offensive," Kindle Worlds nonetheless lays out the terms of its conditional embrace of fan culture.

These guidelines become all the more confounding when we consider the fictional "world" that fans would be writing in. *Gossip Girl*, after all, not only featured sexual encounters between its characters on a near-weekly basis; its entire 2008 marketing campaign featured images of its protagonists engaging in group sex and making out naked in a swimming pool, coupled with cheekily repurposed negative review copy such as "mind-blowingly inappropriate." Thus, in addition to its legalistic efforts to limit fans' transformative impulses, Kindle Worlds also frequently dissuades textual production that canonically or "affirmationally" aligns with the fictional world. Kindle Worlds may deploy "the rhetoric of fans, calling these stories fan fiction and using terms like 'creative community,'"[42] but the inherently gendered terms and conditions the site places on fannish textual production also reflect that what is most "scary about transformative fandom is that it's a place where young women love their media without reservation, and where they can make stories for themselves. [. . .] Because fandom is the province of young women and, culturally, we find young women terrifying."[43]

It is important to, as Mel Stanfill does, situate Kindle Worlds within the context of a broader "fan fiction gold rush" beginning with the 2012 publication of *50 Shades of Grey*, which originated as *Twilight* fanfiction. Stanfill positions this growing array of fanfiction publishing initiatives somewhat hyperbolically, but in no way incorrectly, as a generational "battle for fandom's soul," revealing "tensions between older, more communitarian models of fandom and contemporary, individualistic, market-based ones."[44] The incipient danger, then, is that fans who have come of age within the convergence culture industry potentially lack the institutional memory to fully appreciate the social functionality of fannish gift economies, and may invariably shift fan culture. I agree with Stanfill's sentiment that emergent models are not "inherently bad, unless they crowd out the old one, becoming the only way to be a fan, or unless corporations insist all fanfiction be done in confined, commercial ways. The battle for fandom's soul can only fairly be fought if fans know what's at stake."[45] What is ultimately at stake is a codification of the convergence culture industry's androcentric conception of fan culture. If these initiatives are successful and a generational shift in perspective on the commercialization of fanfiction does occur, it may be at the expense of the facets of the practice that most actively pose a form of feminist intervention. If they are unsuccessful, they risk providing further evidence, however faulty, that women are a niche fan-cultural demographic that is not worth courting.

"Official" Fan Video Contests, Tools, and Provisions

In 2006, *Time* magazine named "you," or Internet users, their "Person of the Year," and Google purchased video-sharing platform YouTube for $1.65 billion. Since launching the year prior, YouTube had become both a significant distribution space for amateur media production and a bourgeoning hub for the fan practice of vidding. Described by Francesca Coppa as "a form of grassroots filmmaking in which clips from television shows and movies are set to music," fanvids use songs "as an interpretive lens to help the viewer to see the source text differently," creating a "visual essay that stages an argument."[46] Vidding originated at a *Star Trek* fan convention in 1975, when Kandy Fong projected a slideshow choreographed to music to tell a story, and evolved in the 1980s and 1990s through laborious tape-to-tape editing facilitated by VCR technology. Fostered by an abundance of new technologies that have eased digital video collection (e.g., file extraction, ripping, storage, and sharing), production (e.g., amateur and affordable editing software), and distribution (e.g., video sharing platforms), vids have grown exponentially as a form of fan production over the past decade.

Historically produced within female fan communities, vids are distinct from other historically male-dominated or gender-neutral forms of fan video production (e.g., fan filmmaking, parody videos, machinima) in both form and content. Importantly, because fanvids tend to use an array of video clips from a selected media property and an entire song in their construction, they stand on more tenuous legal ground than other forms of fan video production, which either have been tacitly endorsed through official contests or are perceived to have stronger fair use claims through their comparatively limited or parodic uses of copyrighted content. Google's acquisition of YouTube thus raised concerns, both because this brought the user-generated-content platform under corporate ownership and also because it signaled the platform's more concerted effort to partner with media industries to control the uses of their copyrighted content. Though the bulk of fanvids qualify as transformative works, and thus are legally protected under fair use doctrine, the introduction of YouTube's Content ID system in 2007 seemed to confirm that the site's primary commitment was to copyright holders.

Content ID is a "video fingerprinting" tool that scans each video uploaded to YouTube against copyright holders' libraries of reference files for any infringing audiovisual content. While it was initially designed to combat piracy (e.g., users uploading an episode of television or a film in its entirety), it has also had a chilling effect on the site's capacity to host fanvids. Because vids tend to use popular songs in full, they are easily scanned and subsequently misidentified as a piratic posting of copyrighted content if the song's use as an interpretive critical lens is not taken into consideration. Alexis Lothian has suggested that fannish "theft" and transformative works represent an "undercommons" in which a fanvid is "neither radically disruptive of, nor fully incorporated into, the media industry's systems of ownership, but simultaneously supports and undercuts them while producing a collectivity of its own."[47] Just as Lothian suggests that "it is worth determining who defines the use as fair, and what it might mean to place a value on unfair uses,"[48] it is important to note that by 2009, Content ID had evolved from a tool to monitor video uploads for pirated content (defining which uses are "fair") to a monetization tool for the platform and copyright holders (placing different values on unfair uses that they deem more or less acceptable).

When Content ID afforded copyright holders the right either to issue a preemptive "takedown" notice for the content or to monetize that content via advertisements, the majority chose the latter. In a support video released by YouTube, this monetization of fan labor is framed as building more reciprocal relationships between content creators and consumers, with the video claiming that "artists can let fans re-use their content, and fans can create promotional and business opportunities for artists, making Content ID a true win-win that enables new forms of creativity and collaboration."[49] The video's careful elision of the institutions that overwhelmingly retain and maintain ownership over an artists' work, and the framing of fannish motivation towards video production as innately affirmational or promotional, clearly explicate what a "win-win" collaborationist relationship between fans and content creators and owners looks like within the convergence culture industry.

The vast majority of industrial efforts to facilitate fan production, either through organized fanvid contests or through devoted archival spaces on official websites to display fan art, replicate these empty "win-win" dynamics, and are prime examples of the conflicted "collaborationist" relationship between content producers and fans that has been cultivated by the convergence culture industry. Even in cases in which transformative fanworks are overtly solicited,[50] the terms and conditions of these contests assure that fan art will remain affirmational. As the official remixing toolkits and contests discussed below suggest, these restrictions are often not as overt as the terms and conditions presented by Kindle Worlds, but are equally designed to subtly stifle the types of fanvids historically produced within female fan communities. Because, as Julie Levin Russo suggests, "[T]he legitimacy and perhaps even survival of forms of vernacular creativity may hinge on the degrees of poaching, hybridizing, and queering that processes of commodification are able to tolerate and incorporate,"[51] an examination of what fans are/are not able or encouraged to "build" with official remixing "toolkits" reveals a great deal about what degrees of transformativity the convergence culture industry is willing to tolerate.

The 2007 launch of the *Battlestar Galactica* Video Maker Toolkit offered an early example of industrial efforts to facilitate the creation of transformative fan works as promotional objects. Russo described the Toolkit, which has unfortunately since been taken offline, thus:

> Its instructions invite fans to "be a part of Battlestar Galactica" by making a four-minute tribute film, the best of which will be selected to air on television. To "help give your videos the Battlestar look and sound," a menu of downloadable audio and video clips is provided, while the rules place a premium on an archaic ex nihilo model of originality by stipulating that the only additional material permitted is what "you created." The

fact that these "tools" are limited to fewer than forty short CGI-based establishment and action sequences indicates that Video Maker's conception of sanctioned derivative filmmaking is extremely narrow, notably excluding the character-based dramatic scenes that make up the majority of the show.[52]

The Video Maker's discursive emphasis on professional affiliation, authenticity, and originality, when coupled with the competitive nature of the exercise, offers an "optimistic fantasy of a warm relationship between media producers and consumers."[53] Importantly, as Russo alludes to here, the lack of raw audiovisual materials featuring characters or conversations, and the overt exclusion of any lyrical music, foreclosed the creation of the types of vids female fans have historically produced. If "vidders incarnate an alternative fantasy of kinship," one that is by design "collective, networked, and unsanctioned, [reproducing] without a patriarchal center,"[54] then the Video Maker Toolkit structurally attempted to institute if not a patriarchal center to fannish video production, then at least a paternalistic one.

In many cases, then, legal terms and conditions only constitute one facet of the "prohibition" of historically female-dominated forms of transformative textual production. Another example of how fanvidding practices might be ostensibly hailed by, but ultimately contained within, the convergence culture industry is Disney and Marvel's partnership with YouTube to create a video remix toolkit to promote the 2012 premiere of *The Avengers*. The title of a *Variety* article announcing this initiative heralded, "Disney, Marvel Offer Do-It-Yourself 'Avengers' Vids: YouTube Software Allows Fans to Craft Legit Remixes from Pic,"[55] seemingly promising a legal and legitimized platform for fanvidders. The toolkit included thirty-two short clips from the film and excerpts of four songs from the film's soundtrack (each track under a minute long), along with clips of dialogue and a variety of SFX and transition options. In theory, this selection, when coupled with the legitimation discourse forwarded by *Variety*, is appealing. At the very least, this toolkit offered the raw audio material, in the form of songs with lyrics, that vidders would need as a lens to stage a particular reading.

Much like the *Battlestar Galactica* Video Maker Toolkit, however, the proffered video clips ensured that vidders would be incapable of building a video that explored character dynamics, (homo)erotic or otherwise. At its core, *The Avengers* is about relationships, but this is not reflected in the range of clips provided: nearly 38 percent just featured explosions (only 15 percent of those featuring a major character), and a whopping 40 percent featured men in some state of action (flying, shooting, fighting). Thus, even with the lyrical content of the songs available as a fannish "interpretive lens," there was little visual fodder to interpret . . . unless someone was angling to compose a riveting commentary on the diversity of explosions in superhero films. The result was a none-too-subtle attempt to overdetermine what "narratives" people used the tool to tell. Part of the rationale for this limited clip selection is understandable: Disney and Marvel probably curated imagery from the film's trailer as a hedge against potential spoilers and to ensure that fans' final products would hew closely to the promotional style of a film trailer in length and content. The vast majority of fan remixes that were made reflect how effective this strategy was, with the toolkit churning out polished videos that reflected a deep understanding of the affirmational aesthetic language of promotional paratexts. As the *Variety* article tellingly noted, "[This] marketing move is seen as the latest way to make moviegoers, especially younger ones, feel as if they're part of a film's campaign."[56] Not a part of the film, or the fan community that surrounds it, but part of the *campaign*.

More often than not, the convergence culture industry's collaborationist initiatives fail to meaningfully reach out to preexisting fanvidding communities, and both overtly and covertly dissuade the forms of remix video that have been historically created by women. This is not to say that many female fans are not using (or enjoying using) these authorized vidding tools, but if this is how "legit" fan remix video is conceptualized, we must also recognize it as part of a broader effort to displace or dissuade those forms the convergence culture industry deems "illegitimate." Efforts like these from Disney and Marvel tend to be discursively framed as a decisive break from the industry's prior prohibitionist response to fan production, taking a more collaborationist approach to fan culture and fan production. While this might mark a step in the right direction, we need to continue to be critical of what modes of creative censure come attached to these collaborationist gestures, and which audiences they court. Much as women continue to be treated as surplus audiences for comic books and superhero franchises, here they are considered surplus remixers as well.

More recently, even historically male-dominated and sanctioned forms of fan video, like fan filmmaking,[57] have become the focus of the convergence culture industry's "collaborationist" crackdown efforts. Though vids often are designed to stage an argument about a media text's narrative, or build alternative narratives through the juxtaposition of preexisting imagery and the song selection, fan films are overtly narrative in design. Like many transformative fan texts, fan films frequently play in the gaps and margins of their source material, or alternately might affirmationally re-create or parody famous scenes or reenact whole films. Aesthetically ranging from delightfully amateurish to decidedly polished and professional, fan filmmaking has been an especially rich form of fan production for franchises with long temporal gaps between installments. This has particularly been the case for the *Star Trek* franchise, with fan filmmaking flourishing within the televisual gap between 2005, when *Enterprise* went off the air, and 2015, when the forthcoming series *Star Trek: Discovery* was announced. Because fan films have historically been semi-sanctioned by media industries via contests, many fans were shocked by a December 2015 lawsuit that targeted *Star Trek* fan filmmakers.

The lawsuit, filed by Paramount and CBS, was directed at a *Star Trek* fan film, *Axanar*, that had crowdfunded over one million dollars with the aim of producing a professional-grade fan film. It was in large part due to this degree of professionalism, which included hiring crew members who had worked on official *Star Trek* productions, that "the studios aimed to convey the message that professional-quality 'derivatives' of its films and series wouldn't be tolerated."[58] On June 23, 2016, CBS and Paramount Pictures released a new set of *Star Trek* fan film guidelines through the franchise's official website to clarify its new policies.[59] In the press release accompanying these "guidelines," *Star Trek*'s corporate owners acknowledged the large role that fans (and fan production, by extension) have played in the franchise's endurance, ultimately claiming that the guidelines were designed to "show our appreciation by bringing fan films back to their roots."[60]

The guidelines themselves opened with the following statement: "CBS and Paramount Pictures are big believers in reasonable fan fiction and fan creativity, and, in particular, want amateur fan film-makers to showcase their passion for *Star Trek.*"[61] The rules that fol-low delimit what CBS and Paramount deem to be "reasonable" forms of "non-professional and amateur" fan creativity, those that they as-sure fans they "will not object to, or take legal action against."[62] Before we even arrive at the terms and conditions, then, we can see a set of discursive contradictions begin to emerge. Fan films are held up as a preferred mode of fan production, perhaps because they tend to cre-atively hew closely to the source material. The guidelines themselves, however, strictly limited the serialized nature of many *Star Trek* fan film projects (limiting each "film" to fifteen minutes and limiting the "parts" of each story to two, meaning that no fannish replication of a television or web series format was feasible). Some of these guidelines seemed to be equally directed at vidding practices, including an em-phasis on wholly original video content and the standard provisions against any content that might not be deemed "family friendly," includ-ing sexual content.

As is typical of these "terms and conditions" statements designed to tacitly endorse but ultimately govern fan production, the closing para-graph of the new guidelines negates its opening assurances that no legal action will be taken:

> CBS and Paramount Pictures reserve the right to revise, revoke and/or withdraw these guidelines at any time in their own discretion. These guidelines are not a license and do not constitute approval or authoriza-tion of any fan productions or a waiver of any rights that CBS or Para-mount Pictures may have with respect to fan fiction created outside of these guidelines.

The *Star Trek* fan film lawsuit was settled on January 20, 2017, just eleven days before its scheduled trial date. In a joint statement, the fan filmmakers and their production company pointedly acknowledged that the planned film was not sanctioned and "crossed boundaries ac-ceptable to CBS and Paramount relating to copyright law."[63] This set-tlement was undoubtedly precipitated by a January 4, 2017, summary judgment, which ruled that the fan filmmakers could not claim fair use as a cornerstone of their defense.[64]

Fair use is a right, one that is vital for all fans to inform themselves about and invoke to protect their cultural production, but several issues hinder this. First, like self-defense laws, fair use is classified as an "affirmative defense," meaning that within "copyright litigation, the first chance to formally invoke fair use comes only when someone accuses you of infringement."[65] The second issue, one that Rebecca Tushnet has extensively discussed in her scholarship on the legalities of fan production, is that fan works are rarely included within broader conversations that recognize transformative reworkings as fair use.[66] When fair use was ruled out as a possible defense in the *Star Trek* case, this effectively ruled out any positive outcome for the fan filmmaker defendants, but it also ruled out an opportunity to stage a high-profile defense of fans' transformative works as exercises in fair use. This incident echoes one of Adorno and Horkheimer's core concerns, namely, that the more forcefully the culture industry "entrenches itself, the more it can do as it chooses with the needs of consumers—producing, controlling, disciplining them; even withdrawing amusement altogether."[67] The more terms and conditions the convergence culture industry places on fannish production, via either prohibitionist crackdowns or collaborationist content guidelines, the more its bias towards affirmational and androcentric modes of fan engagement becomes clear.

Reconsidering Fiske's Taxonomy of Fan Production

Thus far, this chapter has suggested that prohibitionist industrial responses to fan production are alive and well in the convergence culture industry and that they have been merely assimilated, Borg-like, into purportedly collaborationist toolkits and guidelines. It is unlikely that the convergence culture industry will ever wholeheartedly embrace the production of transformative fan works, but it has realized that cultivating certain affirmational forms of fan engagement is in its economic interests. In 1992, John Fiske delineated between three types of fan productivity, while acknowledging slippages among these categories. Semiotic productivity was framed as a product of popular culture broadly, rather than fandom specifically, to characterize how we utilize media as a resource to make sense of our "social identity and [. . .] experience."[68] Fan studies has historically focused on theorizing "textual productivity," the creation and circulation of fans' transformative works such as fanfiction, art, and video. Textual productivity is also, not coincidentally, the form of fan engagement that media industries have historically found most legally and ideologically threatening. Fiske's conception of "enunciative productivity," however, is the form of fan production that has been most readily embraced and fostered by the convergence culture industry. In addition to engaging emergent forms of enunciative fan productivity, like livetweeting or hatewatching (viewing a particular program solely for the purpose of communally mocking it), it is vital to pay particular attention to programming trends through which the convergence culture industry most clearly enunciates its preferred forms of fan participation (and, by extension, its preferred fans).

Defined by Fiske as instances of "fan talk," enunciative productivity describes moments in which semiotic productivity is made visible, either conversationally or sartorially. Matt Hills has argued that within digital fan culture,

> Fiske's categories break down altogether or, rather, are recomposed as a rapidly switching circuit in place of a taxonomy. As fan audiences watch TV and then live-tweet along, they shift "interior" semiotic productivity into socially-shared enunciative productivity that's bound up with a particular moment of broadcast, and immediately switch that into the textual productivity of "narrowcast" (if not actually broadcast) digital mediation.[69]

I do not disagree with Hills's claim that social media have destabilized Fiske's taxonomy, and clearly any application of this term to digitally networked fan culture requires us to amend Fiske's notion that enunciative productivity is bound by space and time, circulating only in immediate social circles and producing limited cultural capital.[70] Still, I believe it is precisely because Fiske's analog terminology does not adequately reflect the fluidity of digital forms of fan productivity that they remain useful for theorizing the convergence culture industry's conditional embrace of digital fan culture.

The convergence culture industry is invested in cultivating enunciative productivity on social media platforms precisely because it is temporally tied to a live broadcast and can be spatially bound to official message boards and Facebook pages, creating clearly demarcated and limited social circles through the deployment of official hashtags. The deterioration of legacy advertising models may have forced media industries to acknowledge and court fans through participatory platforms, but their conceptions of audience engagement remain rooted in nostalgia for analog producer/fan interactions. Enunciative forms of fan participation are legible to the industry, and can be promotionally leveraged in ways that most textual productivity legally and ideologically cannot. Through a consideration of the sanctioned enunciative fan spaces cultivated by the convergence culture industry, and what sort of enunciations are facilitated or contained in those spaces, we might better understand how the industry is attempting to model and mold enunciative fan practices as its preferred mode of fan engagement.

In 2006, the micro-blogging platform Twitter launched, and immediately became a hub for fan discourse and the grassroots development of enunciative fan and anti-fan practices, from livetweeting to hate-watching.[71] The television industry, in the midst of grappling with a crumbling post-network advertising model as time shifting (not watching a program live), place shifting (watching on a device other than a television), and cord cutting (canceling cable subscriptions) became the norm, were quick to facilitate and incorporate these emergent enunciative fan practices. Shows and networks quickly established a presence on the site, promoting official hashtags and encouraging showrunners and talent to engage fans in an unprecedented dialogue. Fans, in turn, alternately relished this newfound intimacy with content creators and endeavored to evade the industry's view by cultivating their own elaborately coded hashtagging systems. By 2013, Neilsen had launched its "Twitter TV Ratings" system, amid a growing effort by the industry to quantify and commoditize social audience metrics.[72] Neilsen's Twitter TV Ratings were less concerned with how many people view a given program, or even their affective reaction to the content, and more concerned with the reach of tweets about a given program through "impressions." Fans, as a vocal audience presence on the platform, were thus revalued as key social "influencers," both through their willingness to conform to analog modes of consumption (namely, watching programming live) in exchange for participating in digital fan communities and via the expansive reach of their preexisting fannish networks.

Ian Ang has noted that the institution of television is "haunted by a constant sense of uncertainty," and that the audience, which is "the *sine qua non* for both television's economic viability and cultural legitimacy, forms its ultimate insecurity factor."[73] Social TV initiatives, ranging from livetweeting and liveblogging to the development of second screen apps like AMC's Story Sync, reflect this anxiety, as well as the related institutional imperative "to 'catch,' 'capture,' or 'lay hold of' the audience."[74] It could be argued that the core industrial appeal of social media platforms like Twitter and fan practices like livetweeting is that it has the capacity to offer a more or less "real-time" answer to this eternal uncertainty, tracking not only whether audiences are tuned in but which elements of the program they are especially responsive to. While the impetus for fans to livetweet might range significantly (or even be considered by some as anathema to a truly fannish form of reverent and/ or close reading), studies have shown that "must-tweet" moments tend to revolve around twists in the plot, moments of grief or humor, and character development.[75] ABC's "Shondaland" block of programming, branded "must tweet TV," suggests that television narratives are now being cultivated to best conform to these findings. In these cases, "Twitter becomes not only a backchannel for the show, but it also becomes a part of the show itself."[76] In rare cases, enunciative fan practices become an entirely new show.

Enunciative Fandom and AMC's *Talking Dead*

Hosted by Nerdist founder Chris Hardwick, AMC's *Talking Dead* premiered as a live half-hour fan chat show in October 2011 following the second-season premiere of *The Walking Dead* and expanded to a full hour in February 2013. The format of the show has remained fairly consistent: *Talking Dead* typically brings together a panel of one or two members of *The Walking Dead*'s creative team or cast, along with one or two "celebrity superfans," to discuss the episode that has just aired. This discussion is supplemented by two to three fan questions per episode, submitted through an array of social media platforms (read aloud by Hardwick off preprinted cue cards or a tablet), via phone, or by a member of the show's live studio audience. The conversation is supplemented with live polls, behind-the-scenes video content and sneak peeks, slow motion in memoriam homages to characters who did not survive the episode, and pop-up trivia about the show. The live show on AMC is immediately followed by an online bonus segment streamed on the show's official website that aims to, in its own words, "continue the conversation."

The industrial appeal of this type of fan-oriented live programming is readily apparent, and AMC executives have acknowledged repeatedly in interviews with the trades that *Talking Dead* was designed to offset the network's original programming costs.[77] In addition to formally harnessing *The Walking Dead's* massive social media presence, the show actively discourages audience time shifting and place shifting, is cheap to produce, and brings in additional ad revenue. *Talking Dead* also provides an ideal platform to cross-promote other AMC shows, such as the repeated synergistic appearances of Kevin Smith from AMC's *Comic Book Men*. Michael Davies, president of Embassy Row (the company that created *Talking Dead*), suggests that fan aftershows require a distinct "volume" and "quality" of conversation on social media, and their success is predicated on the answers to questions such as, "Do social-media monitors find their feeds scrolling frequently? Are hashtags associated with the show used readily? Are viewers asking more questions, no matter whether answers are provided?"[78] Fans are obviously keenly aware that the industrial development of fan talk shows such as these are not strictly (or even primarily) motivated by a desire to start a dialogue. Frequently, industrial efforts to implement and regulate "official" hashtags "are not always adopted by users, particularly if they have been discussing a series long before the 'official' accounts were created."[79] The appeal of *Talking Dead* for fans is that it makes a concerted effort to wed itself seamlessly into fans' preexisting enunciative practices.

For example, Hardwick appears in repeated plugs for *Talking Dead* during commercial breaks for *The Walking Dead* to conversationally introduce specific hashtags timed to narrative climaxes, providing AMC with ever more granular data about which components of any given episode are resonating with fans. These hashtags are notable because they work to obfuscate what are often seen as mercenary efforts by media industries to insert themselves into and guide fan discourse. For example, immediately after a scene in which Carl, in a fit of teenage rebellion, sullenly eats a 112-ounce can of pudding, Hardwick appeared in the commercial break to plug *Talking Dead*. One well-timed joke about Carl from Hardwick, which signal boosted tweets from fans who had already adopted the hashtag to comment on the scene before they were officially prompted to, and #pudding began trending on Twitter. By cultivating these sorts of alternative hashtags that are more closely aligned in tone with the preexisting enunciative practices of fans, *Talking Dead* effectively bridges the gap between official and fannish tagging practices and increases the likelihood that multiple hashtags affiliated with the show will trend simultaneously.

Talking Dead has become a ratings juggernaut and routinely draws between three and six million viewers per week, only being beaten by *The Walking Dead* itself in terms of cable ratings. As the lengthy terms and conditions that govern how fans participate in the show's "conversation" suggest, politicized enunciations by fans (say, a criticism of the show's historically brutal mistreatment of black characters) may be readily available on social media, but are easily muted within the confines of the show itself. *Talking Dead* is, first and foremost, a curator of enunciative fan content, excising any forms of "fan talk" it deems inappropriate and valorizing those that align with the aftershow's affirmational focus on canon and the show's production process. This type of enunciative fan curation is reminiscent of the fan wiki Lostpedia, which caused controversy by first deleting pages related to fan theories and transformative production (e.g., the character "Pairings" page went from documenting both canonical couplings and fan ships, or speculative or desired couples, to just the former) and then restoring them under a page clearly marked "fanon."[80] This was positioned by the site's moderators as an effort to rid the wiki of so-called fancruft, but Jason Mittell notes that the incident functioned more broadly as a "debate over how to appropriately use the site, as well as how best to watch the show itself."[81]

The linguistic significance of deeming feminized fannish content like shipping homoerotic slash pairings of characters "cruft," a term that emerged within hypermasculine tech cultures to describe poorly designed or unnecessary code, quite literally "garbage,"[82] once again points to the gendered valuations undergirding what constitutes desirable fan participation. This also, per Mittell's argument, clearly conveys the "best" ways to watch and engage with the show, legitimating some forms of enunciative fan expression and dismissing others in the process. In the case of *Talking Dead*, questions or social media discourse that might be considered feminine fancruft (representational critiques, speculation about character relationships, romantic or otherwise, etc.) rarely make it to air. Those that do model preferred forms of enunciative fan engagement, often sounding less like authentic fannish expressions of affect than a set of publicist-approved talking points. Though AMC's successful second-screen model and its roots in analog advertising and audience-measurement logics deserves more sustained study, for the remainder of this chapter I would like to home in on how *Talking Dead's* self-identified "celebrity superfan" guests function to model what Melanie Kohnen has called "quality fandom."[83]

In line with *The Walking Dead's* successful effort to recuperate both comic books and the zombie horror genre through AMC's branding as a quality television network, *Talking Dead* attempts to cultivate a vision of quality fandom through the carefully moderated "dialogue" it promotes. Though Hardwick and the panels of "celebrity superfan" guests do indulge in fannish responses to the text (genuinely expressing shock or dismay in response to particular plot developments, giddily discussing favorite characters, and so on), this vision of enunciative fandom is one that is designed to model reverence for the text, creators, and performers, and stress affirmational rather than transformative modes of fan engagement. Like quality TV, which typically foregrounds cinematic production values in order to distance itself from the feminized taint of television, *Talking Dead* distances itself from overly critical, emotionally excessive, or erotic fan enunciations, choosing to mine and present an industrial (and frequently androcentric) vision of the "quality" fan.

Chris Hardwick takes on the role of ur-superfan each week as both *Talking Dead's* moderator and its embodied "quality fan" exemplar. The subsequent chapter discusses Hardwick's fantrepreneurial brand in more detail, but for the purposes of the analysis that follows it is sufficient to state that Hardwick's appeal to both media industries and audiences is rooted in his unabashed and deeply affirmational fannish enthusiasm. If quality fandom is emblematic of broader legitimation efforts that have emerged in the convergence era, in which "masculinized affect is thus embraced as 'quality fandom' that is desirable to the industry, and feminized affect is rejected or simply ignored,"[84] Hardwick embodies an even narrower vision of "quality" enunciative fandom in which "fan talk" that is effusive about media industries and texts is rewarded and rendered visible, and white heterosexual male privilege in fan culture is reaffirmed.

Though it has been clearly stated by the show's producers that the "only requirement for guests is that they be genuine fans of the graphic novel or the show,"[85] female "celebrity superfans" are frequently targeted as disingenuous by *Talking Dead*'s viewers. One potential reason why female guests' fan identities are disproportionately scrutinized is that women are grossly underrepresented on *Talking Dead*, with male "celebrity superfans" outnumbering their female counterparts three to one. Comments on Facebook and Twitter from *Talking Dead* viewers about these female "celebrity superfans" range from questioning their fannish commitment ("It's pretty obvious she's never even seen the show") to indulging in an array of misogynistic slurs ("annoying bitch" being one of the more commonly used). The fact that male and female fans alike engage in this disproportionate boundary policing of female "celebrity superfans" is yet another example of how "fake geek girl" discourses have pervaded fandom's (sub)cultural consciousness. The representation of the show's fans via the studio audience, social media, and phone-in segments tends to be more equitable, but *Talking Dead* still unwittingly props up broader enunciative boundary-policing trends that seek to challenge female fans' authenticity.

It is illustrative to walk through one of these responses to the show's "celebrity superfans" in depth. Responding to an appearance by actress Aisha Tyler in a March 4, 2013, post on *Talking Dead*'s Facebook page, one female fan complained, "Aisha Tyler is obnoxious! Please do NOT bring her back. She hogs the conversation and her energy and enthusiasm is a bit overwhelming. Quite frankly this episode of Talking Dead was more Talking Aisha. With guests like her, I'd not return to watch. no. [sic]." Because all of these complaints might be equally leveraged at Hardwick, it is worth unpacking the significance of directing these complaints at a black female fan. Tyler, more than the vast majority of *Talking Dead*'s celebrity superfans, has a strong claim to that identity, in that her comments on the show frequently exhibit an encyclopedic knowledge of both the comic book and the television series. In other words, her affirmational bona fides are not in question; rather, her mere presence and voice is the issue. While this critique of Tyler's "overwhelming" enthusiasm plays neatly into preexisting gendered fan pathologies, aligning her with the emotionally "excessive" fangirl, the statement that she "hogs the conversation" powerfully suggests that black women, in particular, face difficulty in claiming fannish identity and being accepted as figures of fannish authority.

Actress Yvette Nicole Brown presents another challenge to the conceptual collapse between enunciative and affirmational fandom that is modeled by Hardwick and performed by his various "superfan" commentators. Best known for her role as the maternal, religious Shirley Bennett on the cult television series *Community* (2009–2015), Brown has become one of the most popular guests on *Talking Dead*. As of April 2018, Brown has appeared as a guest eleven times, more than any other "celebrity superfan," and she represents a notable exception to the aftershow's general failure to feature fans of color. Unlike the vast majority of other celebrity superfans appearing on *Talking Dead*, Brown tangibly foregrounds her fannish approach to media consumption: she is frequently accompanied by a thick notebook detailing observations and listing outstanding narrative questions and, occasionally, references to the character Daryl Dixon surrounded by hearts. Brown routinely references her "rewatching" to pick up on additional details and character moments, discusses the difficulties of avoiding spoilers, and so on. Brown is also notably one of the only celebrity superfans whose enunciative contributions actively reflect a deeper literacy in the inner workings of fan platforms, jargon, and practices. In addition to frequently framing her comments with "we," actively aligning herself with the show's broader fan community, she casually invokes the specificities of shipping as a fan practice and discusses particular ships she is invested in. Brown's representative presence as a fangirl, though beloved, has at times made the rest of the panel and Hardwick visibly uncomfortable, in part because these utterances have the potential to undermine *The Talking Dead*'s affirmational investment in authorial intent and canon. Brown may be actively celebrated as a close, fannish reader, but on a show in which fan questions are commonly relayed by Hardwick, only to be diffused with "or is that reading too much into things?" or similar dismissals, she also threatens to disrupt the aftershow's affirmational tone through her potentially transformative enunciative expressions (discussing crushes on particular characters, shipping, etc.).

Because Brown is both the only routinely recurring female celebrity fan on *Talking Dead*, and also a black female fan, she carries an extraordinary burden of representation, particularly because "the stereotype of women in fandom generally precludes women of color as participants and producers of content."[86] Moreover, as a middle-aged black woman, Brown self-reflexively brings a maternal presence to her appearances (for example, offering her sleeve to a cast member whose eyes are watering). Brown's star persona, which for contemporary fannish audiences has been most actively determined by her matriarchal role on *Community*, is also inevitably shaped by her lived identity. The work of scholars like Dayna Chatman and Kristen J. Warner on black female fans' Twitter commentary on the television series *Scandal* provides an excellent starting point for a raced and gendered consideration of how Brown is situated within enunciative fan culture. Because, as Warner notes, "mainstream romance, as a genre, consistently overlooks black women as consumers, choosing instead to envision a 'universal' woman as the reader/viewer where 'universal' becomes a euphemism for normatively white,"[87] Brown's longstanding advocacy for the "Richonne" ship is especially illustrative to consider.

After repeatedly mentioning her affinity for the couple (Rick, who is white, and Michonne, who is black), *Talking Dead* celebrated the moment of the character's canonical coupling with a fan reaction video of Brown. In the video, shot in "night vision" green, we see Brown on her sofa, her fan notebook laid against her chest. At the moment of the "reveal," Brown shrieks with glee, clapping her hands and stomping her feet, a reaction that builds in volume and enthusiasm as the scene progresses and ultimately ends with a triumphant "That's what I'm talking about! That's what I'm talking about!" She shouts "RICHONNE!" raising both fists in the air.[88] Dayna Chatman has argued that online forms of communication like social media "afford Black Americans new counterpublic spheres in which to wrestle with interpretations of texts, and seek to collectively define and police the boundaries of what is acceptable to watch and take pleasure in."[89] Here, *Talking Dead* forwards its own subtle policing strategy, celebrating the moment of canonical coupling in which Richonne is elevated from feminine "fancruft" to a legitimate topic of conversation, simultaneously reveling in and poking fun at Brown's deep emotional investment in the coupling. When we consider Brown's response via Warner's discussion of black women's exclusion from these narratives "about choice, desire, and fantasy," coupled with the misogynoir frequently directed at Michonne as a character,[90] Brown's response becomes decidedly more politicized. *Talking Dead*'s response to Brown's response to this miscegenation narrative, meanwhile, attempts to diffuse the political valences of her enunciative outpouring, as the audible chuckles of *Talking Dead*'s live audience permeate the reaction video's soundtrack.

Hardwick's framing of Brown as *Talking Dead*'s resident "therapist" offers another rich site at which to contemplate the intersection of Brown's star text, lived identity, and fan identity. This designation came about, in part, due to Brown's frequent appearances on *Talking Dead* after significant episodes. This significance is occasionally temporal (Brown frequently appears after the [mid]season premiere or finale episodes) but more explicitly marks her recurring presence after episodes that feature particularly traumatic character deaths, which for a time afforded her the less flattering designation of "grim reaper." The "therapist" title also simultaneously speaks to her maternal visual presence, her feminine/affective connection to the show's characters, and the fact that she ably plays the role of analyst. Brown's prescribed role as fannish "therapist" was arguably cemented by her featured presence on the highly anticipated season 7 premiere on October 23, 2016, which featured the brutal and deeply unpopular deaths of two fan-favorite characters. The installment of *Talking Dead* that followed was anomalous, in that it was broadcast live from Hollywood Forever Cemetery and featured the entire ensemble cast and a massive live audience.

This episode of *Talking Dead*, which functioned as a wake in both locale and tone, only briefly featured two superfans: Brown (dressed appropriately in funereal black and welcomed by Hardwick as a "member of the family") and Greg Raiewski, the winner of an "ultimate *Walking Dead* fan" contest (whom Hardwick introduced as "the *guy* that you *guys* helped select" [emphasis mine]). Raiewski's submission video for this contest, interestingly, focused on how he integrates *The Walking Dead* and *Talking Dead* into his classroom as a high school English teacher. After describing how he "debriefed" students after new episodes of *The Walking Dead*, offering extra credit for answering questions asked by Hardwick on the show, Reiewski praised *Talking Dead* for showing his students "that literary analysis is cool."[91] Considering that Reiewski is the only noncelebrity to be featured on *Talking Dead*, his being selected based on this particular pitch is telling. Held up by Hardwick as the show's "ultimate" fan as well as a representative of the show's fans writ large, Reiewski does not just embody "quality" fandom; he explicitly equates *The Walking Dead* with canonical literature and aligns *Talking Dead* with academic analysis (thereby implicitly aligning enunciative fan practices with masculinized authority and objectivity).

Though Brown and Raiewski appeared only briefly, they both conveyed the emotional devastation that fans experienced with this episode. The typically vocal and articulate Brown found herself at a loss for comforting words. Reiewski also struggled to articulate his response to the episode, noting that "it's nice to be able to get through this with everyone" before echoing an earlier statement from Hardwick that it was "cathartic" to watch the intense episode with other fans.[92] Brown, embracing her role as therapist, closed the segment by stating that the events of the episode would undoubtedly have ramifications on the next several seasons of the show, and assuaging fan anxieties by reasserting, "We know the show we love." Brown is unquestionably able to remain a recurring and well-received guest on the show, and a desirable celebrity representative of the show's fan base, precisely because her presence troubles gendered modes of fan engagement, evoking more transformative forms of fannish meaning making even as she is lauded for her depth and degree of critical analysis.

Still, when Hardwick comments about how happy he is that Brown is "always there for us," and compliments her for "being a wonderful source of positivity and support,"[93] it is never entirely clear whether the "us" he is referring to is AMC and *The Walking Dead* or the show's fan base. Brown's support of Hardwick personally, as well as her potential as a fan moderator, was tested when actress Chloe Dykstra posted a personal essay on June 14, 2018, on *Medium* detailing extensive emotional and sexual abuse by an ex-boyfriend.[94] Though she never named her alleged abuser, it was clear that Dykstra's #MeToo story was in reference to Hardwick. AMC promptly responded to these accusations by suspending Hardwick's hosting duties on *Talking Dead* and pulling his celebrity chat show *Talking with Chris Hardwick*, pending an investigation. With San Diego Comic-Con (SDCC) mere weeks away, many fans' first response to the accusations was to speculate whether Hard-wick would maintain his hyper-visible presence as a moderator at the pop culture convention, and to preemptively express dismay that SDCC would not be the same without him. While this response to such a seri-ous accusation clearly conveys the fan cult of personality that surrounds Hardwick and the convergence culture industry that insulates him, it also signals the significance of moderator figures like Hardwick, and fans' deep investment in them as representatives. Others, many of whom expressed concern about Hardwick's viability as a fan proxy figure in the wake of the accusations, immediately took to social media to rally around Brown as Hardwick's obvious successor. On July 3, 2018, it was confirmed that Brown would replace Hardwick as the moderator for SDCC's "The Walking Dead" and "Fear the Walking Dead" panels, and she was subsequently named the interim host of *Talking Dead* ten days later.

Though Brown remained a vocal supporter of Hardwick during his suspension, insisting via a tweet that she was merely "filling in for a friend," not "jockeying" for his job,[95] many of Hardwick's fans lashed out at Brown on social media and vowed to boycott the show until his return. Following an investigation by AMC that Dykstra did not partici-pate in, Hardwick was reinstated as *Talking Dead*'s host on July 25, 2018, just in time for the midseason premiere of *Fear the Walking Dead* on August 12, 2018. Though Brown ultimately only served as *Talking Dead*'s interim host for one episode, a preview of season 9 of *The Walking Dead* that aired on August 5, 2018, an analysis of Brown's deference to Hard-wick and the panel's response to her as a fangirl moderator in this epi-sode is revealing. The episode opens with Brown directly addressing the audience, joking, "Some of may be thinking, 'Chris Hardwick sure looks different!' Don't adjust your televisions and don't worry, Chris will be back hosting *Talking Dead* when it officially returns. [...] I am honored to be here filling in, just for the week." Brown's explicit reassurance that her tenure as moderator is "unofficial" and temporary, and her repeated calls for fans to not worry or tune out, speak to Hardwick's perceived centrality to the show's appeal.

At various points during the episode, Brown's own gendered fan identity was gently mocked. When Brown became visibly excited about drawing out details of the new season from her guests, actor Khary

Payton playfully chided Brown to "just put your little book away," a reference to Brown's notebook of fan theories (that was notably not present as she took on the role of moderator). Likewise, showrunner Angela Kang jokingly apologized before revealing that one of Brown's longstanding ships, Carol/Daryl, would not be pursued in the upcoming season. Brown moderated the show more or less as Hardwick would have, albeit with a few performative fan flourishes (e.g., gritting her teeth and grudgingly inquiring about Carol's new romantic relationship) that provoked laughter from the in-studio audience. Brown's support of Hardwick and her appearance as *Talking Dead*'s interim moderator ultimately served to reaffirm both the convergence culture industry's preferred forms of enunciative fandom and their preferred moderators. Though Brown proved herself capable beyond any reasonable doubt, the moments of disruption caused by having a moderator engaged in historically feminized fan practices were palpable.

Hardwick opened his return to *Talking Dead* the subsequent week with a tearful speech that made headlines, thanking the fan community for their support and stating, "[T]he show is not just a job to me, this is a vital part of my life, you know? This has been a sanctuary." Expressing gratitude to the fans, producers, and cast members who have allowed him to "be a part of this community every week," Hardwick seamlessly transitioned into teasing the new seasons of both shows, noting, "[W]e're on the precipice of a lot of changes [. . .] in the next few months." By conclusively expressing, "I'm so looking forward to going on that journey with you," Hardwick once again discursively aligned himself with fans, while reestablishing the show's fan enunicative equilibrium as a predominantly promotional space, and his place of prominence within it. Hardwick also expressed his thanks to Brown, returned to her "celebrity superfan" guest status, both for being "a true friend" and for doing an "amazing job" filling in for him in his absence, stressing that she is "a part of this family." The coverage of Hardwick's reinstatement and emotional message overwhelmingly painted a feel-good narrative focused on his connection to *The Walking Dead* fandom, obscuring the fact that several female staffers and an executive producer quit their jobs on *Talking Dead* in response his rehiring.[96] For all of Hardwick's emphasis on the familial bonds of fan community, what was most clearly enunciated by his reinstatement was AMC's enduring commitment to a specific model of enunciative fandom that Hardwick has perfected and come to embody.

Within the convergence culture industry, social media is yet another "significant tool in industry moderation of fan behavior."[97] Shows like *Talking Dead* and figures like Hardwick represent the next level of these moderation efforts, not only curating and making visible those forms of enunciative fandom that they find most desirable but also modeling enunciative fan expression. In this way, the forms of fan control exemplified by shows like *Talking Dead* reaffirm Annemarie Navar-Gill's work on the functionality of television writer's room Twitter feeds: namely, that the convergence culture industry approaches social media and enunciative fan culture as an opportunity "to teach fans about their codes of professionalism, conditioning them not to engage in a way that might damage the brand of the television show."[98] This serves a supplementary pedagogical function, conditioning fans to engage in ways that reinforces the convergence culture industry's branded conception of fan identity.

If, as Fiske suggests, "fan talk is the generation and circulation of certain meanings of the object of fandom within a local community,"[99] I am contending here that shows like *Talking Dead* and figures like Hardwick enunciate and circulate the convergence culture industry's specific and limited understanding of fannish participation. It is precisely the fact that Fiske and subsequent fan scholars have tended to distinguish "consumers" from "fans" through this distinction between enunciative and textual productivity[100] that makes the industry's embrace of enunciative fan practices both appealing and disconcerting. It is possible that, in the future, the convergence culture industry will not only talk the talk but also walk the walk when it comes to fully embracing fan participation. In the meantime, we need to be mindful of how the terms and conditions placed on fannish interaction further support an androcentric framing of fan culture. In Horkheimer and Adorno's view, the culture industry "does not sublimate, it suppresses."[101] Within the convergence culture industry, sublimation has become its own form of suppression for fangirl-dominated forms of critical discursive and transformative intervention. The following chapter returns to Hardwick's branded fan identity to tackle the issue of fan professionalization in more detail, focusing on the fannish figureheads who have been appointed within the convergence culture industry. These emergent hybrid identities of the "fanboy auteur" and "fantrepreneur" not only function to model which forms of fannish affect will be sublimated or suppressed within the convergence culture industry; they powerfully suggest that who is designated to enunciate on fans' behalf is equally as significant as what they say.

5

One Fanboy to Rule Them All

Fanboy Auteurs, Fantrepreneurs, and the Politics of Professionalization

The prior chapter explored how the convergence culture industry has embraced enunciative forms of fan production and disproportionately placed gendered "terms and conditions" on the transformative fan production historically produced by women. This chapter deals with the individuals who are selected to model and moderate the convergence culture industry's newly dialogic relationship between media producers and media fans. By examining how two emergent hybrid identities, the "fanboy auteur" and the "fantrepreneur," are publicized and performed, we can begin to understand the cyclical androcentrism of participation and fan professionalization within the convergence culture industry. The content producers and commentators who have successfully leveraged their own fan identities for professional gain are overwhelmingly white, cishet men who favor the affirmational modes of fan engagement sanctioned by the convergence culture industry. Because gendered tensions surrounding fan professionalization have long underpinned fan cultural production, it is vital to historically situate these concerns before considering how conditions have shifted within the convergence culture industry.

Fannish Gift Economies and the Gender Politics of Professionalization

Long before digital media radically redistributed fans' access to the means of cultural production and the related capacity to capitalize on amateur web content, fan scholars were citing growing concerns about the politics of professionalization within fan communities. In almost all of these cases, the concerns raised focused on the social and communal impact of monetizing fan production. These fannish anxieties ranged from concerns about the consequences of exposure (e.g., that media industries might be increasingly cognizant of and attempt to legally constrain fannish production) to the inevitable social imbalances created when the select few fans moving from "amateur" to "professional" status attempted to mutually maintain their preexisting relationship to a fan community while transitioning fannish peers into followers. As chapter 4's discussion of Fanlib and Kindle Worlds suggests, these concerns have not dissipated, but rather evolved alongside the development of platforms and industrial initiatives to facilitate and monetize fan production.

Early instances in which fans themselves sought to monetize fan works, such as the emergence of semi-professional audiotape producers and distributors around filk (fan folk songs predominantly performed at fan conventions) in the early 1990s,[1] were controversial. Contemporary concerns about the social impact of abandoning fannish gift economies are similar, but require us to distinguish between fan professionalization from within preexisting fan networks and what I have called the convergence culture industry's "regifting economy."[2] Hierarchical visions of fan culture are not always explicitly tied to professionalization, but they are often tacitly connected to a presumed fannish desire for industrial access and accreditation that female and transformative fan cultures have historically eschewed. Fan scholars like Bertha Chin rightly caution that we need a more nuanced consideration of the industrial "exploitation" of fan labor that takes fan motivations into account and recognize that the fan labor that benefits industry (such as the creation and maintenance of "official" fan sites) simultaneously functions as a "gift" or service to other fans.[3] Regardless of intent or functionality, the fact remains that sanctioned and endorsed fan sites like those Chin focuses on tend to view the "rewards" of fan labor as industrial proximity, with the fans who create and run these sites ultimately functioning as gatekeepers, or "acting as intermediaries for other fans"[4] in a similar manner as the fanboy auteur and the fantrepreneur discussed below.

The term "Big Name Fan" (or BNF) emerged in 1950,[5] and continues to be defined loosely as a fan with a large following of fellow fans. Because the term may be used pejoratively, "BNF's are usually far too modest to claim such status themselves, allowing others to categorize them."[6]

Because BNFs expose fallacious conceptions of fan culture as a utopian space in which all fans are created equal, and are a visible reminder that fan communities are "striated by internal hierarchies,"[7] they tend to be a constant source of debate and discord. Certainly, many BNFs become known entities in part because of their various "gifts" (temporal or creative labor) to the fan community. However, because so many BNFs derive their status from the perceived "quality" (e.g., professionalism) of their work, and invitations to become officially and promotionally affiliated with the object of their fandom are explicitly bound up with their *capacity* to professionalize, it is ultimately difficult to divorce the term "BNF" from a broader fannish politics of professionalization.

Of course, some fans are excited when a fanfiction author they have long admired is hired to write a tie-in novel for their favorite franchise, or are happy to donate to a fan artist's Patreon or similar crowdfunding platform to financially support the ongoing creation and circulation of their work. Historically, though, because fandom has operated as a gift economy, most instances of fangirl professionalization within transformative fan cultures tend to be met with skepticism, if not outright antagonism. We need not look further than the common turn of phrase used to describe fanfiction authors who tweak the copyrighted elements of a popular fanfiction story to sell it as an original work to confirm this. When fans refer to these fanfiction authors "filing off the serial numbers" of their fanfic, they knowingly invoke subterfuge and an erasure of the object's past. In most fans' view, this "crime" is not legal (in the text's potential designation as a derivative work), but rather social (tied to a disavowal of both the inspirational source text and the "marks" that various fans have made on the original fanfic as beta readers, commenters, word-of-mouth promoters, and so on). Cases in which fan authors "pull to publish," erasing the digital traces of their stories in order to repurpose and sell them, have resulted in accusations of plagiarism. While one might consider these accusations deeply ironic considering fans' tendencies to poach and remix preexisting media content, the invocation of this academic term reflects both the strict fannish ethics in play and the perceived "codes of conduct" that fan professionalization violates.

The massive popularity of E. L. James's 2011 erotic novel *50 Shades of Grey*, which originated as a popular piece of *Twilight* fanfiction, both exacerbated and complicated these concerns. On one hand, we can read the great success of *50 Shades of Grey* as a rare case in which openly erotic fan content is rewarded rather than contained. The novel's emphasis on BDSM relationships is especially significant because the process of "filing off the serial numbers" almost always refers to heterosexualizing or toning down a fic's erotic or emotional content for greater commercial appeal.[8] When we consider its fannish origins, *50 Shades* is concurrently a natural extension of the controlling and intense pleasure/pain relationship between *Twilight*'s vampire and his human love interest, and an active critique of that franchise's chaste approach to sexuality. On the other hand, *50 Shades* was widely derided within fan communities, alternately for "exposing" erotic fanfiction and for not being an especially polished or interesting exemplar. This reaction neatly encapsulates the doublethink surrounding fan professionalization, the competing desires to keep fan practices isolated from industrial view and co-optation, while championing examples of professional fan production that can most ably speak back to fanfiction's cultural positioning as a denigrated form of writing.

Fans also expressed concerns that the massive success of *50 Shades* would cause publishers to encroach into fan communities and fanfiction archives in search of their next hit novel. One anecdote from digital culture blogger Aja Romano is especially revealing, and reaffirms that media industries rarely have sufficient fannish literacies to understand the communities they are co-opting content from:

> In 2010 right before *50 Shades of Grey* happened I saw [YA author] Maureen Johnson poll a room full of about 500 editors, publishers, and marketing peeps in the publishing industry, and only like 20% of them had ever heard of fanfiction. [. . .] [P]eople just have no idea how insulated the publishing industry has been away from fandom culture until after *50 Shades of Grey* happened, and then they had to immediately and quickly play catchup on this culture that was literally right next to them.[9]

As the discussion of the fantrepreneur and the fanboy auteur below suggests, the inverse is also increasingly an issue, with once-insulated fan communities and practices playing catch-up to learn which facets of fandom the convergence culture industry values. In many ways, this mutual lack of cultural understanding is an essential component of why affirmational forms of fannish production have been historically embraced by the industry, and why fans looking to professionalize have tailored their fan identities and practices to fit this model. Given the complex ecologies in which transformative fanworks are produced and circulated,[10] it is far more temporally and promotionally efficacious for the convergence culture industry to become literate in affirmational modes of engagement.

Analog fan communities' "productive ambivalence" towards professionalization persists within digital fan communities, which are both "productive" in their ongoing interrogation of the merits of "amateur" versus "professional" media production and ambivalent about the fact that it is commonly "those who are already 'credentialized'"[11] who are granted access to fan professionalization and the related cultural and economic capital. Indeed, much of the reason why the conceptual divide over fandom as a gift economy and a space of professional training (acknowledging that for many fans it is both) is so deeply gendered is the prevailing notion that masculinity is a credential in and of itself within the convergence culture industry. Gendered conceptions of which fans are more adept at "going pro" shape media representations of those who have professionalized their fan identities and labor, as well as fannish responses to these representations. Take, for example, the SyFy docuseries *Heroes of Cosplay* (2013–2014) and the fan tumblr "Heroes of Cosplay Confessions," which offered anonymous commentaries on the show's female cosplayers striving to professionalize their fan identities. I have suggested that the show "constructs a narrative in which male friends and partners are presented as the unacknowledged technical brains and fabricating brawn behind [the female cosplayers'] success."[12] The show's subtle messaging that female fans can never fully attain or appreciate professional status is echoed in fan responses to the show on "Heroes of Cosplay Confessions," which overwhelmingly focus on men as invisible, uncredited, or exploited laborers (figure 5.1).[13]

Fan scholars in recent years have adopted their own "productive ambivalence" toward the prevailing conception of fandom as a gift economy, and the feminist implications of retaining this model. In a 2009 exchange, Abigail De Kosnik and Karen Hellekson both addressed the future of fandom's gift economy and the monetization of fanfiction from

some times i feel like this show should be called 'girls who cosplay ~ and the men who do most of the work for them'

~Anon

Figure 5.1. An example of fan responses to *Heroes of Cosplay*'s gendered depictions of male fans as uncredited laborers. Anonymous, *Heroes of Cosplay Confessions,* Tumblr Post, 2014, http://heroesofcosplayconfessions.tumblr.com/post/61472986292.

a feminist perspective. Hellekson framed fandom's gift economy as a form of legal and social protection, contending that fandom constructs "a new, gendered space [. . .] that deliberately repudiates a monetary model (because it is gendered male)."[14] De Kosnik countered with concerns that "women writing fanfic for free today risk institutionalizing a lack of compensation for all women that practice this art in the future."[15] Revisiting this debate in 2015 in the wake of industrial initiatives like Kindle Worlds and the success of *50 Shades of Grey,* Hellekson reasserted that attempts to shift from a fannish gift economy to a commercial model inevitably strive to "legitimize fan activity by subsuming it under the dominant paradigm that fandom is so frequently held up as working against," and that more often than not "this legitimacy is granted on terms that do not benefit the fan."[16] De Kosnik retained her support for women professionalizing and monetizing their fan labor, but expressed reservations about the success of *50 Shades of Gray,* noting that she "did not anticipate that commercial publishing and fan-turned-pro writers would collaborate to strip fan fiction of what makes it new and special, which is precisely that no fan fiction text can be new or special entirely on its own."[17] Productively drawing on Lauren Berlant's concept of "the archive of women's culture,"[18] De Kosnik suggested that it is precisely the archival and communal nature of fannish textual creation that makes it a distinct production culture and feminist space.

In spite of the fact that the monetizing of fans' transformative "labors of love" might be considered a feminist act, the logic persists that "predominantly female [fan] spaces embrace gift cultures while men are more likely to turn their fannish endeavors into for-profit projects."[19] This brings us to a key point, namely, that when contemplating the gendered politics of professionalization within fan culture, we must delineate between the *desire* and the *capacity* to professionalize. Whether or not the presumption that male fans desire to professionalize their fan labor while female-dominated communities tend to actively eschew professionalization is accurate is somewhat beside the point. To my mind, it is more important to consider which fans are or are not able to wield fannish affect as a professional asset within the convergence culture industry. As the rest of this chapter will reveal, the *capacity* to leverage one's own fan identity for professional gain overwhelmingly favors men.

Liminal Fan/Producer Identities

If the prior section contemplated the gender politics of fans going pro, this section considers the inverse, examining what happens when media professionals strategically embrace and perform their identities as fans. Since its inception, fan studies has fixated on the power dynamics between fans and "The Powers That Be" or TPTB (an industrial category that alternately references studio and network executives, creators and showrunners, and cast or above-the-line crew),[20] often characterizing the relationship as "charged with mutual suspicion, if not open conflict."[21] The convergence culture industry's growing incentive to cultivate fan/producer engagement across digital and social media platforms has complicated, but in no way eradicated, these suspicions and conflicts.[22] Authorial engagements with fans in the digital age have more often than not nostalgically attempted to codify, rather than collapse, analog power dynamics between producers and consumers. From early efforts by television showrunners to censor fan discussions on Internet message boards[23] to authorial podcasts that reify the romantic figure of the author-god even as they strike a fannish, dialogic tone,[24] TPTB continue to "imagine participation as something they can start and stop, channel and reroute, commodify and market."[25]

These moments of producorial intervention or fan interaction are typically framed as examples of media creators "breaking the fourth wall." The contextual origins of the "fourth wall," which in classical theatrical terms represents the invisible or unacknowledged barrier that separates the fiction from the audience, are newly resonant given the growing promotional imperative to foster participatory culture. We tend to associate the "fourth wall" with the proscenium arch in theater, or the screen in various media contexts, but when the term was coined by French art critic Denis Diderot in the eighteenth century, it was common practice for some audience members to sit on the stage. The close physical proximity made this "fourth wall" a necessary construct, and to break it risked the reality of the fictional world being compromised and ultimately falling apart. We see a similar movement occur within the convergence culture industry: analog fan communities pointedly built up "fourth walls" between themselves and the creators of their fan object. As creators and consumers increasingly came to occupy the same spaces online (or at least became mutually visible to each other within those spaces), conversations around how these walls should be built, discussions about if/when they should be maintained, and controversies surrounding moments of breakage have increased exponentially. It is in large part because the fourth wall "was established primarily by fans for fans" and functions to mitigate tensions and minimize retaliatory strikes from TPTB[26] that the convergence culture industry's imperative to demolish it is at times met with resistance.

If, theatrically, the fourth wall must be maintained in order to ensure an immersive experience for the audience, the fourth wall of fandom exists to ensure that fan communities are not broken down when The Powers That Be immerse themselves within fan spaces. This is not to suggest that fans have not also embraced the greater intimacy with media creators and stars that social media platforms have afforded. For example, Felicia Day, the creator and star of the popular web series *The Guild*, has built a popular fantrepreneurial brand at the intersection of her social media savvy and her own cult star persona. Elizabeth Ellcessor suggests that Day is a prime example of an emergent "star text of connection,"[27] augmenting what Richard Dyer has called the star text's function of "authenticating authenticity"[28] by skillfully deploying the "illusions of 'liveness' and interactivity presented online, the quotidian rhythms of interaction, [and] the (possible) lack of media gatekeepers such as publicists"[29] on social media platforms to enhance a sense of intimacy and immediacy. Day's efforts to "authenticate authenticity" are immediately visible on her Twitter page, in both her autobiographical self-description as "Actress, New Media Geek, Gamer, Misanthrope" and her insistence that she likes "to keep [her] tweets real and not waste people's time." Day's appeal is not merely her authenticity (she, like her tweets, presents herself as a "real" person rather than a set of promotional talking points) but also in her claim to an authentic "fan" or "geek" identity. This is a core component of Day's appeal, but also central to her business endeavors, including her fantrepreneurial position as the founder and content curator of Geek & Sundry, a popular digital hub for geek culture reporting and content that spans websites, blogs, and a highly successful YouTube channel.[30] Ellcessor concludes that stars like Day are not "merely a product of convergence, but an agent of further convergences, facilitating connections between various media platforms, texts, audiences, and industries [. . .] with the star acting as a uniting force."[31] Likewise, the liminal figures discussed in this chapter are products of the convergence culture industry, presenting themselves as a unifying force for producorial and fan identities.

Another notable figure who successfully oscillates between promotional agent and fan-culture participant via social media is Misha Collins, the actor who portrays Castiel on the long-running cult CW television series *Supernatural* (2005–present). Louisa Ellen Stein suggests that the "double visibility" of creators and fans within shared social media spaces is endemic to Collins's appeal, as "his position as official creator and celebrity certainly propels his popularity on Twitter, but his persona and fan favor are equally shaped by his perceived marginality and transgressiveness."[32] Somewhat ironically, Stein contends that Collins's alignment with female fans comes in the form of satirical performance, with Collins playing "the role of the masculine 'overlord,'"[33] calling his Twitter followers "minions" and playing on the platform's neo-religious connotations of the "follower." Stein suggests, though, that "additional performances of non-heteronormative masculinity render his performance of dominant power strange, and indicative of its opposite—not of a lack of power, but of a non-ideologically-dominant power, through which Collins is aligned with female fans in female/ queer communities."[34] As I will discuss with regard to the "fanboy auteur," these paradoxical performances, the hyperbolic claims to power as a form of deflection or to signal an allegiance with fans, are precisely what makes these liminal producer/fan identities potent and powerful.

Whether they are received warmly or with suspicion, these liminal producer/fan figures present another form of intersectional fan identity that scholars need to grapple with. I have previously put forward actor Orlando Jones as a rich site at which to begin exploring the protectionist gender politics that emerge when a male member of a creative team openly self-identifies as a "fangirl" and embeds himself within the fan community for his own television program.[35] Alongside the 2013 launch of the Fox television series *Sleepy Hollow* (on which he appeared as a supporting character), journalists, fans, and academics alike began to take notice of Jones's efforts to actively participate in (rather than just promotionally interact with) the show's fan base. A wave of celebratory news articles followed, detailing Jones's efforts to "break the fourth wall" and his successful integration into the *Sleepy Hollow* fan community. More often than not, the use of this turn of phrase referenced Jones's efforts either to eschew his position as a creator in order to engage fans as a fan, or to collapse and cohere the conflicting "sides" of producer/ consumer identities. In short, Jones was credited with breaking down the conceptual Berlin Wall between creators and fans, rather than breaking the fourth wall in a traditional diegetic sense of acknowledging or directly addressing the audience through the text itself. It is for this reason, along with Jones's pointed self-identification as a fan, that it is more productive to discursively frame his efforts not as a form of engagement but as immersion.

My use of the term "immersion" might initially seem to break from usages of the term within video game and virtual reality (VR) studies, but I would suggest it is the platform-specific nature of Jones's immersive approach that is significant. Returning to Janet Murray's oft-cited definition of immersion, Jones breaks from prior examples of producorial outreach to fan communities in that he self-reflexively frames fandom as the "sensation of being surrounded by a completely other reality" that has captivated his "whole perceptual apparatus," stressing the necessity of learning and literacy in order "to do the things that the new [participatory] environment makes possible."[36] Murray's emphasis on the need to learn what the participatory environment makes possible is present in many of Jones's Tumblr posts, which frequently feature asides like "BTW, I'm definitely not fishing for compliments here. Am legitimately interested in how this all works. I'm new to this game and just trying to keep up."[37] Alternately, Jones asserted his authenticity as a member of the *Sleepy Hollow* fan community, noting, "I fully understand and embrace the fact that if I'm actively choosing to dismantle the 4th Wall by virtue of how I engage with all of you I need to be accountable for the things I say. But it has to be a two way street."[38] This is a common trope of Jones's immersive efforts—he routinely acknowledges, but ultimately dismisses, the notion that his immersion into fan culture might be problematic or impossible given his status.

In addition to deploying the term to narrativize his fannish roots (e.g., "I've immersed myself in these subcultures throughout my life"),[39] Jones described the chosen title of his Tumblr "The Tumblr Experiment" as an effort to "establish the validity of a hypothesis regarding the creator as fan and the ways in which transformative works can be elevated alongside canon while still existing as its own unique art form."[40] This is a fairly radical mission statement, in both legal, textual, and ideological terms, but it also asserts Jones's attempt to craft a dichotomous persona in which he is both an authentic fan and an authoritative figurehead. In their discussion of micro-celebrity and imagined audiences on Twitter, danah boyd and Alice Marwick suggest that because authenticity is a precious commodity on social media platforms, instances of self-branding are "met with stiff resistance from people used to interactional norms that do not involve the commodification of social ties."[41] This is unquestionably the case with controversies around commercial co-optations of fan culture, which has historically utilized a gift economy. Moreover, Marwick and boyd suggest that the "context collapse" of Twitter, its tendency to flatten multiple audiences into one,[42] makes this authenticity difficult to maintain. In some sense, we can view Jones's "experiment" as centrally interested in the implications of context collapse, as he strives to speak equally to the promotional missives of industry, the subcultural specificity of female fan communities of practice, and the abandoned utopianism of first wave fan studies.

Jones's repeated self-identification as a fangirl, and efforts to immerse himself in the digital spaces and interpretive practices of female fans, have met with some resistance.[43] The tensions that inevitably accompany producers encroaching on (digital) fan spaces were apparent from Jones's first post to his Tumblr account. On September 13, 2013, Jones reblogged a post from a *Sleepy Hollow* fan discussing how Jones, via his Twitter account, was "offering/threatening to prove he reads SH fanfic. By reading it on YouTube."[44] The language of this post is telling, despite its bemused tone, and reflects how anxieties about the growing intimacy between creators and fans online have been compounded by the recent trend of actors performing live readings of erotic fanfiction featuring their characters,[45] and high-profile instances of television series like *Supernatural* and *Sherlock* working in "fan proxy" characters to express their dismissal of, or disdain for, fanfiction and the fangirls who tend to compose and consume it.[46]

Consequently, in addition to general exclamations of shock and/or delight that Jones had "picked up" and reblogged this post from a fan as his initial foray into Tumblr fan culture (which was read by some as an exemplary gesture of his desire to immerse himself in transformative fan cultures), other comments on the post expressed anxieties about the implications of his engagement. One (perhaps jokingly) panicked comment from a *Sleepy Hollow* fan on Tumblr was directed at the initial poster: "WHY DID YOU LET ME WRITE SH FANFICTION HE COULD READ MY SHIT." The original poster responded, "IT'S NOT MY FAULT! I DIDN'T KNOW HE KNEW ABOUT TUMBLR! (But he's requesting Irving/Ichabod, so I'm assuming you're safe . . .)." This exchange simultaneously conveys lingering trepidation about the visibility of fanworks to media creators (e.g., "HE COULD READ MY SHIT"), fannish presumptions and the relative industrial *invisibility* or illegibility of particular fan platforms that render them safe(r) spaces (e.g., "I DIDN'T KNOW HE KNEW ABOUT TUMBLR!"), and the unprecedented nature of Jones's request for homoerotic slash fanfiction featuring his own character.

Though fan response to Jones's presence on Tumblr and his liminal identity has been overwhelmingly positive, some have actively challenged his gendered self-identification as a fangirl. In a March 2014 chat sponsored by the Organization for Transformative Works,[47] Jones and other industry representatives chatted with fans on the topic of "The

Future of Fanworks."⁴⁸ One participant, Laura J., pointedly inquired, "Am I alone in (liking Orlando very much but) not liking his appropriation of 'fangirl'?" Jones's response was typical of previous interactions with fans on this point. After thanking Laura for sharing her perspective, Jones noted that he had "never thought of it as appropriation," but is "mindful that others do." Though Jones relayed that, in his mind, there is a "clear distinction" between fanboys and fangirls, he "think[s] the terms are fair game for either gender," particularly as "we all possess masculine and feminine energy." This remark echoed prior tweets clarifying his self-identification as a fangirl, and one in particular from November 4, 2013, in which Jones wrote in response to a fan, "Fangirl is the correct nomenclature. Fanboys try to hide their feels to 'look cool.' I embrace them."⁴⁹ He closed with the mea culpa that "[e]ither way I realize some may find that response to be disingenuous but I use the term with respect, not derision."

Some fans within the chat were quick to rally to Jones's defense, but Laura J. pressed the point, replying that Jones's stance elided the fact that he was "never going to be shamed for only be[ing] a [fan]girl." Others took issue with Jones's "equation of 'girl' with 'emotional,'" and addressed the political connotations of conflating fannish and lived identities: "I mean, Orlando, if you id as somewhat genderqueer, that's a thing and I would never begrudge anyone's right to self-identify. but if not, then it's side-eye material." Jones stressed that he lacked "the ego or arrogance to suggest I am having the female experience," but maintained that his claim to fangirl identity "applies to my own dynamic in fandom as the term itself is not gender specific in my own mind."

As the prior chapter explores, the convergence culture industry's collaborationist approach deserves further scrutiny, particularly in terms of its gendered marginalization of specific fans and practices. As we move from prohibitionist to collaborationist to immersive industrial engagements with fan culture, new questions arise for fans and fan scholars alike: How do our expectations around producer-fan engagements shift with the adoption of specific social media platforms (e.g., Twitter vs. Instagram vs. Tumblr)? What are the political stakes of a male producer immersing himself within a predominantly female fan community via social media, and/or overtly self-identifying as a "fangirl"? And finally, given the industrial imperative towards soliciting and quantifying audience "engagement," will these efforts towards producorial immersion into fan culture inevitably be viewed as a form of encroachment? Or, to borrow from Michel de Certeau, however sincerely content creators embrace the tactical and transformative space of fan culture, can they ever realistically shed their strategic power?[50] Jones's intersectional identity offers a productive space in which to begin working through these issues, and grappling with fraught moments of engagement between the spheres of industry, academia, and audience.

Even if we accept Jones's claim to fan identity, much less fangirl identity, Jones is always already a "BNF." As Jones himself notes,

> What I'm not as surprised about, but what occasionally makes me sad, is the level of distrust my presence in fandom seems to engender at times. I am sensitive to the concern that people who like things don't want an outsider to come in and pretend to like those things only to turn around and disparage them. Trust is obviously something that needs to be earned, but at a certain point, it starts to become uninteresting to constantly have to prove myself and demonstrate my authenticity.[51]

In a cultural moment in which authenticity policing within fan culture is disproportionately directed at female fans, Jones's statement resonates with his dichotomous identity as a content creator and "fangirl." What Jones fails to acknowledge (or perhaps lacks the institutional memory to fully comprehend, given his relatively recent foray into fan culture) is that this fannish distrust has also been earned, born out of the long history of producer/fan engagements.

It is entirely possible that any effort to perform the dual identity of TPTB and fan will unavoidably suffer from what Erving Goffman calls "discrepant roles":

> Given the fragility and the required expressive coherence of the reality that is dramatized by a performance, there are usually facts which, if attention is drawn to them during the performance, would discredit, disrupt, or make useless the impression that the performance fosters. [. . .] A basic problem for many performances, then, is that of information control; the audience must not acquire destructive information about the situation that is being defined for them.[52]

In other words, in order for Jones's (or Day's, or Collins's) performance as a fan to maintain its immersive state, they must both continuously deflect attention from their alignment with TPTB and reject the
fact that they immediately and invariably hold a position of esteem and
power within the fan community. Jones has proven himself a master of
information control, deftly balancing his dual identities as promotional
agent and fan. Still, the fragility of his fan performance given these "discrepant roles" becomes clear in both fans' occasionally ambivalent responses to his presence, and in his own understandable frustration with
being constantly required to "authenticate authenticity" not just as a fan,
but as a *fangirl*, specifically.

Composing a foreword entitled "Orlando the Fangirl" for a fan studies anthology in 2016, Jones doubled down on his identity as "an unabashed and unafraid fangirl," noting,

> I tried being a fanboy, but it was too limiting. Fanboys are exclusionary.
> Fanboys are guarded. They don't scream loud and refuse to have all the
> feels. And although I've had female fans express concern with my co-
> opting of this chosen fan persona and the implication that I am contrib-
> uting to gender stereotypes, the exact opposite is true. I understand that I
> don't fit the commonly understood description of a fangirl and that's OK.
> It's a role I will continue to embrace as I passionately interact in a com-
> munity that explores and challenges the role that media plays in all facets
> of our connected lives and pursues a version of what the world can be.[53]

As a black, middle-aged man, Jones importantly does not conform to
the "fanboy" demographic crafted by the convergence culture industry,
and accordingly it is understandable that he would find that identity
too limiting. Fans of color undoubtedly find the cultural categories of
both "fanboy" and "fangirl" exclusionary, conceptually connected as
they are to whiteness. Jones is also a notable, and fascinating, exception to the archetypes of the "fanboy auteur" and "fantrepreneur"
explored in the remainder of this chapter. Jones exhibits similar qualities, such as narrativizing and claiming a fan identity to build a liminal
fan/producorial brand, positioning himself as a translator or moderator within fan/industry relations. His self-identification as a fangirl,
however problematic, nonetheless marks a decisive break from the

gendered forms of fan affect and production that are typically embodied by fanboy auteurs and fantrepreneurs.

Fanboy Auteurs

At first glance the archetypal identities conjoined in the term "fanboy auteur," the failed masculinity of the fanboy and the patriarchal omnipotence of the auteur, appear to be diametrically opposed. Any difficulty in reconciling these terms, however, has been mitigated by the convergence culture industry's ongoing integration of the fanboy into hegemonic masculinity, and the parallel cultivation of an androcentric vision of fan culture. The fanboy auteur is constructed simultaneously by author, industry, and audience, with each constituency investing in and wielding this emergent authorial identity to different ends. When cult media properties like *Doctor Who* are rebooted, the fan credentials of each subsequent showrunner are foregrounded in industrial press releases as a point of reassurance that the property is in good hands. When audiences and film critics alternately celebrated or critiqued J. J. Abrams's nostalgic take on the *Star Wars* franchise with the release of *The Force Awakens* (2015), they were ultimately appraising his competence as a fanboy auteur. When superhero movies like *Green Lantern* (2011) flop, articles with titles like "Comic Hero Fanboys Make Terrible Comic Hero Movies" complain that the "fanboy" facet of this authorial identity has won out.[54] In all of these cases the fanboy auteur might evade the paternalism that undergirds most auteurist discourses by painting himself as a relatable "everyman," but it is worth interrogating what imagined "everyfan" this authorial archetype is designed to relate to.

Auteur theory emerged out of writings in the French film magazine *Cahiers du Cinema* in the 1950s and 1960s. Key essays, such as Francois Truffaut's "A Certain Tendency in the French Cinema" (1954), Andre Bazin's "La Politque des auteurs" (1957), and Andrew Sarris's "Notes on the Auteur Theory" (1962), all positioned the director as the core artist responsible for authoring a given film, and as the conceptual link between texts. Similarly, my initial conception of the "fanboy auteur" served a predominantly organizational purpose, namely, as a way of assigning authorship within complex, collaborative, and cross-platform texts. I have suggested that in analyses of the boom in transmedia franchises within the convergence culture industry, "who is designated to speak on behalf of the text is of equal importance as what they say, resulting in a growing reliance on the authorial archetype of the 'fanboy auteur,' or a creator/figurehead of a transmedia franchise who attempts to navigate and break the conventional boundaries between producers and consumers."[55] The fanboy auteur is also a visible and vocal byproduct of the convergence culture industry's competing technological, industrial, and cultural drives to foster closer relationships with media fans and nostalgically retain authorial and interpretive control in the digital age.

In this sense, and in my expansion on the term below, my conception of the "fanboy auteur" is far more indebted to Michel Foucault's discussion of the "author function" in his 1969 essay "What Is an Author?" than to the aforementioned conceptions of the auteur. Foucault's essay emerged amid a shift within literary theory from an emphasis on authorial intent to reader interpretations, perhaps most forcefully marked by Roland Barthes's proclamation in 1968 that "to give writing its future, it is necessary to overthrow the myth: the birth of the reader must be at the cost of the death of the Author."[56] Writing about the function of authorial paratexts, Jonathan Gray suggests the term "undead author" to describe an author figure who, in Barthesian terms, understands that metaphorically "killing himself" is an ideal way to "fashion himself as 'just one of the fans,' when he is decidedly privileged in the relationship."[57] This description echoes the convergence culture industry's paradoxical (dis)empowerment of the fanboy discussed in chapters 2 and 3, but I favor the term "fanboy auteur" rather than "undead author" for two primary reasons. First, there is my desire to explicitly gender the capacity to successfully commit this form of strategic suicide, recognizing that female media creators are far less likely to professionally benefit from an adoption of this authorial persona. Second, my conception of the fanboy auteur as a creator who leverages his fan identity for a preexisting media property as a rationalization for his professional "fit" for the project is more narrowly focused than Gray's conception of undead authorship, which might broadly apply to any media creator who attempts to facilitate a more intimate or dialogic relationship with fans or claim a fan identity.

Just as Foucault situates the author as a product of discourse, the fanboy auteur is a product of the convergence culture industry designed for a very specific discursive purpose. For Foucault, the author is ultimately a psychological projection that will historically "vary according to periods and types of discourse," as well as a product of "the connections that we make, the traits that we establish as pertinent, the continuities that we recognize, or the exclusions that we practice."[58] The fanboy auteur is similarly a product of a distinct period, reflecting the convergence culture industry's efforts to handle the growing discursive power of fans and a more general dissolution of clear boundaries between consumption and production. Because his "fan" identity is his auteuristic trademark, or the point of consistency in his aesthetic brand, the fanboy auteur discursively performs a similar set of connections, continuities, and exclusions at *both* the fan-cultural level and the textual level. In other words, in addition to serving as a point of unification for texts, the fanboy auteur can be performatively wielded to convey which types of fans and/or fan practices will be excluded. Foucault closes his essay by noting that these inquiries are underpinned by "the murmur of indifference: 'What matter who's speaking.'"[59] Though transformative fan culture is to some extent predicated on this indifference, the emergence of the fanboy auteur as an authorial archetype and aspirational form of professionalized fan identity suggests that fans cannot afford to be indifferent about who is speaking, precisely because this figure is presented as speaking for them.

Fanboy auteurs make a point of narrativizing their fan identities as a core component of their creative credentials, a self-promotion that is designed to speak mutually to industry and fan stakeholders. What is being sold is precisely the fanboy auteur's bilingualism, his capacity to reconcile the often-conflicting desires and demands of industrial commodities and fan communities. Thus, the fanboy auteur's "perceived ability to speak fans' 'language,' and his liminal positioning (his ability to present himself simultaneously as one of 'us' and one of 'them,' consumer and producer), is framed as his greatest asset, suggesting that he is an ideal interpreter between text and audience."[60] This conception of the "audience" importantly includes both preexisting fan bases and casual or new fans of a given franchise, and thus the "fan" that the fanboy auteur embodies is amorphous by design. This does not mean that fanboy auteurs are not quick to establish normative definitions of (un)sanctioned fandom, which are frequently predicated on their own preferred modes of fan engagement and their desire to retain artistic and authorial control over the fan object. Unsurprisingly, this routinely results in either representational or discursive dismissals of the forms of fan engagement aligned with transformative textual production. For example, in their discussion of *Doctor Who* fanboy auteur Russell T. Davies, Melissa A. Click and Nettie Brock suggest that one of Davies's primary strategies for broadening the show's appeal and bringing new fans to the rebooted cult series was to publicly express "his disdain for fans whom he feels take things too far,"[61] thereby reinforcing his own carefully calibrated and deeply affirmational fannish connection to the property.

Because the fanboy auteur is often celebrated for having a comprehensive knowledge of and affirmational mastery over a given fictional world or franchise, the fanboy auteur's voice and fannish interpretations are increasingly framed as an essential "text" for fans to consume. These authorial paratexts can range from interviews to DVD commentaries to podcasts to direct interactions via social media. The fanboy auteur's tacit promise of a more dialogic relationship between media producers and consumers more often than not is limited to facile interactions that are carefully regulated and serve a clear promotional function. We need only look at many fanboy auteurs' refusal to engage or their propensity for abruptly leaving social media platforms when their authority is challenged by fans[62] to see a trend emerge. When the fanboy auteur's fan identity is invoked, it is more often than not a means to an end, a display of mastery as a form of fannish certification, designed to definitively end a conversation with fans rather than begin one.

Because the fanboy auteur's distinct author function is wrapped up in the convergence culture industry's broader efforts to support and standardize affirmational modes of fan engagement, it is vital to recall the centrality of the author to obsession_inc's original demarcation between affirmational and transformational fan cultures. In this case, the fanboy auteur's proclamation of fan identity overwhelmingly aligns with the former category, in large part because he benefits from affirmational fans' deference to the author's authority. Industry also benefits, in that "the fanboy auteur models and projects the relationship the industry would like fans to have with their franchises (namely, one of reverential respect for artists and properties)."[63] When fanboy auteurs deploy their own fan identities in order to credential and legitimate their claim to authorship, their alignment with affirmational fan culture's emphasis on canonicity and encyclopedic knowledge plays a large role in this. Consider Zack Snyder's fannishly slavish adaptations and remakes of comic books and cult films (*300*, *Dawn of the Dead*, *Watchmen*, and so on): Snyder's title as a "visionary" filmmaker is ironically derived from his transcriptive storyboarding process and fannish fidelity to the source material, while his subsequent original projects (*Sucker Punch*) critically and promotionally suffered from the lack of an explicitly fannish connection to a preexisting property.[64]

Snyder's (self-)stylization as a fanboy auteur in authorial paratexts like interviews and DVD commentaries functions to carefully craft a "normative" and masculinized vision of fan identity, and each works to foreground one facet of this authorial identity, while mitigating the other. For example, Snyder's DVD commentaries routinely see him adopting a casual tone and geeky jargon, fannishly complaining when an object is on the "wrong" side of the frame than in the source material, or gleefully discussing how fans on message boards are finding the "easter eggs" he's hidden for them.[65] Meanwhile, a profile of Snyder in the *New York Times Magazine* dubbing him "the purest geek-auteur of the geek-film era" is attentive to balancing a celebration of "his ability to speak geek culture's language, both aesthetically and promotionally, and his fearlessness about working on that culture's holiest ground," with reassurances that Snyder is not a stereotypical "fanboy" but rather an "evolved" artist.[66] Much of this is accomplished via the profile's emphasis on Snyder's conventionally masculine physicality (he is described as "handsome" and "compactly buff") and his devotion to his wife and children. In short, Snyder may own a life-size replica of Han Solo frozen in carbonite from *The Empire Strikes Back*, but the profile makes it clear that "he's not the kind of guy who then hangs it over the fireplace."[67] Snyder's positioning as a fanboy auteur, and the construction of fanboy auteurs more generally, tend to reaffirm that "obsessive fandom is acceptable as long as it avoids the unacceptable social types of perpetually single misfit and homosexual."[68]

As a counterpoint, we might consider the misogynist and racist fan backlash to the 2016 *Ghostbusters* reboot as reflective of what happens when a fanboy auteur is perceived as taking too "transformative" an approach. Though screenwriter and director Paul Feig and the actresses portraying the Ghostbusters in the remake all routinely proclaimed their fannish adoration of the 1984 original film, many fans of the franchise viewed the gender swapping of the films' protagonists as antithetical to an authentic fan appreciation of the franchise.[69] While we might view complaints about the all-female *Ghostbusters* remake and subsequent harassment of star Leslie Jones on social media as endemic of the spreadable misogyny and racism of contemporary fan culture discussed in chapter 3, this is also a prime example of the limits of the fanboy auteur identity. Given Feig's perceived failure to affirmationally align his reboot with what were conceived to be the core canonical facets of the original (e.g., the gender of the principal characters, but also the failure to utilize elements like the iconic firehouse headquarters), any and all promotional insistence on his own fan identity was functionally meaningless.

Though the term "auteur" has historically been associated with film, the fanboy auteur is not a medium-specific concept, and can be used to describe transmedia producers, television showrunners, film directors, and so on. With that said, it is vital to acknowledge the paternalistic origins of the term within film studies and cinephilic fan cultures, and the ways in which a default white, cishet masculinity is perpetuated in connection to the term. Who is granted access to the term "auteur" is intractably connected to the paucity of women and people of color in positions of power within media production cultures. However, there is still much to be gained from a contextual consideration of the way fanboy auteurs are situated in a given medium, particularly in terms of how both their own (fan) identities and the presumed identity markers of a given medium's fan culture impact content. For example, Ellen Kirkpatrick's work on comic book fanboy auteurs like Grant Morrison and Frank Miller suggests that they "represent the superhero world (textual and fandom) as they know it and see it, and for some, due to the circles (and cycles) in which they move, it may still appear as largely white and male."[70] Or we might consider Hunter Hargraves's work on "addictive" television spectatorship and binge-watching, which situates the fanboy auteur within the historical feminization (and accordant denigration) of the medium, and how the emergent cultural capital associated with television spectatorship is "steeped in masculinist viewing attitudes."[71]

In discursively extolling their own lived experiences of fan culture and identity, what the fanboy auteur ultimately reinforces is the convergence culture industry's vision of fan culture, and the accordant message that "fan passions should be kept under masculinized control."[72] Particular subsets of fans are emboldened or marginalized by these performances of professionalized fan identity via fans' own "reinforcing practices" within digital forums. Accordingly, the "fanboy auteur also lives in dominant fans, or fans who have established themselves as knowledgeable, respectable, and altogether 'good' fans who reinforce the notions of 'proper' practice."[73] While this might inherently privilege androcentric forms of fan engagement and affect, or affirmational fandom more generally, it begs the question about how this identity might be occupied by women.

Fangirl Auteurs

In his response to my initial conceptualization of the "fanboy auteur," Henry Jenkins inquired about the growing number of "fangirl auteurs," noting,

> Some of them are protégés still finding their voices, often unfairly dismissed when they claim the same authority we easily ascribe to their male counterparts. Some are part of male/female creative teams. Others are taking over existing series. Few are creating their own franchises—yet. But they represent a significant wave of female showrunners and will collectively change the face of genre entertainment. Are they necessarily going to be pulled into established industry conceptions of television authorship in order to prove they can be one of the boys or do they represent the possibility of re-imagining what cult media authorship can look like? If the fanboy auteur embodies a masculine fan culture focused on continuity, mastery, and expertise, might the fan girl auteur reflect the female fan's search for community, reciprocity, and multiplicity? If so, what policies should they adopt or identities should they perform? How will this figure be constructed by fans and by industry to enable a different kind of relationship with the audience?[74]

These remain vital questions, and indeed some authorial figureheads have emerged that fulfill Jenkins's vision of the "fangirl auteur." It is heartening, for example, to witness showrunners like Emily Andras of the SyFy series *Wynonna Earp* (2016–present) be hired from the outset to helm cult programs. Andras has also cultivated a close and mutually supportive relationship with her show's fan community by loudly proclaiming the centrality of feminism to her creative process and being thoughtful and intersectional in her approach to minority representation.[75] However, Jenkins is right to acknowledge just how frequently men remain centered, or alternately are either explicitly or implicitly credited, in these narratives.

For example, a September 2012 *Entertainment Weekly* cover story on the show narrativized the addition of writer Maria Ferrari to *The Big Bang Theory*'s all-male creative team in 2009 by noting that she "wooed her way onto the staff by telling [showrunner Chuck] Lorre how she bought her husband a hard-to-get amulet from the *World of Warcraft* game for their anniversary."[76] Meanwhile, the credentials for the male members of the writing team consisted of things like "being an expert on everything *Star Wars*–related," or being "a Harvard grad who's considered the smartest guy in the room," or having once "attended a costume party dressed as the Doppler effect."[77] Here, we see the Dr. Girlfriend trope discussed in chapter 2 deployed once more: Ferarri's husband is situated as the "real" fan, and her own access to a fan identity (in this case, a core professional "credential") is contained within the feminized and heteronormative act of shopping. The language here is especially telling: whereas male writers are hailed for their intellect and fan expertise, Ferarri must "woo" a male showrunner for a place at the table. We need not look further than the fact that the 2017 reboot of cult television series *The X-Files* initially populated its writers' room exclusively with men to see the persistence of a kind of insidious biological determinism when it comes to hiring creators on fan- and geek-oriented media properties. Though several women were added to the creative team after outcry from fans and public criticism from the show's star, Gillian Anderson, the "change" anticipated by Jenkins has yet to meaningfully come to pass.

Putting the obvious, gender-swapped definition aside, perhaps the more interesting question is, What would a "fangirl auteur" meaningfully look like? While many of the women Jenkins references, such as writer Jane Espenson, do indeed helm cult or fan-oriented series, very few of them are narrativized as fans in the same way as their male counterparts. So, while we might add an array of female showrunners to Jenkins's initial shortlist, from *My Little Pony: Friendship Is Magic*'s Lauren Faust to *Marvel's Jessica Jones*'s Melissa Rosenberg, we must carefully consider how their fan identities are mobilized differently or, in many cases, not at all.

In Faust's case, as a woman rebooting a piece of historically hyperfeminine and aggressively commoditized intellectual property aimed at young girls, her authorial claim to cultural legitimacy was inevitably going to be called into question. Conversations surrounding Faust and the show that sidestepped any discussion of how gender shaped her professional journey or her approach to the reboot nonetheless often credited her husband, Craig McCracken, for the show's more "sophisticated" elements. As Derek Johnson has noted, this is typical of popular discourse that has routinely celebrated male creators "in animation cross-promoting toys and comics targeted at boys and men, but disavowed [. . .] similar attempts to reach girls and women."[78] Complicating this further is the fact that the authorial status granted to Faust was predicated in large part on the emergence of "Bronies" as a surplus audience for the show.[79] Because Bronies (adolescent and adult male fans of show) were celebrated for deigning to consume "feminine" content, and subsequently positioned in narratives about the show as a "co-creative" force, they also played "a key role in [Faust's] construction of authorship, both as participants and props in making claims to cultural legitimacy."[80]

In Rosenberg's case, the head of television at Marvel, Jeph Loeb, is credited with exposing her to the character's original comic, *Alias*, and is described by Rosenberg as "very much my partner and guide into the Marvel Universe."[81] Thus, even in cases such as Rosenberg's, in which a woman expressing an investment in cultivating a female superhero property is hired, and subsequently commits to hiring other women,[82] there frequently remains an articulated deference (however deserved) to men who can more easily and conceptually occupy the label of "fan" within these contexts. The promotional framing of *Wonder Woman* (2017) director Patty Jenkins's fannish history with the property in press releases announcing her hiring and subsequent interviews echoes this. As the trades' coverage of the announcement made clear, "selecting Jenkins helps [Warner Bros.] avoid what some saw as a gender bias against women directors helming superhero tentpoles."[83] In other words,

Jenkins was the right woman for the job first and foremost because she is a woman. When DC Entertainment's president and CCO Geoff Johns touts Jenkins's "deep and meaningful connection" to Wonder Woman, his remark is predicated on Jenkins's emotional and holistic (and thereby feminized) understanding of "the very core of the character,"[84] rather than on a litany of references to Jenkins's comic book collection and worn VHS tapes of the 1970s television series.

Though these pieces do narrativize *Wonder Woman* as a "passion project" for Jenkins over ten years in the making, Jenkins more often than not cites a male superhero property, *Superman* (1978), as the primary influence on both her childhood and the film. Much as "tricky" was discursively deployed by industry insiders to justify *Wonder Woman*'s long tenure in development hell,[85] Jenkins's hiring was described by Warner Bros. as a "gamble," with Jenkins forced to make a "plea" for the opportunity to make the film. In both cases, women are painted as an economic and professional risk, never mind the fact that far more obscure male superhero properties had been greenlit and numerous male directors "have jumped from micro-budget indies to nine-figure blockbusters without anyone batting an eye."[86] In the wake of the film's (surprise) success, Jenkins's warm relationship with the film's fans was often credited as a large part of its appeal, but in the majority of these cases Jenkins is rarely presented as a fan herself.

I would go so far as to suggest that men may, in fact, more easily claim the label of "fangirl auteur" than their female counterparts. Similarly to the ways in which Orlando Jones can claim the label of "fangirl" and reclaim the more stereotypically gendered facets of that cultural archetype in a way that the average fangirl could not, male content creators can more easily situate themselves as fangirl auteurs, or be comparatively celebrated for claiming this identity.[87] *Hannibal* showrunner Bryan Fuller poses an especially intriguing test case for this more flexible conception of the "fangirl auteur," if we deploy the term to reference the rare media creator who actively solicits and celebrates transformative fan culture without any censorial predilection for affirmational or canonical fan works. As Lori Morimoto has argued in her work on Fuller's relationship with *Hannibal* fans, Fuller openly referred to *Hannibal* as his "fanfiction" from the show's inception, thereby aligning himself with the traditions of transformative fan culture. This was an unprecedented move among fanboy auteurs when adapting cult properties, as the term is commonly "used pejoratively in writing by (frequently male) fan critics and media commentators as a way of foregrounding its feminized excesses and textual infidelities,"[88] thereby posing an immediate challenge to their claim to auteurism and/or originality. Fuller also broke ground by openly supporting, circulating, and incorporating fans' homoerotic reading practices and production of slash fanworks into the show itself with regard to the show's core relationship between Hannibal Lecter and Will Graham. Through Fuller's "careful enactment of fan reciprocity" and pointed appropriation of "*women's* commonly maligned fan culture to promote *Hannibal*, the production simultaneously affirmed it."[89] Here, then, "affirmational" takes on a wholly different cadence. The question remains, however, whether a female showrunner would have been capable of embracing transformative fan culture as openly or enthusiastically.

Fantrepreneurs

If fanboy auteurs deploy their fan identity as a cornerstone of their creative credentials to helm fancentric media projects, then the fantrepreneur presents a more flexible conceptual category. I have previously used the term "fantrepreneur" to broadly describe "one who openly leverages or strategically adopts a fannish identity for their own professional advancement."[90] This definition could equally apply to fanboy auteurs or indeed any of the industry publishers or marketers who populate panels at fan conventions to vocally assure "attendees that they only have the fans' best interest at heart since they are geeks themselves and thus know what fans want."[91] For the purposes of the analysis that follows, I would like to home in on one type of fantrepreneur, to better delineate between the fanboy auteur (as a *creator* of mainstream media content) and the fantrepreneur (as a *commentator on* or *curator of* content). Fantrepreneurs, as the term suggests, are adept at capitalizing on the mainstreaming of geek and fan culture, using their preexisting ties to various fan communities to build a network of collaborators and followers. Fantrepreneurs center their fan identities in their self-brand, automatically imbuing their efforts with an "underdog" quality. Like entrepreneurs, they are appealing figures because they have frequently built their reputations and businesses from the ground up, in many cases creating free content for other fans (websites, blog posts, podcasts, etc.) at their own expense before eventually building up enough of a recognizable brand to allow them to monetize their labor.

Like Benjamin Woo's designation of the "alpha nerd" to describe a fan who takes on the role of "cultural intermediary," fantrepreneurs "work between the moments of production and consumption and are concerned with circulation—not only of commodities, but also discourses about their meaning."[92] The fantrepreneur, like the fanboy auteur, thus commonly serves as a liaison between industry and audience, though their connections to "official" industrial fan outreach initiatives can range in degree. One essential point of distinction is that, while presenting liminal fannish identities, the fanboy auteur ultimately serves the interests of industry, whereas it is essential for fantrepreneurs to present themselves first and foremost as fan-cultural agents. Whether sincere or performative, this is often a fraught endeavor that cannot be easily framed as a "bottom-up" or wholly grassroots enterprise considering that many fantrepreneurial brands are founded by industry insiders who use these fan-oriented initiatives to solidify their self-brand: comedian Chris Hardwick's Nerdist Industries empire, actress Felicia Day's Geek & Sundry YouTube Channel, actor Zachary Levi's web content hub and fan convention programming effort The Nerd Machine, actress Ashley Eckstein's fangirl fashion retailer Her Universe, and so on. Thus, when we examine fantrepreneurial business models, there is a discursive imperative not only to articulate the fantrepreneur's own fan identity but to overtly frame fans as having agency over the content or goods created and curated in these spaces.

Consider, for example, a 2015 *Fast Company* profile of Levi's "Nerd HQ," Nerd Machine's off-site programming at San Diego Comic-Con International. Debuting in 2010, Nerd HQ allowed fans to pay to attend more intimate conversations with the stars of their favorite media properties than the convention can provide. Observing that Levi "has used his geek status to build a geek culture brand that fosters greater interaction between fans and celebrities," the profile anecdotally opens with Levi taking the stage and addressing the fans: "'At the end of the day, you guys are the producers,' he says, gesturing to the crowd. 'We get to do this stuff, because you want to buy this shit!' The audience roars." Nerd

Machine has a clearly articulated philanthropic aim, with proceeds from the Comic Con panels going to Operation Smile, but this quotation nonetheless lays bare both the failed promise of fan empowerment and the bottom line underpinning most fantrepreneurial efforts. Indeed, the fact that many of these fantrepreneurial brands are ultimately acquired by larger companies, such as Legendary Entertainment's purchase of Nerdist Industries in 2012 and Geek & Sundry in 2014,[93] and subcultural retailer Hot Topic's acquisition of Her Universe in 2016,[94] suggests that the primary appeal of these fantrepreneurial endeavors is their implicit promise to lead industry "deeper into the fanboy world."[95]

We might look to the startup Legion M, which was founded in 2016 by Paul Scanlan and Jeff Annison as "the world's first fan-owned media company," as a culmination (or industrial codification) of fantrepreneurial efforts over the past decade. In addition to partnering with an array of noted fantrepreneurial brands (Robot Chicken's Stoopid Buddy Stoodios, Geek & Sundry, the Alamo Drafthouse), Legion M has crowdfunded nearly $1.5 million from over two thousand fan investors via WeFunder. With a relatively steep one-hundred-dollar minimum investment and the explicit promise to "open the gates of Hollywood" and give fans input into content creation, Legion M represents a decisive break from prior fan funding or "fanancing" efforts, like the crowdfunded *Veronica Mars* film.[96] Because the U.S. Securities and Exchange Commission's adoption of Title IV of the JOBS Act in 2015 has opened the door for Legion M and other "fananced" media initiatives, the fantrepreneur also forces us to confront a future in which fan "investment" is rendered literal. This sort of emergent "participatory production culture" might be appealing, and Legion M's fans presumably have a (literally) vested interest in the company's productions succeeding. However, while Legion M sells the promise of access to and a tangible sense of ownership over the creative process, what it delivers is a pedagogical vision of corporate fandom, in which the perks of professionalization (e.g., Hollywood parties, access to celebrities, virtual champagne toasts) and fantrepreneurial self-branding practices are valued above collaboration or community.

While the remainder of this chapter focuses on Nerdist CEO and *Talking Dead* host Chris Hardwick, as he is a fantrepreneur par excellence, it is important to note that this hybrid fannish identity may be an easier one for female fans, queer fans, and fans of color to occupy than the fanboy auteur. Echoing a media landscape that has moved increasingly towards catering to niche demographics, and a fan-cultural landscape that has similarly developed digital outlets to speak to a wide array of constituencies within fan and geek culture, there are growing opportunities for grassroots fantrepreneurs (those without preexisiting connections to media industries). For example, Jamie Broadnax, the founder of the geek culture website Black Girl Nerds, was recently named to the SyFy Channel's advisory board, marking a potential space of intervention into content creation and industrial conceptions of desirable fandom. One of the tags adorning the press release was, fittingly, "fantrepreneur," and it went on to detail Broadnax's entrepreneurial ethos, her reliance on crowdfunding and her frustrations with being unable to compensate Black Nerd Girl contributors, and the unwillingness of venture capitalists or mainstream media companies to invest in diversity.[97] The SyFy press release rightly notes that "[a]s genre entertainment has mushroomed in popularity, its producers' traditional focus on white, straight male protagonists—and fans—has come further into focus. Broadnax provides a modicum of relief." Whether Broadnax can make a meaningful industrial impact remains to be seen, but her fantreprenurial brand's focus on inclusion presents a positive intervention even as it powerfully articulates who can more or less easily profit from their fan identity.[98]

Moderating Fan Culture

Horace Newcomb and Paul M. Hirsch's 1983 framing of television as a "cultural forum" remains a conceptually rich starting point for an analysis of contemporary television, even as the Internet has displaced television as our "national medium"[99] and has increasingly become the primary delivery mechanism for "television" content. Numerous scholars, most notably Amanda Lotz, have responded to the difficulty of conceptualizing television as a cultural forum in an era of post-network fragmentation and digital streaming by suggesting that it is perhaps better understood as a "subcultural forum," considering that programming is designed to reach increasingly "smaller and like-minded audiences."[100] As the basis for a consideration of television as a *fan forum* and the place of the fantrepreneur within it, I would like to briefly revisit Newcomb and Hirsch's essay, particularly their claim that television's "emphasis is on process rather than product, on discussion rather than indoctrination, on contradiction and confusion rather than coherence."[101] In addition to articulating my own ambivalence about the convergence culture industry, this conception of the fan forum affords a unique space in which to consider the contemporary slippage between television and Internet content and the fantrepreneur as someone chosen to "moderate" this relationship.

Though we could certainly read the television industry's growing tendency to court and cater to the niche textual tastes and participatory practices of fans as exemplary of television's evolution into a subcultural forum, I have chosen to utilize "fan forum" for a number of reasons. First, while "subcultural forum" and "fan forum" both speak to networks and programming designed to appeal to niche demographics, a contemplation of television as a fan forum additionally allows us to interrogate a post–Web 2.0 television landscape that incentivizes and quantifies audience engagement across platforms. Moreover, the interactive qualities of an Internet fan forum—its production of critical discourse as well as its construction of community—resonate with those qualities of the cultural forum as outlined by Newcomb and Hirsch (namely, an emphasis on procedurality, discussion, and contradiction). A theorization of television as a fan forum also allows us to productively contemplate the role of the moderator, which brings me to the convergence culture industry's most prominent fantrepreneur: Nerdist Industries founder Chris Hardwick.

Hardwick, a stand-up comedian and actor who was previously best known as the cohost of MTV's 1990s dating show *Singled Out*, started Nerdist as a blog and corresponding Twitter account in 2008. Initially conceiving Nerdist as a space for his personal musings on geek and tech culture, Hardwick frequently positions himself as an accidental entrepreneur in journalistic profiles, while simultaneously framing the origins of Nerdist as an explicit self-branding exercise after informing his agent in 2007 that he only wanted to take jobs related to geek culture, science, and technology.[102] Hardwick was an early adopter of podcasting in 2009, and by 2016 the flagship Nerdist Podcast had produced over eight hundred episodes and was downloaded by nearly seven million people each month. Nerdist's merger in 2011 with newsletter publisher

Geek Chic Daily, founded by venture capitalist Peter Levin, helped grow the company's brand. Levin, who had previously worked for Creative Artists Agency (CAA) and the Walt Disney Company, describes the e-newsletter's audience as "primarily young males [. . .] a constituency that advertisers and marketers were very covetous of."[103] While Nerdist's own demographics are more gender neutral, skewing "slightly male, with a median income of $60,000," this "discriminating and desirable demographic"[104] grew exponentially after the merger.

The year 2011 also marked a turning point for Hardwick's self-styling as a fantrepreneur, with both the publication of his playful "self-help" book *The Nerdist Way: How to Reach the Next Level (in Real Life)* and the premiere of the *Talking Dead* aftershow. Hardwick had been a fixture at San Diego Comic-Con for several years as a panel moderator prior to his hiring by AMC to host *Talking Dead* and, subsequently, *Talking Bad* (the fan aftershow for *Breaking Bad*). As the head of programming for AMC, Joel Stillerman has noted of Hardwick's appeal, "[A]udiences can smell a rat a mile away. The people who watch the *Talking* shows are true super-fans, and it doesn't work unless you are talking to them on a level they respect."[105] Precisely because it is Hardwick's perceived authenticity that is at the core of his (and, arguably, every) fantrepreneurial brand, it is significant that he routinely self-identifies as an "unashamed fanboy," rather than a fan, modeling not just an affirmational but an effusively uncritical mode of fannish engagement.

This gets somewhat more complicated when Hardwick, industry executives, and journalists present him as mainstream fan culture's "attractive, welcoming emissary," framing his "celebratory tendencies" as a bid for greater inclusivity in geek culture.[106] Thus, in the span of one profile, Hardwick's bona fides as an affirmational fan are foregrounded (he is not "a fake nerd" and is "worthy of attention" precisely because he knows "as much as his fans [or more] about the their favorite TV shows, movies, comics and other hallmarks of geek culture") and his wholly celebratory take on geek culture properties is presented as striking back at the "walled garden and exclusionary behavior" that mars mainstream geek culture. This flattening of affirmational and inclusive fandom in profiles of Hardwick is doubly ironic, considering that these are the only forms of fannish expression that the convergence culture industry has adopted an inclusive attitude towards. It is precisely because Hardwick is the reigning "ringmaster of nerd culture" that it is vital to consider how he directs the performance of contemporary digital fan culture, making it legible (and, more importantly, lucrative) to legacy media industries.

In 2012, Hardwick sold Nerdist to production company Legendary Entertainment for an undisclosed sum of money. What Legendary Entertainment ultimately purchased, in addition to Nerdist Industries' audience base (which aligned with the company's investment in geek culture IP), was Hardwick's fantrepreneurial expertise and identity. In describing the Legendary Entertainment acquisition, Levin framed Nerdist as a scrappy start-up, the "bottom-up voices" to Legendary's "top-down" approach to fan culture, noting that "[w]hen you can make those two meet, things get real interesting."[107] Because fantrepreneurs are, more often than not, both the site and the embodiment of this merger, their functioning as (sub)cultural interpreter for industry becomes paramount. Specifically, what was being sold and why it was appealing to Legendary Entertainment was a monetizable fan-culture model predicated on unabashedly celebratory and voracious consumption across platforms.

Just as Newcomb and Hirsch were interested in how content creators responded to technological shifts, functioning both as "cultural interpreters" and *bricoleurs*, I am interested in Hardwick as a prominent moderator of geek culture generally, and his self-branding as both an interpreter and *bricoleur* of socially mediated digital fan culture for television specifically. My use of the term "moderator" references Hardwick's primary role as the moderator of televised fan aftershows and game shows, as well as of panels at various fan conventions, but it also evokes the function of an Internet forum mod. The duties of a digital fan forum mod (moderator) typically include overseeing and facilitating communication, making decisions about which topics are (in)appropriate, and directing conversation to keep topics organized. In short, a mod occupies an empowered position within a fan forum, but is also a participant who endeavors to create coherence from contradiction, product from process. Importantly for the purposes of this argument, moderators are often viewed as moving beyond their role as curators or facilitators of discourse, abusing their power to ban users or delete threads that they determine violate community standards and norms.

I also pointedly use this term to imply that Hardwick's self-presentation as an arbiter of fan culture is one that is inherently moderate, if not expressly hegemonic. Not unlike a moderator who might step in to douse a flame war or delete a controversial thread, Hardwick curates and broadcasts a branded and coherent vision of digital fan forums, turning the process of digital fan participation into fixed products (in this case, television programs), and collapsing discussions into subtle indoctrinations about which modes of fan engagement are recognized and rewarded within the convergence culture industry. Newcomb and Hirsch close their essay by noting that they are "far more concerned with the ways in which television contributes to change than with mapping the obvious ways in which it maintains dominant viewpoints."[108] Because I am deeply ambivalent about these emergent forms of fantrepreneurial "brandom," I begin this analysis of Hardwick and the two television shows he hosts, AMC's fan aftershow *The Talking Dead* and Comedy Central's social-media-fueled game show *@midnight*, by noting that I am far more concerned with the ways in which television as a fan forum might maintain dominant viewpoints by imbuing its moderator with too much power.

It is difficult not to draw parallels between Dykstra's accusations of Hardwick's allegedly "controlling behavior,"[109] discussed in the prior chapter, and the ways in which his controlling presence as a fan moderater has been widely celebrated by the convergence culture industry and fans alike. While, in our current geek-culture-saturated landscape, fan culture moderators like Hardwick are not in short supply, fans are deeply and at times disconcertingly invested in Hardwick's fantreprenurial identity. A Change.org petition that was started shortly after Hardwick's initial suspension by AMC, fighting to "Bring Chris Hardwick Back!" ultimately gathered over forty-four thousand signatures,[110] and fan activist hashtags like #IstandwithChrisHardwick mobilized Hardwick's self-proclaimed "Army" of followers on Twitter. Hardwick's most vocal defenders in the wake of Dykstra's accusations were overwhelmingly white women.[111] While this is perhaps unsurprising, given the fact that 52 percent of white women voted for Donald Trump in the 2016 presidential election, it nonetheless paints a very different picture of the ongoing #MeToo movement and powerfully suggests that in particular cases, white female fans may be equally invested in, or responsible for, maintaining the supremacy of white men in fan culture.

Alternately, and certainly less politically, we can read fans' efforts to reinstate Hardwick and restore his reputation as reflective of their deep and enduring loyalty to his carefully cultivated form of brandom. Sarah Banet-Weiser has argued that brands are increasingly "about *culture* as much as they are about economics," that brands are not mere products but rather "the essence of what will be experienced [. . .] a promise as much as a practicality."[112] I am conceptualizing brandom similarly: to demarcate both spaces in which fan identity is capitalized on and those products that promise the essence of a fan experience while eschewing any components that legally or ideologically challenge the convergence culture industry. Like the post-network televisual landscape, digital fan culture is both vast and fragmented. Nerdist's industrial appeal as a geek culture content hub is that it strives to present a branded, coherent vision of fan engagement from the contradictions and chaos of digital fan forums. In Hardwick's tongue-in-cheek self-help book *The Nerdist Way: How to Reach the Next Level (in Real Life)*, he narrates the 2008 birth and branding of the Nerdist empire as follows:

> I wanted the idea that Nerds now owned popular culture to be an ideology to which anyone could subscribe, therefore the "ism" of it all. [. . .] Since that time, Nerdist has sprouted a bunch of different heads, but it's all pieces of the same voice, which is mine. [. . .] To paraphrase [Sir Richard Branson], "It wasn't the product," he would tell them. "It's the Virgin Experience." The important factor was that the point of view was consistent.[113]

I am tempted to spend the remainder of this book just unpacking this statement, but it will suffice to home in on Hardwick's use of the term "ideology," which is paradoxically framed as inclusive and pluralistic, while remaining decidedly autocratic. The language here is telling: anyone can subscribe (literally in the case of Hardwick's podcast) to the *idea* that nerds own popular culture, but Hardwick effectively owns and actively shapes that idea as Nerdist's brand ambassador.

This remains the case even though Hardwick has professionally parted ways with Nerdist. In February 2018, Hardwick rebranded the Nerdist Podcast as "ID10T with Chris Hardwick," named after his new business endeavor. In addition to Id1otfest, an annual music and comic "conival," which launched in June 2017, Id1ot primarily functions as a web store that sells Hardwick- and geek culture–related merchandise. Per the website's "about" page, composed by Hardwick,

> ID10T is a joke IT code that essentially means "user error." I like it because it reminds us that we can take responsibility for our own crap. As a rabid consumer of nerd-centric pop culture goods, it recently occurred to me that I could also take responsibility for MAKING my own crap. Anything you see in the coming months on this site will be meticulously designed, carefully curated and will be items that I personally wanted to exist so I could own them. Please understand that while I love you, I'm KIND OF doing this whole exercise for me (insert winky emoticon here).[114]

What Hardwick positions as an exercise in personal responsibility is, in fact, an incredibly savvy business decision, bringing his fantrepreneurial brand entirely under his control. Far from an example of "user error," Hardwick's framing of his play to remove the middleman from his efforts to capitalize on his own fan identity is telling.

Here, and in countless interviews, Hardwick stresses that it is his own fan identity and voice that are central to Nerdist Industries' (and, later, Id1ot's) brandom. He is appealing as a fantrepreneur precisely because he is at once an Everyfan and a Big Name Fan, whether discursively claiming a need to sell merchandise predominantly so that he can personally buy it, or embodying the liminal power of a fan forum moderator in his simultaneous claim to "love" his community while centering himself ("I'm KIND OF doing this whole exercise for me"). This is reinforced by Nerdist's advertising partners: to quote just one, the core appeal of partnering with Nerdist is an "alignment in ideology in the way Chris Hardwick redefines what a nerd is."[115] The best way to exemplify the ideological underpinnings of Nerdist's brandom and Hardwick's fantrepreneurial role in redefining digital fan engagement is to quickly analyze two Hardwick-hosted television series that are programmatically designed to hail and interpellate fans: AMC's fan-oriented aftershow *Talking Dead*, and Comedy Central's purportedly "live" geek comedy game show *@midnight*.

As discussed in the prior chapter, AMC's *Talking Dead* is moderated by Hardwick and brings together a panel of *The Walking Dead*'s creative team, along with "celebrity superfans," to discuss the episode immediately after it airs. This discussion is supplemented by fan questions submitted through an array of social media platforms, via phone, or by the live studio audience. *@midnight with Chris Hardwick* was a half-hour-long game show that aired five nights a week on Comedy Central. From its premiere in 2013 until its cancellation in 2017, its format was relatively consistent: three comedians compete in a series of challenges drawing on digital culture to earn points from Hardwick and symbolically "win the Internet" for the night. Though *@midnight* was predominantly aimed at comedy fans, the content of the challenges frequently drew on geek and fan culture, as well as Hardwick's own fanboy identity.

Both shows have been celebrated for their ability to cultivate and capitalize on digital participatory culture. *Talking Dead* has become a ratings juggernaut, and in addition to winning the 2015 Emmy for Outstanding Social TV experience, *@midnight* distinguished itself as the most social late-night talk show, generating an average of around 250,000 social media mentions per week and routinely ranking in the top three shows in its time slot with men aged eighteen to thirty-four.[116] The industrial appeal of these programs is apparent, as they both nostalgically rely on and actively augment watching television programs as they air. The shows' appeal for fans is that they programmatically cultivate "technoprosociality," or "the integration of social media technology to maximize audience engagement and interpersonal relationship development between celebrities and fans."[117] The success of these programs thus relies on minimizing the "social distance" between Hardwick and the programs' audience.

Beyond Hardwick's presence, there are some notable corollaries between these two shows. First, liveness is essential to both shows' appeal. However, because *Talking Dead* airs immediately after *The Walking Dead*'s East Coast feed and is rebroadcast, only a small percentage of fans can participate in the show's interactive elements, such as polls and phone-in questions. Ironically, because *Talking Dead* is notorious for featuring actors immediately after their character is killed, it has forced many fans to stay off social media entirely, for fear of being spoiled, thereby potentially disincentivizing participation in digital fan forums. *@midnight*, alternately, is prerecorded but presented as airing live, with Hardwick performatively beginning each show by stating "It's 11:59 and 59 seconds and this happened on the Internet today." The title's "@" symbol thus serves a dual function, marking both the show's air time and its claim to liveness and signaling the dominant mode of interacting with the show via Twitter's "@" mode of directing comments to particular user accounts. The façade of liveness is essential to the show's appeal, as the comedians are presented as improvising their answers on the spot. The show even goes so far as to label one segment the "live challenge," insinuating that the contestants only have the time span of a commercial break to compose their answers. Because each forty-minute taping is cut to twenty-three minutes, it is common to see point totals inexplicably shift, resulting in the facsimile of liveness breaking down for the viewer in spite of all Hardwick's rhetorical framing to the contrary.

This claim to liveness is directly connected to each show's desire to harness the liveliness of digital discursive spaces like Twitter or other fan forums. More importantly, the premium that these shows place on liveness allows them to structurally and seamlessly facilitate the audience's movement from digital to televisual spaces and back again. *Talking Dead* accordingly urges fans to "continue the conversation" by watching additional footage on the show's official website, and *@midnight*'s audience is prompted by Hardwick to "keep the game going" each night online by using promoted hashtags and occasionally competing to be featured as a contestant on the show. Though the emphasis is on a sustaining audience interaction, ironically, neither show offers fans any meaningful opportunity to engage with or shape the content of the programs themselves.

This brings us to each show's framing of fan participation. At its best, *Talking Dead* replicates the kind of impassioned textual debates that occur within fan forums. At its worst, it models and attempts to mold a vision of fan discourse that is both carefully controlled and corporatized. This vision of fan engagement aligns its "brandom" with both AMC's identity as a quality television network and Hardwick's identity as a quality fan: brandom is passionate but not excessive. It is deeply analytical but never overtly critical, reflecting Hardwick's own effusively affirmational fan identity. Thus, the format and tone of *Talking Dead* is ultimately closer to something like *Inside the Actor's Studio* than the average digital fan forum. Hardwick himself describes the show as "a little therapy," equating it to "a cigarette after the sex" for the fans who "can't shut their brains off."[118] Just as the prior chapter discussed the implications of assigning this "therapeutic" work to a maternal black actress, the explicit framing of the aftershow as simultaneously a space to capture, quantify, and ultimately diffuse fans' participatory impulses, to help them "turn off their brains," is troubling.

@*midnight* similarly situates Hardwick as the avatar of the show's desired audience, to the extent that the entire show is designed around topics and jokes that resonate with Hardwick's fan persona. According to one @*midnight* participant I interviewed on the condition of anonymity, each contestant is assigned show writers who "are acutely aware of what jokes will fly, and which won't. They guide you through what they think Chris will like." When I inquired whether contestants were expected to engage fan "players" on Twitter, my source noted that "[c]ontestants are expected to have a social media presence of some sort and are asked to tweet [to promote] their appearance," but "that's the extent of what is requested." This, in some sense, reflects the relatively low level of engagement for fans of the show, who are encouraged to "play along" albeit in limited and structured ways, and always with an eye towards garnering the approval of Hardwick (via likes and retweets from the show's official account). Audiences are most actively encouraged to participate in the Hashtag Wars, a rapid-fire segment in which contestants come up with as many humorous answers as possible to a hashtag prompt in sixty seconds. At the end of each segment, one audience tweet from the prior night's Hashtag Wars topic is featured, thereby incentivizing audience participation. Here, we see clearly that it is not just the answers that are pitched to what the writers think Hardwick will like; the prompts are commonly rooted in juvenile fanboy humor in both concept and tone (e.g., a #sexystarwars prompt might provoke responses like "Blow me, Wan Kenobi").

Whether simply a byproduct of Hardwick's fan identity shaping content, or part of a more systemic effort by the convergence culture industry to cultivate a brandom aligned with its desired fan demographic, both shows present a decidedly androcentric vision of fan culture. Hardwick's fantrepreneurial persona and his personal narrative of leveraging his fan identity into vast professional success lauds fan engagement that is able to be contained and commercialized, and ultimately reaffirms fan culture as a space of white heterosexual male privilege. Just as women are underrepresented as "celebrity superfans" on *Talking Dead*, 70 percent of the comedians featured on *@midnight* are men, but because the contestant with the lowest score is eliminated before the final "for the win" round, these statistics become more interesting. Female contestants are disproportionately eliminated before the final round to the extent that it became something of a running joke on the program for the eliminated comedienne to make a parting crack about Hardwick's or the show's inherent sexism.

A further consideration of television's functioning as a fan forum would certainly consider brandom in its myriad forms, for example, Bravo's Andy Cohen and shows like *Watch What Happens Live*, which speak to different niche audiences and tonally encourage more stereotypically "feminine" or "gossipy" (if similarly limited and illusory) modes of participation. To conclude, though, I want to turn back to Hardwick as a model of emerging fantrepreneurial identities and how they are situated as moderators of fan culture. In a March 2015 interview with *Forbes* magazine, Hardwick stressed the importance of integrating fan interactions into the programs he helms, noting, "I wanted it to feel like Comic Con where everyone's involved in the conversation. [. . .] A lot of the vibe of the show relates to the Comic Con subculture and the second people realize what they're watching is fake, or not authentic, the show doesn't work. It's insulting to the fans."[119] This analogy is, of course, as problematic as it is perfect in its articulation of Hardwick's own carefully cultivated fantrepreneurial brand: Comic-Con is, first and foremost, a promotional space driven by the interests of media corporations. It is also inherently contained, both as a physical space with a limited number of attendees and thus inaccessible to many either geographically or financially and as a discursive space in which few if any fans have the opportunity to pose questions or join panel conversations. In short, Hardwick in his role as a moderator of fan culture is perhaps the only person who can claim that "everyone's involved in the conversation," because he is always already at the center of it.

Adapting Adorno's claim that the "consensus which [the culture industry] propagates strengthens blind, opaque authority,"[120] this chapter's survey of liminal and hybrid producer/fan identities like the fanboy auteur proposes that this authority has been maintained through these fannish figureheads' perceived transparency, accessibility, and relatability. Likewise, if "the entire practice of the culture industry transfers the profit motive naked onto cultural forms,"[121] the figure of the fantrepreneur represents a concerted effort to transfer the subcultural form of one's fan identity into profit. Because this chapter and indeed this entire book have suggested that it is far easier for fanboys to leverage their identities for visibility and professional gain, the final chapter trains its focus on where fangirls are rendered visible and economically viable within the convergence culture industry.

6

From Poaching to Pinning

Fashioning Postfeminist Geek Girl(y) Culture

The prior two chapters have focused on what John Fiske termed "enunciative" fandom, considering how media industries have alternately fostered and attempted to constrain, monetize, and model forms of "fan talk." Given the industry's frequent equation of fan participation with enunciative productivity, as well as what types of fans tend to be elected to speak on fandom's behalf, these visible "moderators" of fan culture inevitably elevate affirmational fan voices, identities, and modes of engagement, potentially silencing others in the process. If fanboy identities and masculinized modes of fan engagement have been overwhelmingly and systematically privileged, it begs the question: Where *does* the convergence culture industry carve out space for female fans, and must we view any acknowledgment of female fans as inherently positive or progressive?

To begin answering this question requires that we return to an oft-overlooked facet of Fiske's initial definition of "enunciative participation," namely, that it encompasses sartorial as well as verbal forms of expression. These enunciations, which might include "styling of hair or make-up, the choice of clothes or accessories," were conceived by Fiske as public efforts to construct a social identity, or assert the fan's membership in a broader community.[1] If this book has heretofore traced the interrelated ways in which women's membership in geek culture or their claim to the social identity of "fan" have been strategically foreclosed by the convergence culture industry, then this final chapter examines the one space wherein women have historically been and continue to be hailed as legitimate and valued consumers: fashion and beauty culture. Being careful to delineate between the lived identities of geek girls, and the "geek girly" lifestyle identities that are curated and sold through social scrapbooking platforms like Pinterest and fangirl-centric clothing retailers like Her Universe, this chapter turns a critical eye toward hy-perfeminized expressions of fannish affect. These spaces may envision female fans as a postfeminist target market, or problematically conflate fan participation with pinning or purchasing, but that does not render them inherently unproductive or depoliticized. Just as Fiske suggests that enunciative performances of fan style might have an empowering social purpose, moving from affiliation to provocation by "deliberately challeng[ing] more normal social values and the discipline they exert,"[2] these calculated efforts to appeal to the female fan consumer are com-plex. Fan fashion and its relationship to the gendered fan body might afford a potent site to challenge the androcentrism of the convergence culture industry. First, however, we must contemplate gendered fan merchandise more generally, and confront the postfeminist vision of fan identity it frequently represents.

Gendered Fan Merchandise

Despite being central to both fannish consumption and the performance of fan identity, fan merchandise remains undertheorized. One reason for this is that the study of fans' economic (rather than affective or temporal or creative) investment in various media texts conceptually threatens the framing of fans as "resistant" consumers. Though "incorporation" in the vast majority of fan scholarship tends to be used to describe those fans as consumers who do not actively ideologically challenge or critique media objects through their own textual production, "incorporation" takes on a slightly different valence in Dick Hebdige's work on subcultural style. Suggesting that all subversive subcultural performances are ultimately incorporated or domesticated, thereby robbing them of their political potency, Hebdige identifies two key forms of incorporation: the ideo-logical form and the commodity form. The former refers to a dominant group's efforts to label and redefine the subculture in question via two pri-mary ideological strategies for dealing with the subcultural threat: either transforming the Other into "meaningless exotica," a spectacle, or denying the difference of the Other, rending the Other "trivialized, naturalized, domesticated."[3] We can see this strategy deployed in the pathologized por-traits of fans that inspired the first wave of fan studies, and that continue to linger despite their incorporation into the convergence culture industry.

The commodity form of incorporation recuperates and domesticates a subculture by converting its signs into mass-produced objects, removing them from their "private contexts" so that they might be "codified, made comprehensible, rendered at once public property and profitable merchandise."[4] It is this second strategy, "the subtler mechanisms through which potentially threatening phenomena are handled and contained,"[5] that poses greater concerns, as the convergence culture industry has, above all, worked to naturalize and standardize particular fan identities. It is this attempted "domestication" of fan culture and the efforts to contain or trivialize female fans and transformative practices that have been the focus of this book thus far. Hebdige was referring to the literal transition of subcultural style into commodities, such as the safety-pin-riddled punk style being mass produced and sold. We could certainly make a similar case about how fan subcultures have come to popularize a growing array of "geek chic" merchandising outposts ranging from big box stores like Target to more niche chain retailers like Hot Topic or digital sites like ThinkGeek, all of which enable fans to quite literally purchase and physically enunciate an array of subcultural and fannish identities. In line with the prior chapters' examination of how the convergence culture industry has cultivated an androcentric vision of fan culture, this chapter is less interested in decrying the incorporation of fannish subcultural style than in considering how this incorporation functions differently for women than for men.

Like the bulk of the cultural studies work emerging from the Birmingham School in the 1970s, Hebdige's analysis of the connections between identity and the subversive dimensions of subcultural style within male-dominated music subcultures focused predominantly on class. While it is clearly impossible to divorce class from any conversation about fan merchandise, I am more invested in filling what Avi Santo identifies as a gap in the theorization of fan merchandise, namely, how it poses "sites of struggle and negotiation over what constitutes fandom and who can gain access to/status within a particular community."[6] If fandom is increasingly packaged and sold by media industries "as a lifestyle category rather than a communal experience,"[7] then fan merchandise might offer a space in which the convergence culture industry's androcentric packaging of fan culture is beginning to break down. However, there are still issues with the ways female fans are being positioned within this emergent "lifestyle category" via fangirl-oriented merchandise and fashion.

One version of this chapter's argument would contend that outreach to female fans via fan fashion functions to cultivate a postfeminist fan subject, a natural extension of the convergence culture industry's neoliberal conception of the media fan. Until relatively recently (and still to some extent), fan merchandise has reinforced androcentric conceptions of the fan, with merchandise aimed at female fans routinely failing to address them as a part of the preexisting fan demographic for the franchise in question. When fangirls were hailed, it was commonly through t-shirts in conventionally feminine hues of pink and lavender, often bedazzled with glitter or crystals, displaying slogans in feminized cursive script like "Training to Be Batman's Wife." Another heterosexist favorite, "I only date superheroes," is emblazoned on baby onesies, girls' t-shirts, and women's tank tops, clearly conveying that women are socialized early to internalize, and never sufficiently "age out" of, this messaging. In other cases, female characters are entirely erased from merchandise or textiles featuring a superhero "team," instead relegated to beauty products like shampoo and make-up.[8]

This has changed somewhat, due in part to fan activism, and one positive ramification of the convergence culture industry's embrace of fan culture is that female fans now have a far greater array of merchandise to choose from. In this sense, it is tempting to read some forms of "incorporation" via fan merchandise, however problematically postfeminist, as a potential "win" for fangirls. Or, as Elizabeth Affuso notes, we might positively view the "move of branded fan merchandise into this feminized market" as speaking simultaneously to "the dominance of female fans in contemporary fan cultures and the distinctive needs of this group."[9] Simultaneously, though, Affuso cautions that this growing array of female-oriented fashion and beauty projects "speaks to the ways that fandom can be indoctrinated into cultural values, such as those related to appearance, and also illuminates that as fan practices become more gender inclusive they often simultaneously reinforce gender divides."[10] The analysis that follows, focusing on Pinterest as a feminized fan platform, everyday cosplay trends that encourage female fans to embody male characters, and fan art that transformatively critiques sexualized superheroine costuming, thus strives to balance considerations of how

androcentric conceptions of fan culture are challenged with considerations of how they are upheld. Gendered fan merchandise is positioned
less as a "way out" of the convergence culture industry in this model
(particularly because it is a cornerstone of it) than as a potent and potentially feminist space for fan criticism of standardized and gendered
conceptions of fan culture.

Pinterest and the Politics of Pinning

Since Pinterest launched in 2010, it has distinguished itself within the
social media landscape through its rapid growth and branding as a
decisively gendered digital space. According to a 2015 study by the Pew
Research Center, Pinterest is second only to Facebook in unique visitors,
with an estimated 31 percent of adults who are online using the site.[11]
Building on earlier studies claiming that Pinterest has a broader gender
gap than any other social media site, with female users outnumbering
male users five to one,[12] the 2015 study reaffirms the site's demographics
as overwhelmingly female, and skewing younger (with the bulk of its
users in the eighteen to twenty-nine age range), middle-class, and subur-
ban.[13] Immediately upon joining Pinterest, one is taken to an "interests"
page and required to check various boxes to begin developing a user profile. Nestled among the topics one might expect from a contemporary
social "scrapbooking" or "vision boarding" site aimed predominantly
at affluent young women (such as beauty, fashion, yoga, and antique
mansions) are a range of fannish media properties, companies, celebrities, and practices from *Star Wars* to Marvel Comics, Tom Hiddleston to
cosplay. The site also prominently features "geek" as a lifestyle category
in its dropdown menu, immediately marking the platform as a fangirl-
friendly space. It also clearly identifies the site as a hyperfeminine fan
space, in which discourses around beauty, fashion, and fandom are
designed to cross-pollinate.

As a platform for fan engagement, Pinterest aesthetically and conceptually echoes the migration of fan communities from text-driven
platforms (like LiveJournal or Dreamwidth) to image-driven sites like
Tumblr over the past decade. After initially checking boxes for fannish
properties and companies when registering, Pinterest curates a page
of related pins, or images coupled with descriptive text, hashtags, or

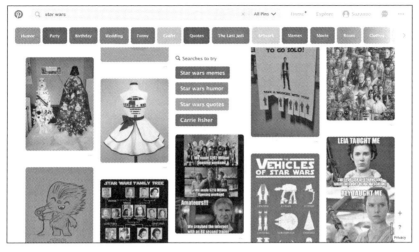

Figure 6.1. An example of fannish pinning on Pinterest, including examples of fan fashion, fan art, and feminist fan memes. Screengrab from Pinterest, https://www .pinterest.com/search/pins/?q=star%20wars&rs=typed.

hyperlinks. When broadly searching fannish tags (for example, *#Star-Wars*), the Pinterest interface will intermingle fan art, images and GIFs, quizzes and commentary, and both fan-crafted and commercially licensed merchandise (figure 6.1). Pinterest's branding as a social lifestyle scrapbooking site means that images pertaining to fan fashion tend to be featured more prominently than on Tumblr, to the extent that fashion retailers with no explicit connection to a particular franchise frequently co-opt these hashtags and related image boards to promote their products (for example, an array of pastel frilly prom dresses posted under the #marvelcomics tag). More often than not, however, the forms of fan merchandise that are the most prominently and prolifically "pinned" fall into gender-normative consumer categories: geeky housewares, hyperfeminine fan fashion (dresses, high heels), and licensed beauty products and jewelry derived from mainstream media franchises.

It would be easy to contend that Pinterest as a platform is designed to contain fandom's feminist potentialities, or at the very least reroute them through an unabashed celebration of the postfeminist consumer subject. Indeed, most marketing researchers emphasize (and, more often than not, celebrate) the site's capacity to do just that, contending that Pinterest functions as a form of digital "daydreaming out loud," in which users' ability to "explore new tastes before risking [purchasing items or crafting their own] in reality" is "supercharged" by the site's socially networked capabilities.[14] I would also like to daydream out loud for a moment, to contemplate a different way we might conceptualize Pinterest as a consumer daydreaming space. Specifically, I would like to suggest that geek girly culture on Pinterest (in the form of image boards, tags, or pinned content) presents a vision board on a broader cultural scale, reflecting and refracting concerns over the frequent erasure of women within the convergence culture industry's construction of fan identity.

It would be far easier to claim Tumblr as the social media platform most actively asserting fandom's feminist politics and empowering minority fans within the convergence culture industry. Scholars have convincingly argued that Tumblr as a platform is "optimized for alterity,"[15] exhibiting a form of "queer reverb" in its design that can structurally "buoy an antinormative or resistant politics,"[16] making it a popular and comparatively "safe" space for minority fans and transformative practices. Comparatively, the feminist potentialities of Pinterest as a platform are difficult to defend, or even readily observe, particularly when one is "examining the assumptions built into interfaces as the normative or 'correct' or path of least resistance."[17] Even when approaching platforms that "may not be particularly empowering, or particularly liberating to women as subjects of feminism, they create a space for new idioms of intimacy"[18] and may always be used in ways not initially intended by the designers. For the purposes of this analysis, then, I am less interested in analyzing Pinterest's functionality as a social media platform than in considering the affordances and limitations of "pinning" as a fan practice. By analyzing the broader politics of moving from fan poaching (as a creative mode of feminist intervention) to pinning (as a feminine curatorial exercise), we can begin contemplating what might be gained or lost through these intersections among fandom, fashion, and (post) feminism.

Initially drawing on Michel de Certeau's description of readers as textual travelers, moving "across lands belonging to someone else, like nomads poaching their way across fields they did not write,"[19] Jenkins's "textual poaching" remains central to theorizations of participation and transformative textual production within fan communities. What this

poaching looks like, however, has invariably shifted alongside the development of digital fan culture and fan-cultural platforms, and with
this shift questions about the parameters of "poaching" inevitably arise:
Does simply reblogging or retweeting existing content to form a person-
alized feed count as contemporary "poaching"? Is some sort of textual
contribution or commentary a prerequisite? Can "poaching" still function as a dominant lens to consider fan engagement, when so much of
contemporary media affirmationally situates fans more as "information
hunters and gatherers"?[20] Pinning functions similarly as a "hunting and
gathering" process but also constitutes a sort of "poaching," personal-
izing a vast sea of digital content into clearly demarcated "boards" to
potentially political ends.

In moving from a discussion of textual poaching to what I am calling strategic pinning, I am drawing on Ellen Gruber Garvey's historical work on scrapbooking and the "strategic scrapbooks" created by
women's rights activists in the early nineteenth century. Garvey suggests, "Like diaries, scrapbooks can be intended for self-reflection or for
an audience," but are composed by "cutting and pasting mass-produced
public materials, not by inscribing in the maker's own hand."[21] In other
words, women's rights activists were rewriting a cultural narrative in
their scrapbooks much as fans do in their production of transformative
works. Resonating with Jenkins's description of fans as textual poachers,
Garvey frames the creators of strategic scrapbooks as pointedly constructing "records of their activism using articles from newspapers they
did not control."[22] Contemporary fans, whether poaching or pinning,
are not operating from the same "position of cultural marginality and
social weakness"[23] as they were in the 1900s or even the 1990s, but they
continue to be in a constant negotiation with the ideological strictures
of both media industries and social media platforms.

I would like to suggest that fan-oriented image boards on Pinterest,
and pinning as a fan practice, might serve a similarly feminist function
as Garvey's "strategic scrapbooks," either explicitly or implicitly. Garvey's
description of feminist "strategic" scrapbooking practices may hew more
closely to de Certeau's characterization of tactics, a "maneuver 'within
the enemy's field of vision,' [. . .] and within enemy territory," an "art of
the weak,"[24] but my use of the term "strategic pinning" gestures to my
own ambivalence about whether Pinterest can ever operate as a truly

tactical space outside of its strategic postfeminist branding and platform design. Still, I would suggest that the panoptic practices that de Certeau associates with strategic power, which transform "foreign forces into objects that can be observed and measured, and thus control[led],"[25] might ultimately serve a tactical function when we consider the intersections among fashion, feminism, and fan culture. Because mass-produced fan merchandise functions as an arm of the convergence culture industry, it conveys powerful messages about which fans are being hailed, mobilized, or marginalized.[26] Strategically pinning fan fashion on Pinterest might function to help include female fans in the scope of the convergence culture industry's vision. More importantly, it can fill that vision, on image board after image board, with fan fashion designed and sold by women.

But what happens when we move away from a characterization of Pinterest as an artisanal support network for female fan crafters to engage the most explicitly hyperfeminized and mass-marketed pins appealing to fangirls? Can we make similar claims about pins that translate the aesthetic of *Star Wars* stormtroopers into nail art or the perfect smokey eye, or seem to spatially limit a woman's expression of fannish affection for a media property to the domestic sphere via housewares? It is generative to take a cue here from Mary Celeste Kearney's nuanced analysis of "sparkle," which simultaneously recognizes its inevitable linkage to postfeminist and neoliberal values while still suggesting that the "ironic knowingness of postfeminist glamour" has the capacity to deploy "self-consciously spectacular performances as weapons against normativity."[27] A space like Pinterest, precisely because it speaks the commoditized language of the convergence culture industry's vision of fan culture, might be similarly mobilized against the convergence culture industry's normative (e.g., masculine) conception of fan culture.

Pinterest presents a compelling, albeit conflicted, site at which to address fandom and femininity. It also, perhaps unconsciously, opens a generative space to consider broader feminist endeavors to expose and critique the gendered assumptions that are baked into mass-produced and licensed fan merchandise. The platform may relentlessly reinforce gendered ideologies and norms, but given the convergence culture industry's reticence to acknowledge female fans, Pinterest's unruly collection, curation, and circulation of content also has the capacity to "enter into, punctuate, and impact women's daily lives, tweaking, exacerbating, or revising how women move through and feel everyday experiences."[28] Thus, even as Pinterest visibly seems designed to contain female fandom through the conventionally gendered scripts of shopping and crafting, I want to consider what it might reflect about how fangirls move through and experience mass-produced fan fashion, and how in turn the presence of geek girl(y) culture on Pinterest and the development of strategic pinning practices might enter into or punctuate the convergence culture industry's valuation of female fans.

Over the past several years, there has been a boom in hashtag activism around the systemic erasure of female characters from mass-marketed fan fashion. Shortly after the release of Marvel's *Guardians of the Galaxy* in August 2014, the hashtag #wheresgamora appeared on Twitter, alongside images of fan merchandise lacking the lone female member of the superhero team. Responding to a similar absence in merchandise for *The Avengers*, actor Mark Ruffalo, the Hulk himself, tweeted in April 2015, "@marvel we need more #BlackWidow merchandise for my daughters and nieces. Pretty please." This sentiment gestures to the major critical through line of these hashtag campaigns, namely, that mass-produced fan merchandise might have a marginalizing effect on younger fangirls. In the instances in which companies have responded to these inequities, this systemic erasure of female characters on fan merchandise is most frequently explained through a combination of target demographics and the socially engrained gender biases of young boys. Here is where strategic pinning might cultivate productive intersections between feminism and fan fashion, both in curating image boards explicitly critical of these trends and in circulating alternatives to this officially licensed fan merchandise.

In all of these cases of hashtag activism, the stakes are framed as far larger than the equal right to purchase t-shirts and action figures, and are actively tied to broader feminist fan critiques surrounding media representations and producorial parity. Many examples, like the #wheresNatasha hashtag, make explicit connections among the erasure of Black Widow from *Avengers* merchandise, the ongoing unwillingness to create merchandise for female fans that is not pink or about the desire to date a superhero, and Disney's and Marvel's unwillingness to give Black Widow, the most prominent female member of the Avengers, her own stand-alone film. Thus, the critiques are not strictly relegated to branded merchandise but allude to broader concerns about how the convergence culture industry is branding fandom. These instances of hashtag activism that speak back to branded fan merchandise, and the branding of fandom by extension, are an explicit effort to both tell fangirls' stories and comment on the frequency with which fangirls are written out of the cultural narrative of the ascendance of geek culture. These campaigns have accordingly coalesced around the hashtag #IncludeTheGirls, with the "girls" in question referencing both female characters and the female fans whom these products actively alienate. Pinterest, as a space that not only includes girls but overtly caters to them, presents an opportunity for a sort of curatorial poaching, with fans utilizing pins and image boards to stitch together the elements of popular objects that resonate with their identity politics, and excise those elements they find problematic.

Pinterest is a vital space of future fannish study precisely because of the frequent failure of the convergence culture industry to meaningfully establish dialogues with female fans via promotional discourse. Sarah Banet-Weiser has argued that through "social media, marketers increasingly assume (and exploit) the existence of consumers' dialogic relationship with cultural products and emphasize an affective exchange between corporations and consumers."[29] Pinterest not only facilitates these affective exchanges in the platform's design but also can make these failures visible through its proliferation of pins (figure 6.2). Pinterest's self-branding as a fannish space is unquestionably problematic, and my framing of it as a potential space of commodity activism perhaps even more so. Like Banet-Weiser, I am intrigued by the "contradictions, contingencies, and paradoxes" of commodity activism, and also the connections it produces "between merchandizing, political ideologies, and consumer citizenship."[30] Though the convergence culture industry will never unilaterally succeed in standardizing fan culture or fan identity, we would be wise to begin identifying ways to resist within these spaces of incorporation.

So, where does this leave the concept of strategic pinning as a fan practice, much less a feminist fan practice? In order to gesture simultaneously to Pinterest's feminist fannish potential and postfeminist appeal, I would like to return to Dick Hebdige's *Subculture: The Meaning*

Figure 6.2. Pinterest's capacity to curate and organize a wide array of digital content allows for strategic pinning as a form of feminist commentary. Accessed at https://www.pinterest.com/pin/134756213822784024/.

of Style. On one hand, we could choose to view fan fashion image boards on Pinterest as a textbook example of Hebdige's claim that subcultural style is ultimately incorporated via the ideological form or the commodity form.[31] Geek girly culture on Pinterest is designed to embrace the commodity form—collecting, circulating, and celebrating "the conversion of subcultural signs [. . .] into mass-produced objects"[32] via pins and image boards—and is intimately bound up with trends towards licensed, female-oriented fan fashion sites (like Her Universe), clothing lines (such as the Limited's *Scandal* collection), and beauty products (*The Hunger Game*'s "Capitol Colours" make-up line). It is Pinterest's approach to ideological incorporation that poses a more interesting point of conflict. Pinterest clearly attempts to domesticate the productive feminisms of fan culture through its emphasis on beauty and fashion, routing female fans towards "normative" modes of engagement. However, it in no way trivializes female fans, and potentially offers the flexibility as a platform to speak back to more insidious industrial incorporation attempts and to the erasure of female fans within the convergence culture industry more generally.

As Hebdige notes, "[I]t is through the distinctive rituals of consumption [. . .] that the subculture at once reveals its 'secret' identity and communicates its forbidden meanings."[33] Pinterest as a platform, and strategic pinning as a distinctive ritual of consumption, have the capacity to make this revelation and communication of forbidden, perhaps even feminist, meanings happen on a much larger cultural scale. I acknowledge that fashion is a fraught space in which to locate this argument, as fashion is a core component of the "post-feminist masquerade" that more often than not reifies hegemonic masculinity and heteronormativity.[34] However, given the recent growth of social media activism around fan fashion, and its connection to broader feminist fan campaigns, I would echo that "it is at the meeting point between pockets of everyday life and packets of online data that digital media are imbued with power,"[35] and suggest Pinterest as an optimal space in which to supplement these efforts to expose and critique the hegemonic masculinity of fan and geek culture. If Pinterest is, as many have argued, an aspirational space, it might also be wielded to offer an aspirational vision of the convergence culture industry's valuation of female fans.

Her Universe and Everyday Cosplay

Moving from Pinterest as a platform to curate and potentially critique fan fashion to a notable designer and retailer of fangirl fashion, Her Universe, the following sections will explore the ways in which clothing designed for fangirls alternately challenges and reinforces androcentric conceptions of fan identity. Her Universe was established in 2010 with the stated mission of carving out a space for "fashionable, feminine products for fangirls" and to "give these fans a voice and affirm they play an important role."[36] Like the fantrepreneurs discussed in the prior chapter, the site's founder, actress Ashley Eckstein, has deep ties to Hollywood. Prior to launching the Her Universe fashion brand, Eckstein was best known for voicing the lead role of Ahsoka Tano on the animated series *Star Wars: The Clone Wars*, affording her a place of prominence within one of the most insatiable consumer fan bases as well as insider access to the most powerful fan merchandising license in the galaxy. Thus, while it is tempting to unabashedly celebrate Eckstein and Her Universe as a counterpoint to Chris Hardwick and Nerdist, we need to be mindful that other female fantrepreneurs will not be similarly positioned to be personally handed a license to produce *Star Wars* merchandise by George Lucas after complaining about a lack of t-shirts featuring their character on a hit television series.[37] Likewise, women crafting artisanal fangirl fashion will rarely have access to the promotional placement that Her Universe and Eckstein benefit from in fan spaces like San Diego Comic-Con, including a prime retail location within the sprawling *Star Wars* booth and sponsored events like the Her Universe "Geek Couture" Fashion Show.

A collection of high-end *Star Wars* fashion designed for Hot Topic helped secure the subcultural chain retailer's acquisition of Her Universe in 2016. There are two notable aspects of Her Universe's 2016 Hot Topic collection. First, the collection featured winning designs from the 2015 Her Universe fashion show at San Diego Comic-Con. Since 2014, Her Universe has offered an opportunity for designers to submit their fan-oriented fashions and compete for a space on the runway at the annual show. The winner(s) are subsequently given the chance to design a fashion collection for Hot Topic. The fan designs featured in the show not only stress the inclusivity of Her Universe's brand (making a point of utilizing diverse models in terms of race, body type, and ability) but also present a rare professionalization opportunity for female fans. The second notable point is that the Hot Topic collection featured wearable versions of character costumes from *The Force Awakens*. Some items, like Poe Dameron's leather jacket, required minimal adaptation from screen costume to commercial fan fashion. Others loosely evoke a character's costume in color palate, textiles, and pattern, such as the dresses designed to reference BB-8 and Kylo Ren. Part of the appeal of this form of character-based fangirl fashion, as well as its potential as a form of political commentary, is the explicit feminization of iconic male characters.

Over the past decade, as fan scholars have increasingly turned a critical eye towards instances of media industries co-opting or commercializing fan practices, there has been minimal engagement with fan fashion's capitalization on cosplay as a fan practice. This lack of engagement is perhaps unsurprising when we consider that cosplay has historically faced comparatively little controversy surrounding fans monetizing and professionalizing their labor. Through a taxonomic examination of the emergent "everyday cosplay" clothing category that fangirl retailers like Her Universe have helped popularize, this section homes in on one specific fan fashion trend: trompe l'oeil dress designs that replicate male character costumes. Cosplay, or the fan practice of constructing costumes inspired by fictional characters and embodying those characters in real-world spaces, is notably not only a prime example of a gender-neutral fan practice; it productively complicates the binaristic logics of "affirmational" and "transformative" fan production.[38] Cosplay also opens up a unique conceptual space in which to explore fan merchandise in relation to both fan identities and fan practices. Everyday cosplay, as the consumer category suggests, temporally and spatially dislodges the fan practice of cosplay from the places where it is accepted and expected (e.g., fan conventions, or culturally specific sites like the Akihabara district in Japan). The pleasures of embodiment remain, but the conveyance of fan identity and affiliation is coded and, thus, more culturally acceptable. We need not look further than Barbara Adams, the Whitewater juror who was mocked on the national stage for wearing her *Star Trek* Commander's uniform while performing her civic duty, to make a conceptual distinction between cosplaying every day and everyday cosplay.

The everyday cosplay merchandising category emerged alongside the growth of fancentric retailers such as Hot Topic, Think Geek, and Her Universe. Over the past several years, "cosplay" has also been increasingly deployed as a retail category by chain stores like Torrid that, while not primarily fan retail spaces like Her Universe, offer trend-based merchandise. In all of these cases, what is being sold to fans is the promise of embodiment and identification, a fact that is often explicitly reflected in the ways in which items are categorized in dropdown menus (such as We Love Fine's "I am+" cosplay category) or in the naming of individual items (e.g., the "I Am Han Solo Skirt," or the "Captain Picardigan"). Everyday cosplay is thus predicated on selecting recognizable characters, but it is also importantly about recognizing female fans' identification with the male protagonists of fan franchises, and the representational lacks that might force that identification, much in the same way that slash fiction does.

Before we delve into the one prolific subgenre of everyday cosplay merchandise (trompe l'oeil dresses that visually mimic the costuming or armor of male fictional characters), it is important to break down the concept of "everyday cosplay" in more detail. Though the term is used broadly to categorize clothing that straddles the conceptual boundaries between casual wear and costume, I would suggest the need for a more nuanced taxonomy. In contemplating both aesthetic and contextual dimensions that shape these fan merchandising categories and what they reveal about the place of fangirls within the convergence culture industry, we need to distinguish between types of garments and the gendered markets they might signify (t-shirt vs. dress). We also need to remain attentive to production contexts (fancrafted vs. licensed and mass produced) and price point (such as the recent trend of luxury brands like Christian Louboutin and Rodarte working fannish items into their ready-to-wear lines). Even within one distinct form of everyday cosplay, within one specific website, there is significant semiotic complexity. Take these two suggested "everyday cosplay" options for *Star Wars* bounty hunter Boba Fett from the website Disneybounding, a Tumblr started by Leslie Kay in 2012 that mashes up ready-to-wear clothing items to evoke a particular Disney character (figure 6.3).[39] We can see some immediate aesthetic corollaries between the two, such as the gray bodycon dresses, leather-studded bracelets, and tan booties. Alternately, there are

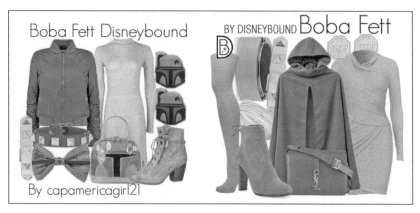

Figure 6.3. Two examples of "everyday cosplay," each offering a distinct take on *Star Wars* bounty hunter Boba Fett. *Left image*: Capamericagirl, *Thing's* [sic] *A Geek Girl Loves*, November 26, 2015, https://capamericagirl.tumblr.com/post/134030525180/boba -fett-disneybound-by-capamericagirl21. *Right image*: Leslie Kay, *DisneyBound*, 2016, http://disneybound.co/post/135474713458.

items that on the surface seem similar (e.g., army green outerwear) but carry very different connotations in their design: the hooded cape on the right might be selected to evoke Boba Fett's iconic Mandalorian helmet, whereas the selection on the left more generally references a military flight jacket. Then there are the class considerations: while a luxury handbag might nicely evoke Boba Fett's bottom-line-oriented approach to bounty hunting, it is safe to guess that one could purchase the entire outfit on the left for less than the cost of the Yves Saint Laurent bag featured on the right. Then there is the question of how overt or explicit the evocation of the character is designed to be, with the outfit on the left utilizing an array of licensed merchandise aimed at fangirls (specifically, the earrings, hair bow, and purse) to clearly reference the character.

One way we might further explicate the complexity of everyday cosplay as a fan fashion category is to take a taxonomic approach. For example, subcategories of everyday cosplay might include the following:

- *Authenticated Everyday Cosplay*: This category of everyday cosplay might range from auctions of items of clothing that particular characters have worn on screen to an array of industry-affiliated or fan-run websites, or apps like Spylight, which directly link fan consumers to where they can buy the clothing featured in a given media property. As Josh Stenger pointedly noted in his analysis of a *Buffy the Vampire Slayer* eBay auction in 2003, "Authenticity and proximity cost far more than mere dress-up; that is, dressing like Faith and having the clothes Eliza Dushku actually wore involved two vastly different sums of money."[40] While fans utilizing sites like "Worn on TV" might not have the same issues with scarcity as a fan bidding on a one-of-a-kind item worn on screen, they nonetheless will frequently be routed to luxury clothing items well outside both the fan's and the character's budget. Fan merchandise generally, and this category of everyday cosplay most specifically, productively opens up an underdeveloped space to address how class shapes the capacity to sartorially enunciate fan identity.

- *Covert Everyday Cosplay*: More "covert" forms of everyday cosplay would be those that do not immediately visually code as a form of fannish dress-up. Paul Booth, who devotes a chapter of *Playing Fans* to similar practices on Polyvore, calls this "digital cosplay," or "costuming without physicality, drag without performance."[41] Though Booth's work on digital cosplay has been foundational to my thinking, particularly around the neoliberal and performative dimensions of these practices, I am not utilizing his term here for a number of reasons. First, Booth views this practice of curating character outfits as rarely leaving the digital realm (in other words, they are conceptualized but never worn), and I am more invested in how actualized examples of everyday cosplay function as embodied and public performances of fan identity. Second, Booth suggests that this is perhaps more an exercise in fashion selection than a fannish practice, or perhaps an exercise in "trying on" a fan identity in the anonymous and disembodied safety of digital space. My proposed category of "covert everyday cosplay" draws on similar themes of minimizing the ties between fan performance and pathology. To wit, a *Time* magazine article headline on Disneybounding proclaims it as a "New Kind of Disney Cosplay Slightly Less Embarrassing Than Original."[42] Though frequently lumped into the category of "casual cosplay" by retailers and fans alike, "covert cosplay" marks both the subtlety and the relative social acceptability of the form, in which the cosplay component is more or less camouflaged. Accordingly, we might also consider something like the *Scandal* clothing line produced for The Limited in 2015 within the "covert everyday cosplay" category, in which no specific character costumes are replicated, but rather the clothing aims to holistically capture a character's aesthetic. The *Scandal* clothing line was pitched to fans as things Olivia Pope *might wear* (and, of course, eventually did wear on the television series for cross-promotional purposes), but were not designed to be worn as an Olivia Pope costume.

- *Evocative Everyday Cosplay*: This category is distinct from "Covert Cosplay" in the sense that the connection to a fictional character is more visibly marked. This is commonly accomplished through color schemes, through the cut of the garment (e.g., evoking Wonder Woman's bodice), or via iconic reference (e.g., the trim on a dress created from the silhouette of Loki's horned helmet).

- *Artisanal Everyday Cosplay*: This subcategory can be used to delineate fancrafted clothing items from those that are licensed or mass-produced.[43] Artisanal examples of everyday cosplay are unique, in terms of both the retail spaces in which they are sold (most prominently sites like Etsy) and the challenges to licensed fan merchandise that they represent. Consider, for example, 20th Century Fox's crackdown on *Firefly* fan knitters and the sale of handcrafted Jayne hats in 2013, in large part due to the launch of a competing licensed iteration on Thinkgeek. Fans subsequently renamed and continued to covertly sell these fancrafted items, but this category nonetheless opens up new lines of inquiry around the shifting legalities of contemporary fan production and the monetization of fan labor. This category of everyday cosplay is accompanied by greater expectations that the crafter will also be a self-identified fan of the given media object, and will be more engaged with and responsive to their customer base, in line with the reciprocal ethos of a fan community.

Everyday Crossplay and Trompe L'oeil Character Dresses

Finally, we arrive at the subcategory of everyday cosplay that I wish to focus on: *everyday crossplay*, and the symbolic significance of trompe l'oeil dresses within this category (figure 6.4). Just as "crossplay" describes instances in which a cosplayer embodies a character of a different sex, "everyday crossplay" is used here to conceptualize fan merchandise that facilitates a fan dressing as a character of the opposite sex (or as a robotic or inanimate object, such as R2-D2 or the Tardis) in its design. Crossplay is a rich concept, both in its evocation of genderswap and drag and in its

Figure 6.4. Two examples of Her Universe's "everyday crossplay" trompe l'oeil dresses that iconically mimic Boba Fett's armor. *Left*: "Star Wars Boba Fett A-Line Dress," Her Universe, https://www.heruniverse.com; *Right*: "Boba Fett Tunic Tank," ThinkGeek, https://www.thinkgeek.com.

exploration of the relationship among clothing, the body, and identity performance. It also opens up a productive and intersectional space in which we might engage multiple "crossings" and identity play not exclusively around gender but also race, sexuality, age, and so on.

Importantly, as Theresa Winge notes in her history of cosplay, "crossplay may portray the opposite gender with accuracy or may have humorous intentions within its display."[44] Similarly, just as female fans purchase these dresses for a variety of reasons, they will code differently when viewed by different publics or in particular contexts. Everyday crossplay might simply convey a fannish appreciation of a male character, or could subtly function as a wearable commentary on the historic lack of compelling female protagonists or heroes within canonical fancentric media properties. Outside of spaces such as fan conventions, screenings, or meet-ups, these dresses might be mistaken for or conflated with the hypersexualized genderswap costumes that dominate Halloween stores.

Or, perhaps even more problematically, the visual dissonance between the masculine costume or armor and the feminine cut of the dress might read as inherently humorous, drawing on or devolving into transphobic stereotypes. In all of these cases, the character's masculinity shapes the decoding, even when the character in question has subsequently become canonically female (see: Thor, The Doctor).

It is for these reasons that we need to be especially attentive to the textual, industrial, and historical contexts of the characters women are encouraged to embody through these trompe l'oeil dresses. For example, the popularity of Boba Fett as a character for everyday cosplay aimed at women simultaneously resonates with and capitalizes on female *Star Wars* fans' Campaign for a Female Boba Fett from the 1980s onwards. Though eventually quashed by the reveal that Boba Fett was, indeed, male, this campaign was positioned as an explicitly feminist intervention by its organizers: "*Star Wars* series is a cultural event with the capacity to make a significant impact on the prejudices of its viewers. Acknowledging this, its almost exclusively white and male human population is a disappointment."[45] The focus on the gender rather than the race of Boba Fett was rationalized through the series' female characters' tendency to "fall prey to female stereotypes," but was more actively positioned as an opportunity to acknowledge preexisting fangirls as well as welcome new ones to the franchise.[46] Because the campaign blamed "[t]he force of female exclusion from *Star Wars*" on a lack of compelling female characters, it reasoned that the "casting of a female actor in the role of Boba Fett would demonstrate that women are not a forgotten or negligible demographic, as well as provide evidence that women can serve a cinematic purpose other than romance and reproduction."[47] Some of the issues raised in the Campaign for a Female Boba Fett in the nascent days of digital fan culture have since been resolved, both as fangirls more forcefully assert their identities as *Star Wars* fans and as the franchise itself becomes more attentive to diversity in its casting. I bring up this campaign both to historicize the desire of female fans to inhabit this character and to suggest that much of the popularity of figures like Fett or anthropomorphized robots like R2-D2 is due to the fact that they are canonically less rigidly gendered.

It is also useful to consider the common cuts and styles of these trompe l'oeil character dresses, which overwhelmingly tend towards the tube dress and skater skirt styles (figure 6.4). Though in theory the appeal of these dresses resides in their playful verisimilitude, and the attendant ability of the public to recognize the fannish referent, the cut of these dresses often pointedly fails to assist in this goal. For example, why not a bubble skirt design to echo the bulbous silhouette of BB-8, or a long A-line skirt to evoke a Dalek, or a shift dress to capture the lines of R2-D2? The pragmatic answer may well reside in price point, that these favored styles can be produced cheaply and many different characters can be easily mapped onto these cuts of dress, thereby cutting costs for retailers. Nonetheless, the fact that these styles not only are designed to cling to the female form but are linked to a decidedly youthful form of femininity should not be overlooked. Just as embodiment is a core pleasure of cosplay, these dresses might offer a different type of pleasurable embodiment, quite literally shedding Fett's Mandalorian armor to reveal the feminine form beneath.

An even more interesting reading of the skater skirt as a preferred cut for these dresses might address the historical shift of figure skating from a sport designed to display the grace and expressiveness of upper-class masculinity in the eighteenth and nineteenth centuries to its current denigration as a "girls' sport."[48] At the risk of pushing an analogy to its breaking point, we could perhaps positively map the growing visibility of fangirls within the convergence culture industry via fan fashion with the evolution of the skater skirt from the early twentieth century to the present. Formerly ankle-length to promote modesty, as "women's status advanced and their place in sport widened, skirts became shorter and necklines lower."[49] Contemporary skater skirts outside the realm of athletic competition might be viewed as provocatively short, but they can also be theorized as allowing the body to be more active, much as their everyday cosplay counterparts do.

We can best assess these particular dress designs as a mode of fannish commentary, as well as the political capacity of commoditizing crossplay, by drawing on theories of drag, camp, and the subversive potentialities of cross-dressing from Esther Newton, Judith Butler, and J. Jack Halberstam, among others. In *Vested Interests: Cross Dressing and Cultural Anxiety*, Marjorie Garber begins by acknowledging that for generations it was commonplace for children to be clothed in "frocks," often making it difficult to immediately distinguish young boys from girls.[50]

Similarly, prior to the 1940s, it was common for boys to wear pink. Garber frames the subsequent entrenchment of pink/blue gendered color schemes as destabilizing "feelings of tradition, continuity, and naturalness."[51] Trompe l'oeil crossplay dresses can have a similarly destabilizing effect, upending longstanding presumptions about the masculinity attached to fancentric franchises and fan culture more generally.

Garber viewed cross-dressing as progressively confronting "easy notions of binarity, putting into question the categories of 'female' and 'male,' whether they are consider essential or constructed, biological or cultural."[52] We could perhaps make a case that these everyday crossplay dresses function similarly, putting into question the convergence culture industry's binaristic construction of fanboys and fangirls. Writing in 1992, Garber situated the growing popularity of cross-dressing as a theme in popular media within a broader cultural critique of binarism in its myriad forms (male/female, but also black/white, Republican/Democrat, self/other, and so on). It is in large part because the convergence culture industry, and indeed to some extent the culture at large, seem so nostalgically fixed on maintaining these binaries, and further endorsing a white-male-supremacist vision of (fan) culture, that I find it difficult to share Garber's optimism for the disruptive potentialities of everyday crossplay as a more socially acceptable form of cross-dressing.

Given that these trompe l'oeil dresses based on male characters' costumes function as a form of female-to-male crossplay, Halberstam's work on drag kings perhaps affords a more fruitful point of origin. Within Halberstam's own taxonomic approach to the performed masculinities of drag kings, butch realness and the femme pretender occupy opposing ends of the continuum. Crossplay offers a similar continuum of performed masculinities, with some cosplayers aiming for screen-accurate verisimilitude (e.g., fully "passing" as a differently sexed character, or achieving "an authentic, unadorned, or unperformed masculinity")[53] and others playing the role of femme pretender, often rooting their performance in camp, irony, or parody, calling attention to the gender play. In these cases, according to Halberstam, the performance revolves around

> a consolidation of femininity rather than a disruption of dominant masculinity. The femme pretender actually dresses up butch or male only to

show how thoroughly her femininity saturates her performance—she performs the failure of her own masculinity as a convincing spectacle. [. . .] [T]he femme pretender offers a reassurance that female masculinity is just an act and will not carry over into everyday life.[54]

I want to suggest that everyday crossplay has the capacity to function similarly, offering reassurance that female fan identity is ultimately just a performance. This particular form of masquerade is more likely to consolidate than to meaningfully disrupt the convergence culture industry's androcentric conception of fan or geek culture. As Halberstam notes regarding the differences between male and female impersonators, "[W]ithin the theatre of mainstream gender roles, femininity is often presented as simply costume whereas masculinity manifests as realism or as body," and thus "if masculinity adheres 'naturally' and inevitably to men, then masculinity cannot be impersonated."[55] In the case of these dresses, the failure to impersonate is always at risk of moving beyond character identity to fan identity.

It is precisely the inherently playful but ultimately deceptive quality of the "trompe l'oeil," the fact that it is an optical illusion, that makes these everyday crossplay dresses significant. To my mind, the deception occurs on two distinct levels. First, unlike the other examples of everyday cosplay that mask their connection to character costumes, these trompe l'oeil dresses momentarily trick the eye. Quickly the deception becomes clear: this is cosplay without materiality, cosplay without labor. Secondly, and arguably more importantly, when the trompe l'oeil design is coupled with both the element of crossplay and the pointedly feminine style and cut of these dresses, it has the potential to suggest that the wearer is deceptive in their performance of fan identity writ large. Just as Baudrillard described the trompe l'oeil as an "enchanted simulation" that is "more false than false,"[56] trompe l'oeil everyday crossplay dresses potentially suggest that what is more false than false is female fans' capacity to authentically occupy a fan identity.

Here is where the current boom in fancentric merchandising converges with the rise of "fake geek girl" accusations, many of which hinge explicitly on the apparent cognitive dissonance of seeing emblems of geek culture on a female body. Because everyday crossplay commonly designs outfits for female fans based on male characters, Derek Johnson's work on the problematic postfeminism of fangirl retailers like Her Universe (one of the primary producers of these trompe l'oeil dresses) is instructive in helping us begin to consider the affordances and limitations of everyday crossplay as a mode of fan expression or performance of fan identity. Building on Angela McRobbie's work on the place of fashion in postfeminist masquerade, Johnson argues that while Her Universe "carves a small space for female 'empowerment' within a popular culture marketed primarily for boys and men," in doing so it "doubles down on heteronormative ideologies."[57] Her Universe has, over time, moved away from Eckstein as its lone model to be more inclusive (both in offering plus-size options and in casting racially diverse models), but Johnson's critique that the site "ushers female consumers into a hegemonically aged, gendered, and sexed iteration of [. . .] fandom"[58] remains valid.

Indeed, one could easily make a case that much of the licensed merchandise aimed at female fans, as well as the bulk of the pins pertaining to fan fashion on Pinterest, fall into the same trap that Johnson describes in relation to Her Universe, namely, that the "appropriation of once marginal feminine subjectivities" ultimately works "to realign female fandom to objectification by and for that core male audience."[59] Carving out clearly demarcated "fangirl" spaces has the capacity to credential, but perhaps might ultimately function to further cordon off, women within contemporary fan and geek culture. In other words, rather than recognizing fangirls' preexisting place within the broader fannish ecosystem and rendering them more visible, fangirl-oriented retailers like Her Universe and geek girly spaces like Pinterest might instead function as a natural extension of the convergence culture industry's efforts to commoditize and contain female fans and feminine/feminist forms of fan expression. Because fangirl fashion has the ability to expose, but perhaps is unable to meaningfully disrupt, the androcentric biases of the convergence culture industry, I would like to close this chapter with an example of feminist fan intervention that conceptually draws on "crossplay."

Pinning Down/Pinning Up Transformative Feminisms in Fan Culture

Just as scholarly work on drag and cross-dressing might productively open up a consideration of "everyday crossplay" as a site at which to potentially destabilize rigidly gendered conceptions of fan identity, it is illustrative to consider fan activism that utilizes similar transformative tactics. Much as the prior section focused on one particular strain of everyday crossplay, this section focuses on a particular subgenre of transformative fan art, in which male superheroes are parodically styled in the costumes and poses of their female counterparts. Fan studies' preoccupation with fan art has never fully manifested into a robust theorization of the practice, with fan scholars instead paying disproportionate attention to fanfiction and fanvids as objects of study.[60] The relative lack of scholarship on fan art (which, broadly defined, would include fan drawings and painting, as well as digital image manipulations, mashups, and even potentially animated GIFs) is particularly confounding given fan culture's migration to platforms like Tumblr that trade in spreadable fan-produced imagery. Through an analysis of one transformative superhero fan art site, *The Hawkeye Initiative*, the remainder of this chapter considers the transformative potential of crossplay fan art within comic book fan culture.

The crowdsourced fan art site *The Hawkeye Initiative* was founded in December 2012 on a simple premise: "How to fix every Strong Female Character pose in superhero comics: replace the character with Hawkeye doing the same thing."[61] The "initiative" referenced in the site's title is to "illustrate how deformed, hyper-sexualized, and impossibly contorted women are commonly illustrated in comics" by redrawing comic book panels featuring superheroines with the Marvel character Clint "Hawkeye" Barton, while retaining the superheroine's hypersexualized costume and pose (figure 6.5).[62]

Though fan texts are in no way medium specific (e.g., one might write textual fanfic about an audiovisual fan object, like a television show), the sequential art form of comics lends itself to both a proliferation of fan art and a more robust collection of terminology and scholarship to theorize it. Because superhero narratives complicate the notion of a "true" identity by design, and likewise drag "subverts the distinction between inner and outer psychic space and effectively mocks both the expressive model of gender and the notion of a true gender identity," we might couple these theories towards a better understanding of the camp humor that *The Hawkeye Initiative*'s fan art employs.[63] The fact that comic book fandom remains one of the most inhospitable fan cultures for women

Figure 6.5. A typical example of the transformative fan art submitted to *The Hawkeye Initiative*. *The Hawkeye Initiative*, Tumblr Post, 2014, http://thehawkeyeinitiative.com /post/74992098472/moneynolaundry-submitted-to.

within the convergence culture industry only compounds the capacity of crossplay superhero fan art as a feminist project.

The bulk of the reporting on *The Hawkeye Initiative* has defined the images as examples of "genderswap" fan art.[64] Though fans have a long history of producing "genderswap" art in a variety of forms (fanfic, cosplay, and fan art most prominently), the label itself can be slippery in its definition and problematic in its application. "Genderswap" is broadly used to classify fanworks in which "characters have become differently sexed."[65] Kristina Busse and Alexis Lothian contend that these "sudden re-embodiments," particularly those "forcing male characters to experience the social and cultural, physical and emotional realities of life in a female body," are "connected to feminist concerns with the cultural meanings and effects of gendered bodies."[66] The fan art featured on *The Hawkeye Initiative* may be designed to provoke male readers of comics to experience the realities of viewing comics as a female reader, and is mutually invested in commenting on the materiality of the superhero body (or how it is artistically rendered) and the performance of gender it enacts, but technically speaking they are not examples of genderswap. When Hawkeye is redrawn in the costume and pose of a superheroine, he does not become a female version of himself. Because crossplay may alternately strive for accuracy or comedy, the term resonates with *The Hawkeye Initiative*'s emphasis on the humorous absurdity of accurately costuming men in superheroine garb.[67] *The Hawkeye Initiative* aims to be both playful and political in its commentary, a dichotomy that is embodied in the fannish concept of crossplay. I reference "genderswap" and "drag" here not to dismiss them in favor of "crossplay," but to suggest rich alternate frameworks for understanding the appeal and subversive potential of this fan art. I have also chosen to characterize this as "crossplay" fan art to make an explicit connection between the transformative feminist fan art featured on *The Hawkeye Initiative* and the "everyday crossplay" fan fashion trends discussed above.

The site stresses that it aims to be not just illustrative but transformative: a "way that people can express the desire for [a change in the extreme sexism of modern comics] in a way that is both compelling and fun."[68] Similarly, I would like to position *The Hawkeye Initiative* as illustrative of a broader trend in comics fan art towards "crossplay" renderings of characters as a mode of transformative intervention, "turning the male gaze of comic book culture back on itself and holding the industry accountable for the paltry number of women being hired to work on mainstream superhero titles."[69] Both the formal dimensions and cultural implications of superhero crossplay fan art gesture to its transformative capacity for superhero representations specifically, and androcentric comic book culture more broadly.

The Hawkeye Initiative

The Hawkeye Initiative represents a more organized, thematically cohesive iteration of a long tradition within comics fandom of calling attention to sexist costuming and posing practices. Each post on *The Hawkeye Initiative* is fairly uniform in design: the original image and crossplay fan art are positioned side by side, arranged horizontally or vertically. The fan art ranges in aesthetic prowess and professionalism, from sketches that roughly evoke the original image to those that aesthetically echo it in minute detail. The contributor will frequently cite the title and issue number of the comic the original image is derived from or offer some brief textual explanation of the fan art and what inspired the parody. As the site has grown in popularity, it has begun to feature the occasional image of male fans cosplaying as "The Hawkeye Initiative," either at fan conventions or as "live action" embodiments of a particular comic book panel.[70] An immediate question that the project provokes, but refuses to concretely answer, is, Why Hawkeye? *The Hawkeye Initiative*'s "Origins" page links to four Tumblr posts, all focused on archer Clint "Hawkeye" Barton. These posts include an analysis of the cinematic costuming of Black Widow and Hawkeye, a doodle celebrating Hawkeye's derriere and Jeremy Renner (the actor who portrays him) as a "Strong Female Character," and the inaugural example of Hawkeye Initiative fan art.[71] Though other superheroes, such as Thor and Spider-Man, are routinely "dressed down" on the site, the titular and visual emphasis on Hawkeye deserves further unpacking.

We might choose to read Hawkeye's selection as a byproduct of the massive success of *The Avengers* (2012), as it was released seven months prior to *The Hawkeye Initiative*'s debut and served as the introduction of the character to the Marvel Cinematic Universe (MCU).[72] Because Hawkeye is presented as physically and mentally vulnerable in the film (he is the only nonempowered male "Avenger" and is immediately brainwashed and rendered servile to the villainous Loki), it is easy to suggest that he presents a comparatively "feminized" member of the team. A more simplistic explanation for Hawkeye's selection is that he poses a "lower stakes" satirical option than, say, Iron Man, as a site of critical commentary, while still being iconically legible to a wide audience because of his ties to *The Avengers* franchise. As the only male Avenger without a solo film franchise (or related merchandise) to support, Hawkeye is an ideal satirical subject for fans precisely because his status as a superhero is mocked within the films themselves. To wit, in promotional trailers for *Avengers: Age of Ultron* (Joss Whedon, 2015), each member of the superhero team is introduced by name with a title card and footage of superheroic feats (flying, throwing motorcycles, summoning lightning, etc.). The trailer concludes with Hawkeye, crouching in hiding and fatalistically quipping, "We're fighting an army of robots, and I have a bow and arrow."

A more compelling rationale comes from the *Hawkeye* comics, particularly the run by writer Matt Fraction and artist David Aja that launched four months prior to *The Hawkeye Initiative* in August 2012. This run of *Hawkeye* comics, which has been incredibly popular with female readers, is unique in that the superhero mantle of "Hawkeye" is simultaneously held by a man (Clint Barton) and a woman (Kate Bishop). Without delving into the complexities of comic book continuity, the comics' equal treatment of these two characters (Kate is not "Hawkgirl" or "She-Hawkeye") both is an anomaly and also functions as a representational respite from the issues that *The Hawkeye Initiative* seeks to expose and critique.

Superhero(ine) Physicality, Costuming, and Posing

Before considering how superhero crossplay fan art might function as a transformative feminist intervention into comics culture, we need to address the semiotic significance of superhero physicality and costuming. As Trina Robbins has noted, by the late 1980s both male and female superheroes were no longer just "physically flawless human beings" but exaggerated fantasies designed for the presumed male, adolescent comic book reader.[73] In order to show off these new, "bizarrely morphed" female bodies that featured "balloon breasts and waists so small that if they were real humans they'd break in half," comic book artists "clothed the women in bottom-baring thong bikinis, with as little as possible on top."[74] Moreover, as Carolyn Cocca's quantitative analysis of the portrayal of women in mainstream superhero comics bears out, "[F]emales are posed in ways in which males simply are not. [. . .] In the most extreme version, a female character's back is drawn unnaturally twisted as well as arched, displaying all of her curves in front and back simultaneously."[75] As I have discussed elsewhere, much of the transformative fan art focused on superheroine representations focuses on the physical impossibility of these proportions and poses.[76]

Superheroines may be physically powerful, but they are not always empowered. They are drawn in action, but frequently contained by a (presumed) male gaze. Their costumes protect their identities, even as they expose their bodies. Peter Coogan utilizes the triptych of mission, powers, and identity to classify the superhero, but it is the identity category (jointly comprised of "the codename and the costume") that is of importance here. Identity is what marks superheroes as distinct from other heroes, and is the most significant in terms of ruling particular characters in or out of "superhero" status.[77] Not only do the superheroes' code names "externalize either their alter ego's inner character or biography," but their costumes function to "emblematize the character's identity."[78] One of the primary issues with superheroines is that they are routinely "spun off" from male superhero franchises. Thus, their code names (Batgirl, Supergirl, etc.) inevitably render their own inner character and biography as secondary to the originating male superhero's identity. Their costumes function similarly, subsuming the superheroine's identity by using variants on the male superhero's immediately recognizable emblem (Superman's "S," Batman's bat silhouette, and so on). It is simple enough to argue that what is really being externalized and emblematized are franchising logics. However, when these superheroine identities are always already embedded in another man's origin story, it is difficult not to read the choices surrounding superheroine costuming as, first and foremost, emblematizing the comic book industry's ongoing commitment to a white, male, cisgender, heteronormative readership and the presumption that this demographic desires (or demands) sexual objectification of female characters. Thus, despite the superhero's potentiality as a "culturally produced body that could potentially defy all traditional and normalized readings," predominantly "super-sexuality has been carefully constructed according to highly visible binaries."[79]

Comics scholar Scott Bukatman notes that superheroes, "invariably denied the expressivity of the face [due to their masks], must rely on the boldness of bodily presentation. Posture, kinesis, and pose structure the theatrics of superheroic performance."[80] When these bodily presentations and poses are isolated from the rhythmic structure of surrounding comics panels and pages, as they are with *The Hawkeye Initiative*, their resonance with pin-up iconography becomes more pronounced. The digital age has seen a resurgence of pin-up art, marked by a nostalgia for the 1940s even as they inject "a wider range of explicit sexual representation into the mostly soft-core vocabulary of the genre,"[81] and we can certainly locate *The Hawkeye Initiative* within that trend. Likewise, the comics panels parodied in fan art on

The Hawkeye Initiative tend to conform to the two primary stylistic features of pin-up art: (1) one body, depicted in its entirety and not engaged in a sexual act with another body, and (2) a focus on the potential sexual energy of the pin-up, through a "direct eye-line connection to the implied viewer."[82]

The bulk of the images that fans choose to parody on *The Hawkeye Initiative* are, not coincidentally, those that most visibly resonate with pin-up or erotic art, particularly in terms of the subject's pose and look.[83] Here, Richard Dyer's work on the instability of the male pin-up, and its resonance with the images that fill *The Hawkeye Initiative*, is illuminating. Male pin-up images, Dyer suggests, produce a paradoxical effect, in that they are simultaneously designed to be looked at by women and yet this act of looking "does violence to the codes of who looks and who is looked at (and how), and some attempt is instinctively made to counteract this violation."[84] This "attempt," for Dyer, is made through the male pin-up's own gaze and pose. Unlike the direct eye-line connection and inviting smile of the female pin-up, the male pin-up either avoids looking at his implied viewer or "stares at the viewer [. . .] as if he wants to reach beyond and through [the camera] and establish himself."[85] Likewise, while female pin-ups poses suggest that they are just there to be looked at, the male pin-up either is commonly in the middle of some action or "promises activity in the way he is posed."[86] Dyer places emphasis on the way in which the specific pose "tightens and tautens his body so that the muscles are emphasized, hence drawing attention to the body's potential for action," while broadly theorizing the ways in which this muscularity "legitimizes male power and domination."[87] These distinctions, between "being looked at" and "staring," physical "passivity" and "activity," Dyer suggests, mean that what is at stake with pin-ups is "not just male and female sexuality, but male and female power."[88] This is where the fannish canard of "but male superheroes also have hypermasculine physiques, and are costumed in skintight outfits" breaks down, and the feminist potential of a site like *The Hawkeye Initiative*, or crossplay fan art generally, reveals itself. It is not simply about making visible the amount of skin superheroine costumes reveal but also about noting the subtle distinctions between how the equally muscular and kinetic bodies of male and female superheroes are posed, and what their gaze implies.

Figure 6.6. These images, created nearly thirty years apart, suggest how deeply entrenched hypersexualized depictions of women in comics are. Jill Pantozzi, "Marvel, This Is When You Send an Artist Back to the Drawing Board," *Mary Sue*, August 19, 2014, https://www.themarysue.com.

The aesthetic correlations between superheroine art and soft-core pornography have been made more tangible in recent years. One visible, and vociferously critiqued, example from August 2014 was Milo Manara's variant cover for the relaunch of *Spider-Woman #1*, which was aesthetically reminiscent of a panel from Manara's erotic comic *Click!* (1983). These images, when arranged side by side (figure 6.6), simultaneously evoke the aesthetic of posts on *The Hawkeye Initiative* and illustrate the necessity of the project's feminist intervention. The cover's sexual objectification of the female body is disconcerting, but what is perhaps more disturbing is what the now invisible or implied audience present on the *Spider-Woman* cover suggests about the comic's presumed target market. The fact that many of the images that contributors choose to parody on *The Hawkeye Initiative* are comic book covers is significant. The cover is not just the most visible frame (in that it hails the reader, specifically a presumed male adolescent reader); it implies that the images within will representationally or ideologically "cooperate" with the cover. It also clearly frames which comic book fans the convergence culture industry values.

Crossplay Superhero Art as Transformative Intervention

In *The System of Comics*, Thierry Groensteen identifies six functions of the frame to consider the effect of these functions on both the panel's contents and the cognitive experience of the reader.[89] Of these six functions, two are especially significant to understanding why sites like *The Hawkeye Initiative* harbor the capacity to transform comics culture: the rhythmic function and the readerly function. Groensteen's engagement with the rhythmic function suggests that the comic book, "in displaying intervals (in the same way as persistence of vision erases the discretization of the cinematic medium), rhythmically distributes the tale that is entrusted to it," but there is not "an automatic correspondence between the form and the dimensions of the frame, and the length of the supposed action that it enframes."[90] For Groensteen, the "peculiarity" of comics' cadence is that "each panel hastens the story and, simultaneously, holds it back," with the frame functioning as "the agent of this double maneuver of progression/retention."[91]

As we can see, this "function" within Groensteen's model is implicitly connected to the "readerly function."[92] If we should not, as Groensteen suggests, overdetermine how the formal properties of a panel or arrangement of panels represent diegetic time, then the rhythm (of both narrative time and the time spent consuming each panel) is ultimately determined by the reader. Groensteen's explicitly gendered introduction of the "readerly function" has a decidedly romantic quality to it: "When he 'meets' a frame, the reader is taken to presuppose that, within the perimeter that has been drawn, there is a content to be deciphered. The frame is always an invitation to stop and to scrutinize."[93] This readerly function, according to Groensteen, "goes beyond the semiotic function inherent in framing because, since the panel contributes to a sequential discourse, its frame calls for not only a contemplation but also a *reading*."[94]

Like all fannish transformative works, submissions to *The Hawkeye Initiative* decontextualize, and then recontextualize, images and moments from media texts, but it is the focus on a single frame or panel of

Figure 6.7. In this submission to *The Hawkeye Initiative*, the mirror image constructed by the artist also effectively holds a mirror up to gendered posing conventions in comics. *The Hawkeye Initiative*, Tumblr post, 2014, http://thehawkeyeinitiative.com /post/73351462778/nathan-morton-tigra-and-hawkeye -just-hanging.

a piece of sequential art that is significant. It is not a romantic invitation to peruse the frame; it is a demand to deconstruct it. The images in each submission to *The Hawkeye Initiative*, as evidenced by figure 6.7, often lack a gutter or border; they sit uncomfortably close to one another, bleed into one another, and reflect one another as a mirror image much as they strive to hold a mirror to comics creators and culture. Here, the rhythms that would typically be established by the reader moving from panel to panel are replaced by scrolling through submissions. Looking at an individual submission might be humorous, but when submissions are scrolled through in sequence, when the proliferation of this imagery in comics is made clear, the site takes on tragicomic dimensions. Much as Groensteen contends that, "bound to the contents that it encloses, the [comics] frame is no less attached to the frames that surround it," *The Hawkeye Initiative* binds its commentary to the political lineage of transformative fan works, and to the broader frames of comic book art and culture.[95]

As Carole Stabile has suggested, "[S]uperhero narratives provide important places for imagining different here-and-nows; for defamiliarizing social problems and exploring them in a context that offers fresh insights and radical visions of the future."[96] *The Hawkeye Initiative* is one of many notable spaces in which this defamiliarization and reimagining is occurring within comic book culture. And there has been a tangible, transformative impact of these sorts of "initiatives" in the turn towards more pragmatic costuming for Batgirl and Spider-Woman in 2014.[97] But in celebrating the transformative potentiality of crossplay fan art, we should be mindful of the necessity for the legal origins of this term. In August 2014, the Tumblr site *Escher Girls* received a DMCA takedown notice from comic artist Randy Queen, on the grounds of copyright infringement and defamation.[98] *Escher Girls*, which in name applies the confounding constructions of M. C. Escher to representations of the female form, has a similar mission to *The Hawkeye Initiative*, though with an emphasis on critically analyzing comics images (in addition to other media) rather than producing fan art parodies.[99] Despite the fact that Queen ultimately retracted the legal threat and apologized, this incident represents more than just an attack on fair use doctrine or transformative fan criticism. It suggests that feminists' critiques of gendered superhero iconography, and their efforts to imagine a different "here-and-now" for comics culture, are perpetually in danger of being taken down, even as they are pinned up.

Conclusion

Fan Studies' OTP: Fandom and Intersectional Feminism

The fannish concept of a "One True Pairing" (or "OTP") describes "the sole or primary pairing someone is interested in for a given fandom. Someone with an OTP may have little or no interest in reading or creating fanworks for other pairings."[1] Emerging out of fanzines in the mid-1980s, the term "OTP" is conceptually bound up in the fan practice of "shipping" (short for "relationshipping"), or preferring particular romantic pairings of characters that may never be canonically realized within the media text. Indeed, the *Fanlore* page on OTPs stresses that, "while one may ship more than one pairing in any given fandom, OTP is used to single out a fan's favorite pairing in that fandom."[2] With fan studies becoming an increasingly promiscuous field, both topically and methodologically, this conclusion strives to make a case for fandom and intersectional feminism as fan studies' OTP. Explaining why this is an essential pairing requires us to acknowledge that we cannot afford to limit our discussions of fan identity to gender or ignore other "pairings" that can enrich our understanding of who has been marginalized by the mainstreaming of fan culture.

When we talk about OTPs, what we are really talking about is a sliding scale of privilege: what elements of the text a fan might privilege or, in my case, what a scholar chooses to privilege in his or her understanding of a particular cultural moment. "Privilege," of course, has another meaning deeply connected to this book's focus on the ways in which women are systematically alienated or rendered less visible within geek and fan culture, and my own privileging of a vision of fan studies that remains centrally invested in questions of identity and power. When we consider how privilege functions within fan culture and fan studies, it is perhaps science fiction author John Scalzi's 2012 analogous definition that is most appropriate:

> In the role playing game known as The Real World, "Straight White Male" is the lowest difficulty setting there is. [. . .] The default barriers for completions of quests are lower. Your leveling-up thresholds come more quickly. You automatically gain entry to some parts of the map that others have to work for. The game is easier to play, automatically, and when you need help, by default it's easier to get. [. . .] The player who plays on the "Gay Minority Female" setting? *Hardcore.*[3]

While this has certainly been the case for fans within the convergence culture industry, Scalzi emphasized that the lowest-difficulty-setting analogy was useful in large part because it avoided "invoking the dreaded word 'privilege.'"[4] Those playing on this "lowest difficulty setting" like to claim that social justice activists discursively invoke the term to derail conversations, conveniently deflecting from their own efforts to avoid discussions of systemic bias and who benefits from it. I begin this conclusion by hauling out the dreaded "P" word with the opposite intent, to close this book by opening up a conversation about the importance of intersectional identity politics to fandom and fan studies.

This book has broadly examined fan privilege through three primary lenses: the convergence culture industry's privileging of particular types of fans and/or fan practices, the intra-fannish privileging and subsequent policing of fan identities, and what we as fan scholars privilege in our work. I turn most actively to this last lens here, but not as an attempt to offer a definitive "state of the field." I prefer to think of it as a simple privilege check. In 1988, Peggy McIntosh famously unpacked what she called her "invisible knapsack" of white privilege, containing "special provisions, maps, passports, codebooks, visas, clothes, tools, and blank checks [. . .] that I can count on cashing in each day, but about which I was 'meant' to remain oblivious."[5] If, as McIntosh suggests, the mere act of describing privilege makes one newly accountable, unpacking fan studies' own invisible "bag of holding" (to borrow an appropriately geeky term from Benjamin Woo, who has also adapted McIntosh's work to engage fandom and fan studies' troubling "color-blindness"[6]) can have a similar effect. In discussing some of the contents, this conclusion suggests that we need to hold ourselves newly accountable at this moment in history to considering fan privilege in all of its incarnations, and actively ship intersectional feminism and fan studies as, if not our OTP, then one of our privileged pairings.

Fan culture and fan studies as a field has undergone exponential growth and diversification over the past decade. Much like a bag of holding, our understanding of the fan as a cultural subject is concurrently (and occasionally maddeningly) fixed and flexible, clearly demarcated and ostensibly limitless. As chapters 1 and 2 outlined, we see this negotiation in ongoing debates about how scholars, journalists, and media representations conceptualize the "fan." We see this paradox play out in the gendered boundary-policing practices within fan communities documented in chapter 3, which attempt to conceptually manage fan culture's digital sprawl and the newfound power of fan demographics by identifying pockets of "authentic" fandom. Similar tensions are laid bare in the convergence culture industry's gendered valuation of particular fans and fan practices, addressed in chapter 4. Likewise, we can see how particular fan identities can be mobilized for professional gain (chapter 5) or rerouted into potentially postfeminist or heterosexist consumer spheres (chapter 6).

Though I am thrilled to be witnessing the rapid expansion of our field, and excited to see what different methodologies and perspectives have to offer, this book presents compelling evidence of how easy it is to fall prey to fannish "OTP" tendencies. I am admittedly unwilling to let go of foundational scholarly conceptions of fandom as both a feminine and a potentially feminist space, particularly within a cultural moment in which antifeminist sentiment and androcentric conceptions of the "fan" conspire to erase and exclude women from the fan-cultural landscape. For women within the convergence culture industry, fan identity is not easily claimed, and is routinely contested outside of female-dominated fan communities, cultures, and platforms. Studying male-dominated fan communities and "masculine" modes of fan engagement, as well as toxic masculinity within geek culture,[7] is essential to this work. My call, then, is not to forward feminism and fandom as fan studies' *one* true pairing, but to reassert it as an *original* true pairing, one that we must be attentive to evolving as the field itself evolves. Reinvesting in and reimagining the core concerns of first wave fan studies of the late 1980s and early 1990s is essential as we consider who is privileged within contemporary fan culture, and what we privilege as fan scholars.

Vitally, McIntosh stressed that privilege is a matrix of interlocking advantages and oppressions, and accordingly this conclusion addresses the need for a more intersectional conception of fan identity within our field and highlights the intersectional feminist work that is already being done. Echoing the Vulcan adage popularized by *Star Trek*, the Infinite Diversity in Infinite Combinations of contemporary fan culture has never been more vibrant. Still, considering fan studies' foundational investment in identity politics and power dynamics, our field has been slow to engage race as a critical axis, and has only peripherally begun exploring axes of identity such as age, ability, sexuality, nationality, and class. Fandom was initially conceptualized, and continues to be for many fan scholars, as "a vehicle for marginalized subcultural groups [. . .] to pry open space for their cultural concerns within dominant representations."[8] As fan scholars, however, we have been historically reluctant to interrogate our own privilege, or tendencies towards dominant representations within our construction of fans' marginality. In other words, we are quick to foreground our own self-identification as fans in our work, but are less inclined towards being similarly forthcoming about how our lived identities and fannish predilections shape the work we do. While these issues are being debated with more frequency by fans and fan scholars alike, and are certainly in the process of changing, it is important to briefly engage some of the barriers that remain.

On Fan Fragility

Similar to Richard Dyer's argument in *White* that we must engage in "the project of 'making whiteness strange,'"[9] that "as long as whiteness is not seen or analyzed, it will continue to function as the norm,"[10] it is necessary to interrogate our attachment to a certain brand of "feminist fan studies." In both cultural and scholarly conceptions of the fan, whiteness and straightness are often problematically assumed, and thus inherently privileged. Throughout this book I have made a conscious choice to focus on both the explicit and the implicit androcentrism of the convergence culture industry's conception of fan culture, frequently at the expense of documenting the failings of (white) feminism in fandom and the study of it. Moreover, in relegating this point to the book's conclusion, I risk replicating the tendency of first wave fan scholars to treat discussions of identity markers outside of fan studies' "key axes of discrimination" of gender or age or class, such as race and sexuality, as something to be focused on in the future, rather than foregrounding them as vital to the book's central argument. Fiske rationalized his focus on particular "axes of subordination" through the lack of "scholarly studies on non-white fandom."[11] Because this book has predominantly focused on how the fan is demographically conceptualized and hailed, my own foregrounding of gender as the most visible and prominent axis of subordination is similarly predicated on a lack of diversity and imagination within the convergence culture industry's conception of desirable fan identities. As I noted in the introduction, the convergence culture industry's efforts to standardize fan identities and privilege affirmational fan practices does not exclusively impact fangirls, but rather negatively impacts a wide array of marginalized fan identities, communities, and cultural practices.

Beginning a more constructive conversation about intersectional axes of both privilege and subordination requires that we confront the fan fragility currently operating within the convergence culture industry.[12] My conception of fan fragility builds on Robin DiAngelo's work on white fragility, which describes "the anger, withdrawal, emotional incapacitation, guilt, argumentation, and cognitive dissonance" that manifest when white people are confronted about racism and their own institutionalized privilege. This response is due, in part, to the fact that white people in the West "live in a social environment that protects and insulates them from race-based stress," which ultimately "builds white expectations for racial comfort while at the same time lowering the ability to tolerate racial stress."[13] Importantly, DiAngelo conceives of white fragility as a decidedly nonpartisan quality, with "so-called progressive whites" also suffering from "the reduced psychosocial stamina that racial insulation inculcates."[14] This lack of stamina ultimately provokes a set of "defensive moves" that range from argumentation to abandoning the conversation entirely, all of which ultimately "function to reinstate white racial equilibrium."[15] Fan fragility, in its scholarly and fannish and industrial incarnations, manifests as a similar series of "defensive moves" and likewise nostalgically attempts to reinstate a predigital equilibrium in its conception of the "media fan."

Given the vastness and mutability of contemporary digital fan culture, and the challenges inherent in participating within it, much less monetizing or studying it, this desire is understandable. But, not unlike Fiske's stated but unfulfilled desire to engage race as an axis of subordination within fan culture, much of the issue resides in the fact that white fragility has rendered whites "at a loss for how to respond [to racism] in constructive ways."[16] Similarly, media producers, fans, and fan scholars often have trouble grappling with perceived bias (either positive or negative) towards particular fans and fan practices, resulting in a similar series of "defensive moves." For fans, this often manifests as an effort to reinstate a cultural moment in which fan culture was less accessible and fan identities could be more easily authenticated. For the media industry, and legacy media in particular, this often means responding to the disruptive nature of digital participatory culture by retreating to what is familiar (e.g., pathologized fan representations and updated "audience commodity" initiatives to contain, count, and monetize fans for advertisers). For fan scholars, this has manifested in both the defense of a vision of the field that continues to center transformative (and, thus, predominantly female) fan cultures and practices, and debates surrounding the affordances and limitations of a more inclusive definition of "media fandom" as an object of study.

Of the various factors that DiAngelo claims inculcate white fragility, ranging from segregation to psychic freedom, two are particularly germane to a conceptualization of fan fragility. The first is the competing forces of universalism and individualism, in which whiteness is constructed as the "norm" (a form of universalism deployed "to deny the significance of race and the advantages of being white"), and yet white people are taught to "see themselves as individuals rather than as part of a racially socialized group" (which elides conversations about the generational accumulation of wealth and its perpetuation of white privilege).[17] DiAngelo also suggests that representation plays a role, consistently reaffirming the message that whites "are better and more important than people of color" by placing them at the center of a range of cultural narratives, from history textbooks to advertisements to popular media texts.[18] Fan fragility also resides at the intersection of these two factors, and has been forged in large part by the convergence culture industry's efforts to construct androcentric and affirmational fandom as the "norm."

This book has touched on three distinct (if at times ideologically divergent) forms of fan fragility, all of which can be viewed as reactions to the growing diversification of fan-cultural identities and the concordant efforts by the convergence culture industry to entrench androcentric conceptions of the "fan." The first strain, emerging from particular corners of fan culture, is a response to the longstanding hegemonic construction of white, cishet men as the "norm" in terms of who can most easily occupy fan identities, and the perception that fannish "social justice warriors" are challenging this norm. Interestingly, the defensive moves displayed by a small segment of predominantly white, straight male fans are not in direct response to fan-based stress. On the contrary, the stress that provokes their "defensive moves" is derived from the attendant *lack* of stress that has accompanied the mainstreaming of fan culture, a nostalgic longing for the stress that once accompanied the subcultural claim to otherness. The issue is that this obscures the fact that they were always already privileged, and counterintuitively manifests as a crackdown on the inclusivity they claim that they have been historically denied. This backlash is undergirded and emboldened by the convergence culture industry's affirmation of their claim to "universal" fan identity.

The strain of fan fragility specific to media industry has similarly endeavored to create a "universal" conception of the fan that can be most effectively and efficiently wedded to the media industry's evolving business models. While the media industry's reticence to embrace transformative fan cultures is rooted in legitimate legal and economic concerns, it has cumulatively and consistently communicated the primacy of male-dominated fan practices, and male fans by extension. The most intriguing manifestations of this industrial strain of fan fragility appear in those producorial figures who are either promotionally tasked with balancing or personally strive to balance their own fannish identities with their industrial affiliations. In addition to emerging archetypes like the fanboy auteur or the fantrepreneur that gesture toward industrially intersectional fan identities, we might consider the growing number of media creators who have previously participated in digital and transformative fan cultures. In these cases, it will be markedly more difficult to perform "defensive maneuvers" or deflect conversations surrounding the conditional embrace of media fans, precisely because they will have previously been on the receiving end of those defections and deferred conversations.

The third strain of fan fragility within fan studies is a response to the idea that the rapid growth of both fan culture and the field might erode the field's originating foci on power and identity politics. This series of defensive moves may be preemptive, or even wholly unnecessary considering the preponderance of fan studies work that continues to explore these topics. However, I believe that this iteration of fan fragility speaks to broader concerns about the rising tide of spreadable misogyny and toxic masculinity within fan and geek culture and growing antifeminist sentiment in our current sociopolitical moment. This book has endeavored to explore some of the factors that have led to the development of these three strains of fan fragility within the convergence culture industry. In part because I do not have any easy answers for how to best confront fan fragility at the fan-cultural level (resolving the growing issue of toxic masculinity within fan and geek culture) or the industrial level (envisioning a future in which content creators and owners wholly embrace transformative fans and their practices), the remainder of this conclusion focuses on fan fragility within fan studies. While still advocating for the centrality of feminism to both fan culture and the study of it, I want to engage some of the blind spots that have been an unfortunate byproduct of my own aca-fannish fragility. Because this book has only periodically modeled what shipping intersectional feminism and fan studies might look like, it seems only fitting to conclude by acknowledging those already modeling this work.

Towards an Intersectional Fan Studies

Because first wave fan studies was informed by both feminist and queer theory, and initially trained its focus on transformative fan cultures that are overwhelmingly populated by women, gender has historically been and continues to be the axis of identity privileged by fan scholars. It is not my intent to critique our ongoing scholarly investment in the gender politics of fan culture, and indeed this book is predicated on the claim that these discussions are more crucial now than ever before. However, in this moment of convergence for both fan culture and fan studies, it is increasingly important to interrogate convergent fannish identities as we reinvest in and reimagine discussions of identity and power. Revisiting first wave fan studies also returns us to the cultural moment when the term "intersectionality" was coined by Kimberlé Crenshaw, and to her call to "summon the courage to challenge groups that are after all, in one sense, 'home' to us, in the name of the parts of us that are not made at home."[19] Only then, Crenshaw suggests, can we "speak against internal exclusions and marginalizations, [and] call attention to how the identity of 'the group' has been centered on the intersectional identities of a few."[20] I wish to recognize the frequent failure of fan scholars (myself included) to critically examine our privileging of the identities of a few at the expense of developing a more intersectional conception of fan identity.

Intersectionality better allows us to theorize what Patricia Hill Collins calls the "matrix of domination,"[21] and though this book has focused predominantly on gender, the convergence culture industry poses a similar "matrix of domination" for minority fans. It is precisely because fannish boundary policing and the conditional industrial acceptance of fans remains so deeply and disturbingly gendered that I am unwilling to abandon gender as fan studies' conceptual "home" despite its potentially problematic comforts. If first wave fan studies' utopian depictions of fan communities and creative works have been glibly referred to as the "Fandom Is Beautiful" phase, then the ugliness of contemporary fan culture (what I have perhaps equally glibly called "Fandom's War on Women") demands that we reprioritize analyses of power, reassert fan studies' feminist project, and holistically consider fan privilege within the convergence culture industry. If, as the old saying goes, "fandom is a way of life," then so is fan studies. Developing a more intersectional fan studies means checking our own privilege and confronting the issues of whose stories are told or obscured within cultural narratives of progress, who is telling them, and how they are told. It also requires us to examine how fan scholars' own adoption of "boundary policing" practices shapes the field in this moment of expansion and branding for fans and fan studies alike.

In order to do this, fan scholars need to be attentive to building coalitions across institutions, disciplines, nations, and identities as we collectively brand the field of post-convergence fan studies. Per Crenshaw, intersectionality "requires that we first recognize that the organized identity groups in which we find ourselves [. . .] are in fact coalitions, or at least potential coalitions waiting to be formed."[22] Whenever fan scholars meet, on Twitter or Tumblr or at academic conferences, we have the opportunity to recognize and form these coalitions, to dump out the contents of our bags of holding and interrogate the contents. I am painfully aware that this book might read to some as an extended exercise in aca-fannish boundary policing, hypocritically privileging older or more "authentic" critical investments over emergent lines of inquiry in the field. However, in performing my own aca-fannish privilege check, I do not see first wave fan studies' emphasis on gender as too limiting or, in postfeminist terms, so pervasive as to be irrelevant. Rather, I choose to see it as a coalition waiting to be both reformulated and reformed to better engage intersectional fan identities and address bias within fan culture.

As Rukmini Pande has rightly noted, there is a tendency among fan scholars to "default" to a particular demographic conception of the media fan, avoiding conversations about race, nationality, or other factors in order to paint fandom as an "inclusive" space.[23] It is in part because this desire to frame fandom or fan identities as inclusive too often devolves into universalism that Bertha Chin and Lori Morimoto's recent framing of fandom via Benedict Anderson's concept of "imagined communities" offers a productive parallel framework through which we might explore forms of fan fragility around issues of (trans)national identity.[24] Because the convergence culture industry constructs an even narrower vision of the imagined community of fan culture, there is a growing imperative to work on transcultural fandom and concordant efforts to "de-Westernize" fan studies.[25]

Even those axes of identity that have been comparatively present within fan studies since its inception, such as sexuality or class, remain at the peripheries of the field. For example, considering the preponderance of work on (straight) fans' queer reading strategies and textual production, too little attention has been paid to femslash (or slash fanworks that feature F/F pairings) as a transformative practice populated by (and focused on) queer women.[26] In the introduction of their recent special issue of *Transformative Works and Cultures* on queer female fandom, editors Eve Ng and Julie Levin Russo offer a similar argument as my own about the underrepresentation and marginalization of femslash and "the primacy of slash as the unmarked term" within both fandom and fan studies.[27] In other words, in addition to continuing to theorize how fandom might broadly function as a queer female space,[28] we would do well to turn our attention more actively to queer fans and their experience of mainstream fan culture. Rukimini Pande and Swati Moitra's interrogation of fannish investment in racialized femslash pairings on the television series *Once upon a Time* (ABC, 2011–present) offers one rich intersectional example.[29]

Then there are the axes of fan identity, such as ability, that have received comparatively little scholarly attention. A handful of scholars have tackled the issue representationally, analyzing documentaries that feature disabled fans[30] and examining fan criticism surrounding the casting of able-bodied actors as disabled characters[31] or "rebooted" characters whose disabilities are removed.[32] Others have considering how transformative fan production,[33] as well as fan platforms and interfaces,[34] address disability. Other identity markers, like size, have not received a robust theorization by fan scholars, which is especially surprising given how many of the bodily stereotypes about fans are rooted in their failure to conform to hegemonic standards of masculinity and femininity and pernicious conceptions of the fanboy's "failed masculinity" and the fangirl's "excess." Theories of the body are essential to future discussions of gendered fan culture, from studies of cosplay as a fan practice to considerations of fan merchandise. Alternately, we might look to Mary Ingram-Water's fascinating and self-reflexive work on interviewing female authors of male pregnancy fanfiction (or "m-preg") while she herself was pregnant as a model for future considerations of how our own physical presence as researchers shapes our relationships to the fans we are studying or interviewing.[35]

There is also emergent work on undertheorized axes of fan identity that are ripe for future intersectional applications: take, for example, the growing body of scholarship on how both age and aging shape fan identities.[36] The work of Denise Bielby and C. Lee Harrington most actively gestures to the potential complexity and diversity of these emerging lines of inquiry, which might include the analysis of "fandom and life milestones, changes in the fan self over time, age norms within fandom, and changes in the fan object over time."[37] This work will be especially pertinent to longitudinal studies that explore either the generational shifts from analog to digital fan culture, the migration of fans to particular digital platforms, or the impact of the convergence culture industry on those who were initially exposed to fan culture in this period. Louisa Stein's book *Millennial Fandom* and its examination of the intersection of "feels culture" and fan culture models one such approach, remaining mindful of how digital platforms shape and are shaped by generational fan performances and practices.[38] We would also benefit from extending analyses of "gender-plus" forms of fan bias that denigrate both feminine media objects and its fans based on their "age or generation"[39] to a "gender-plus-plus" analytic to address those fans who do not conform to the convergence culture industry's limited conception of the fan along multiple axes of identity.

Perhaps fittingly, given the aforementioned discussion of "fan fragility," race remains the largest blind spot in contemporary work on fan identity and culture. Though this is currently in the process of changing, there have been a number of telling "false starts" in expanding this body of work, most notably in the wake of RaceFail '09, a series of heated blog posts and exchanges between science fiction and fantasy fans and authors that broadly addressed race and racism in both media objects and fan culture. RaceFail '09 remains a touchstone for discussions of intersectional bias within fan culture, with many "debates about race, cultural appropriation, and related discussions about class, disability, language, and gender"[40] citing the conflict. Race is once again poised to be a growth area within the field of fan studies, with forthcoming journal issues, monographs, and anthologies devoted to fans and fandoms of color, and intersectional work already being done.[41] The work of Mel Stanfill and Benjamin Woo has also been vital in broadening conversations about whiteness in both fandom and fan studies, while effectively modeling intersectional approaches that also consider gender, sexuality, and class.[42]

In a book that so frequently decries the erasure of transformative fan cultures and practices from the convergence culture industry's conception of fan identity and participation, I have spent little space celebrating these transformative fan works, as well as those who produce and circulate them. Because these transformative impulses and practices undergird many contemporary forms of fan activism, we might look to scholarly work on racebending as a model for how fannish production might evolve into interventionist and intersectional feminist politics.[43] Alternately, Kristen J. Warner's work on fans advocating for the canonical casting of a black woman to (continue to play) Iris West in the forthcoming *Flash* feature film maps a more intersectional fan studies both in its focus on these black female "defense squads" and in the ways it troubles a clear delineation between affirmational and transformative modes of fan activism.[44] We can also look to the growing body of work on fan activist responses to queerbaiting as a model for enacting change and raising consciousness around the longstanding mistreatment of queer characters.[45] In all of these cases, it is important to stress that fan activism frequently echoes historical and contemporary political movements, in the sense that they are frequently spearheaded by queer women and women of color.

This conclusion can only offer a woefully incomplete overview of the intersectional work already being done within fan studies. By returning to many foundational fan studies texts over the course of this book, I intended to suggest that many of these issues not only remain unresolved but in many cases have been compounded by the convergence culture industry and deserve renewed consideration. Racism and sexism and homophobia within fan culture are interrelated issues, and fans are often quicker than scholars in identifying and subsequently "calling out" instances of bias within media objects, industries, and fandom itself. The colloquialism "your fave is problematic," frequently utilized as a form of fannish shorthand to identify fannish blind spots, might be similarly applied to feminist fan studies. In a March 2015 blog post, Ijeoma Oluo forthrightly notes, "[T]hat your fave is problematic isn't a big deal—the big deal is if we ignore it. [. . .] Our feminism is racist, classist and transphobic. Our anti-racism is sexist. Our LGBT rights movement is racist and classist. They are all ableist. Acknowledging this isn't divisive: ignoring it is."[46] If the convergence culture industry's favored conceptions of fan culture are problematic, then so is fan studies' frequently limited vision of "fangirls" and feminist fan culture. This does not mean, however, that we should unilaterally dismiss feminist fan studies as our OTP. I will always ship feminism and fan culture. This OTP is my personal fave, and although I am conscious of the fact that it may at times be problematic, it is also increasingly necessary.

ACKNOWLEDGMENTS

It is only fitting that a project about fan culture concludes with me unabashedly fangirling the community of family, friends, mentors, scholars, and colleagues who have inspired this project and supported it from its inception. I am forever indebted to my family, including my amazing mother, Gail (for being an endless source of moral support, angel food cake, and occasionally forced, but always much-needed, exercise), my father, Steve (who instilled in me at a young age that you must be passionate about your chosen profession), and my sister, Gretchen (who is wiser and cooler than any younger sibling has the right to be). My gratitude also goes out to the entire Pebler clan, who are the antithesis of every media narrative about horrible in-laws.

I feel incredibly privileged to have been taught and mentored by some of the most brilliant media scholars in the world, first as an undergraduate at New York University and later as a graduate student at the University of Southern California. Matt Fee, thank you for modeling pedagogy before I even knew the term and for not talking me out of writing my grad school admissions essay on Wes Craven's *The People under the Stairs*. I owe a life debt to my dissertation committee at USC, professors Ellen Seiter, Tara McPherson, and Henry Jenkins, for their thoughtful guidance and unwavering support throughout my years as a doctoral student and beyond. Tara's graduate seminar on shopping and beauty culture, as well as her own work on technology and gender, is a continued source of inspiration. Working with Henry was a professional goal I had harbored since first encountering *Textual Poachers* as an undergraduate, and the experience far exceeded my (perilously high) expectations. I will never be able to adequately convey what it means to me to know Henry is in my corner, or sufficiently thank him for championing my earliest publications. Last but certainly not least, my deepest gratitude to Ellen for all of her advice and for never mincing words. If or when future students thank me in their acknowledgments, they will be indirectly thanking you for providing me with a model of mentorship that I will carry with me throughout my career.

To the incredible group of scholars and friends I met as a graduate student at USC, you will always be my favorite people to have beers and share ideas with. Particular kudos to Elizabeth Affuso, Kate Fortmueller, Kristen Fuhs, Julia Himberg, Chris Hanson, Dave Lerner, Patty Ahn, Daniel Chamberlain, Jorie Lagerwey, Daniel Herbert, Janani Subramanian, Taylor Nygaard, Jennifer Rosales, Robert Buerkle, Bella Honess-Roe, and Paul Reinsch, who have heard me rant about this topic for over a decade and not yet de-friended me. I am also deeply appreciative of the people who are a consistent source of stimulation and sanity in my life: Michael C. Bolton for being the Ravenclaw to my Slytherin; Michael Koresky and David Connelly for bringing two things; Huriya Jabbar and Joshua Roebke for the euchre tournaments; Rich Murphy for forming kowchkru; Jennifer K. Stuller for her feminist fangirl solidarity; and the first wives club for *Castle* nights.

This book is also profoundly beholden to all my fellow fan scholars, who have offered an endless stream of inspiration, feedback, and friendship since I entered this field over a decade ago. When we extol the virtues of fan community, I can think of no more illustrative group than this scholarly network, and I am honored to be a part of your Scooby Gang. I would like to specifically acknowledge Kristina Busse, Melissa A. Click, Mel Stanfill, Julie Levin Russo, Derek Johnson, Melanie Kohnen, Louisa Stein, Derek Kompare, Alexis Lothain, Bob Rehak, Francesca Coppa, Will Brooker, Katherine Morrissey, Lori Morimoto, Sam Ford, Bethan Jones, Dan Hassler-Forest, Lucy Bennett, Bertha Chin, Paul Booth, Anne Gilbert, Karen Hellekson, Kristen Warner, Tisha Turk, Mark Stewart, and Lesley Willard for conversationally beta editing the ideas contained in this book at various stages of the process.

I could not imagine a better set of colleagues than those I have the good fortune to work with at the University of Texas at Austin, particularly Alisa Perren, Mary Beltran, Caroline Frick, and Cindy McCreery. Special thanks to Kathy Fuller-Seeley for calling my attention to the early poem about fans featured in the introduction, and for always having your door open when I needed advice. To all of the brilliant undergraduate and graduate students I have taught over the years in courses on fan culture, transmedia storytelling, video games, comic books, and remix culture, you are the reason I got into this profession, and the reason I stay in it. I cannot wait to see everything you accomplish.

Innumerable thanks to my editor, Eric Zinner, for shepherding this project from our earliest meetings at SCMS through its final revisions, and to the entire team at NYU Press for their guidance and work on this project. I am also deeply appreciative for the feedback from my outside reviewers, who inarguably made the book better, and to the editors of the Critical Cultural Communication series, Jonathan Gray, Aswin Punathambekar, and Adrienne Shaw for their confidence in both me and the project.

Finally, to all the wonder(ful) women who have made my experiences in fan culture transformative, in every sense of the word, this book is for you.

NOTES

INTRODUCTION

1　Milton Griepp, "Marvel's David Gabriel on the 2016 Market Shift," *ICv2*, March 31, 2017, https://icv2.com.

2　Alex Brown, "Let's Talk about Marvel Comics, the 'Diversity Doesn't Sell' Myth, and What Diversity Really Means," *Tor.com*, April 5, 2017, http://www.tor.com.

3　Asher Elbein, "The Real Reasons for Marvel Comics' Woes," *Atlantic*, May 24, 2017, https://www.theatlantic.com.

4　Jude Terror, "Possibly Hungry for Meat and Potatoes, Axel Alonso Remarks, Marvel 'Never Lost Sight of Our Classic Characters,'" *Bleeding Cool*, December 30, 2016, https://www.bleedingcool.com.

5　Griepp, "Marvel's David Gabriel."

6　MaNishtana, "The New Nazi Captain America Is the Hero That Bigoted Comic Book Fans Deserve," *Tablet Magazine*, June 15, 2016, http://www.tabletmag.com.

7　Mia Consalvo, "Confronting Toxic Gamer Culture: A Challenge for Feminist Game Studies Scholars," *Ada Journal* no. 1 (2012), http://adanewmedia.org.

8　Karen Hellekson, "A Fannish Field of Value: Online Fan Gift Culture," *Cinema Journal* 48.4 (Summer 2009): 113–14.

9　Julie Levin Russo, "The L Word: Labors of Love" (paper presented at Console-ing Passions Conference, Santa Barbara, CA, April 26–24, 2008), http://community .livejournal.com.

10　Ibid.

11　Ibid.

12　See: Suzanne Scott, "Authorized Resistance: Is Fan Production Frakked?" in Tiffany Potter and C. W. Marshall (eds.), *Cylons in America: Critical Studies in Battlestar Galactica* (New York: Continuum, 2008), 210–23; Suzanne Scott, "Who's Steering the Mothership? The Role of the Fanboy Auteur in Transmedia Storytelling," in Aaron Delwiche and Jennifer Henderson (eds.), *The Participatory Cultures Handbook* (New York: Routledge, 2012), 43–52; Suzanne Scott, "Battlestar Galactica: Fans and Ancillary Content," in Jason Mittell and Ethan Thompson (eds.), *How to Watch Television: Media Criticism in Practice* (New York: NYU Press, 2013), 320–29.

13　Rebecca Wanzo, "African American Acafandom and Other Strangers: New Genealogies of Fan Studies," *Transformative Works and Culture* 20 (2015), http:// journal.transformativeworks.org.

14 See: Lori Kendall, "Nerd Nation: Images of Nerds in US Popular Culture," *International Journal of Cultural Studies* 2.2 (1999): 260–83; Ron Eglash, "Race, Sex, and Nerds: From Black Geeks to Asian American Hipsters," *Social Text* 20.2 (Summer 2002); Mel Stanfill, "Doing Fandom, (Mis)doing Whiteness: Heteronormativity, Racialization, and the Discursive Construction of Fandom," *Transformative Works and Cultures* 8 (2011), http://journal.transformativeworks.org; Benjamin Woo, "The Invisible Bag of Holding: Whiteness and Media Fandom," in Melissa A. Click and Suzanne Scott (eds.), *The Routledge Companion to Media Fandom* (New York: Routledge, 2018), 245–52.

15 Throughout this book, I frequently use the terms "fan," "geek," and "nerd" interchangeably, or draw on literature addressing one to theorize another. It is not my intent to flatten these cultural identities, as they have discrete etymological origins and are unique social categories with varying degrees of cultural capital over time. However, because the terms have become more fluid during the historical period this book addresses, and are frequently conflated, I occasionally follow suit.

16 Henry Jenkins, *Convergence Culture: Where Old and New Media Collide* (New York: NYU Press, 2006), 12.

17 Ibid., 18.

18 Ibid., 19.

19 Ibid., 23.

20 Ibid.

21 Matt Hills, *Fan Cultures* (New York: Routledge, 2002), 31.

22 Max Horkheimer and Theodor W. Adorno, "The Culture Industry: Enlightenment as Mass Deception," in Meenakshi Gigi Durham and Douglas M. Kellner (eds.), *Media and Cultural Studies: Keyworks*, rev. ed. (Indianapolis: Wiley-Blackwell, 2009), 43.

23 Jenkins, *Convergence Culture*, 247.

24 Henry Jenkins, *Textual Poachers: Television Fans and Participatory Culture* (New York: Routledge, 1992).

25 Jenkins, *Convergence Culture*, 133.

26 Theodor W. Adorno, "Culture Industry Reconsidered," in J. M. Bernstein (ed.), *The Culture Industry: Selected Essays on Mass Culture* (London: Routledge, 2003), 98.

27 Dougles Kellner, "Media Industries, Political Economy, and Media/Cultural Studies: An Articulation," in Jennifer Jolt and Alisa Perren (eds.), *Media Industries: History, Theory, and Method* (Indianapolis: Wiley-Blackwell, 2009), 96.

28 David Hesmondhalgh, *The Cultural Industries*, 3rd ed. (Thousand Oaks, CA: Sage, 2013).

29 John Hartley (ed.), *Creative Industries* (Malden, MA: Blackwell, 2005).

30 Hesmondhalgh, *The Cultural Industries*, 25.

31 Adorno, "Culture Industry Reconsidered," 105.

32 Jenkins, *Convergence Culture*, 247.

33 Ibid., 248.

34 Adorno, "Culture Industry Reconsidered," 98.

35 Ibid., 99.

36 Horkheimer and Adorno, "The Culture Industry," 53.

37 Ibid., 69.

38 Ibid.

39 Adorno, "Culture Industry Reconsidered," 105.

40 Horkheimer and Adorno, "The Culture Industry," 63.

41 Kristina Busse, "Geek Hierarchies, Boundary Policing, and the Gendering of the Good Fan," *Participations* 10.1 (May 2013): 76.

42 Stanfill, "Doing Fandom, (Mis)doing Whiteness."

43 Ibid.

44 Willie Osterweil, "What Was the Nerd?" *Real Life Magazine*, November 16, 2016, http://reallifemag.com.

45 Kyle Wagner, "The Future of the Culture Wars Is Here, and It's Gamergate," *Deadspin*, October 14, 2014, http://deadspin.com.

46 Matt Lees, "What Gamergate Should Have Taught Us about the 'Alt-right,'" *Guardian*, December 1, 2016, https://www.theguardian.com.

47 Ian Sherr and Erin Carson, "GamerGate to Trump: How Video Game Culture Blew Everything Up," *Cnet*, July 8, 2017, https://www.cnet.com.

48 Emanuel Maiberg, "Under Trump, Gamergate Can Stop Pretending It Was about Games," *Motherboard*, February 9, 2017, https://motherboard.vice.com.

49 Allum Bokhari, "Leftists Think GamerGate Caused Donald Trump: Maybe They're Right," *Breitbart*, June 22, 2017, http://www.breitbart.com.

50 See: Janine Fron, Tracy Fullerton, Jacquelyn Ford Morie, and Celia Pierce, "The Hegemony of Play," *Proceedings, DiGRA: Situated Play*, Proceedings of DiGRA Conference, Tokyo, Japan, September 24–27, 2007, ist.usc.edu; Anastasia Salter and Bridget Bloggett, "Hypermasculinity and Dickwolves: The Contentious Role of Women in the New Gaming Public," *Journal of Broadcasting & Electronic Media* 56.3 (2012): 401–16; Shira Chess and Adrienne Shaw, "A Conspiracy of Fishes; or, How We Learned to Stop Worrying about #GamerGate and Embrace Hegemonic Masculinity," *Journal of Broadcasting & Electronic Media* 59.1 (2015): 208–20.

51 La Touche Hancock, "The Motion Picture Fan," *Motion Picture Story Magazine*, April 1911, 93.

52 Charlotte Brunsdon, *The Feminist, the Housewife, and the Soap Opera* (Oxford: Oxford University Press, 2000), 29.

53 Janice A. Radway, *Reading the Romance: Women, Patriarchy, and Popular Literature* (Chapel Hill: University of North Carolina Press, 1984), 18.

54 Ellen Seiter, Hans Borcher, Gabriele Kreutzner, and Eva-Maria Warth, "Introduction," in Ellen Seiter, Hans Borcher, Gabriele Kreutzner, and Eva-Maria Warth (eds.), *Remote Control: Television, Audiences, and Cultural Power* (New York: Routledge, 1989), 1.

55 Derek Johnson, "Devaluing and Revaluing Seriality: The Gendered Discourses of Media Franchising," *Media, Culture, and Society* 33.7 (2011): 1080.

56 Adorno, "Culture Industry Reconsidered," 100.

CHAPTER 1. A FANGIRL'S PLACE IS IN THE RESISTANCE

1 Angela Watercutter, "Princess Leia Gave the Women's March a New Hope," *Wired*, January 23, 2017, https://www.wired.com.

2 Hannah Shaw-Williams, "Rogue One: *A Star Wars Story*'s 'Sexist Backlash' Is Not Newsworthy," *Screenrant*, April 8, 2016, http://screenrant.com.

3 Todd McCarthy, "'Rogue One: A Star Wars Story'; Film Review," *Hollywood Reporter*, December 13, 2016, http://www.hollywoodreporter.com.

4 See: Radway, *Reading the Romance*; Ian Ang, *Watching Dallas: Soap Opera and the Melodramatic Imagination* (London: Methuen, 1985); Nancy Baym, "Interpreting Soap Operas and Creating Community: Inside a Computer-Mediated Fan Culture," *Journal of Folklore Research* 30.2/3 (1993): 143–76.; C. Lee Harrington and Denise D. Bielby, *Soap Fans: Pursuing Pleasure and Making Meaning in Everyday Life* (Philadelphia: Temple University Press, 1995).

5 Alexander Doty, *Making Things Perfectly Queer: Interpreting Mass Culture* (Minneapolis: University of Minnesota Press, 1993), 3.

6 Rukmini Pande, "Squee from the Margins: Racial/Cultural/Ethnic Identity in Global Media Fandom," in Paul Booth and Lucy Bennett (eds.), *Seeing Fans* (New York: Bloomsbury Academic, 2016), 209–10.

7 Constance Penley, "Brownian Motion: Women, Tactics, and Technology," in Constance Penley and Andrew Ross (eds.), *Technoculture* (Minneapolis: University of Minnesota Press, 1991), 138.

8 Constance Penley, "Feminism, Psychoanalysis, and the Study of Popular Culture," in Lawrence Grossberg, Gary Nelson, and Paula Treichler (eds.), *Cultural Studies Now and in the Future* (New York: Routledge, 1992), 491.

9 Ibid., 492.

10 Ibid.

11 Louisa Ellen Stein, *Millennial Fandom: Television Audiences in the Transmedia Age* (Iowa City: University of Iowa Press, 2015), 11. See also: Abigail De Kosnik, *Rogue Archives: Digital Cultural Memory and Media Fandom* (Cambridge, MA: MIT Press, 2016); Lyn Thomas, *Fans, Feminism, and "Quality" Media* (New York: Routledge, 2002); Rhiannon Bury, *Cyberspaces of Their Own: Female Fandoms Online* (New York: Peter Lang, 2005).

12 Michel de Certeau, *The Practice of Everyday Life* (Berkeley: University of California Press, 1988), 40.

13 Penley, "Brownian Motion," 138–39.

14 Penley, "Feminism, Psychoanalysis, and the Study of Popular Culture," 479, 490–91.

15 Joanna Russ, "Pornography by Women for Women, with Love," in Karen Hellekson and Kristina Busse (eds.), *The Fan Fiction Studies Reader* (Iowa City: University of Iowa Press, 2014), 94.

16 Patricia Frazer Lamb and Diana L. Veith, "Romantic Myth, Transcendence, and *Star Trek* Zines," in Karen Hellekson and Kristina Busse (eds.), *The Fan Fiction Studies Reader* (Iowa City: University of Iowa Press, 2014), 99.

17 Russ, "Pornography by Women," 84–85; Lamb and Veith, "Romantic Myth," 101–2.
18 Lamb and Veith, "Romantic Myth," 101.
19 Russ, "Pornography by Women," 94.
20 Karen Hellekson and Kristina Busse, "Fan Identity and Feminism," in Karen Hellekson and Kristina Busse (eds.), *The Fan Fiction Studies Reader* (Iowa City: University of Iowa Press, 2014), 79.
21 Camille Bacon-Smith, *Enterprising Women: Television Fandom and the Creation of Popular Myth* (Philadelphia: University of Pennsylvania Press, 1992), 17.
22 Ibid.
23 Ibid., 18.
24 Axel Bruns, *Blogs, Wikipedia, Second Life, and Beyond: From Production to Produsage* (New York: Peter Lang, 2008).
25 For a discussion of how male academics have strategically recuperated "fanboy" identities in response to feminism's perceived colonization of the margins, see: Jacinda Read, "The Cult of Masculinity: From Fan-Boys to Academic Bad-Boys," in Mark Jancovich, Antonio Lázaro Reboll, Julian Stringer, and Andy Williams (eds.), *Defining Cult Movies: The Cultural Politics of Oppositional Taste* (Manchester: Manchester University Press, 2003), 61.
26 De Certeau, *The Practice of Everyday Life*, 36–37, 174.
27 Jonathan Gray, Cornel Sandvoss, and C. Lee Harrington, "Introduction: Why Study Fans?" in Jonathan Gray, Cornel Sandvoss, and C. Lee Harrington (eds.), *Fandom: Identities and Communities in a Mediated World* (New York: NYU Press, 2007), 2. The quoted reference to the "power bloc" is from John Fiske, *Understanding Popular Culture* (Winchester, MA: Unwin Hyman, 1989).
28 Matt Hills, *Fan Cultures* (New York: Routledge, 2002), 30.
29 Cornel Sandvoss, *Fans* (Cambridge: Polity, 2005), 11–43, 42.
30 Nicholas Abercrombie and Brian Longhurst, *Audiences: A Sociological Theory of Performance and Imagination* (London: Sage, 1998), 15.
31 Matt Hills, "Negative Fan Stereotypes ('Get a life!') and Positive Fan Injunctions ('Everyone's got to be a fan of something!'): Returning to Hegemony Theory in Fan Studies," *Spectator* 25.1 (Spring 2005): 36.
32 John Fiske, *Understanding Popular Culture* (New York: Routledge, 1991), 18.
33 Henry Jenkins, "Afterword: The Future of Fandom," in Jonathan Gray, Cornel Sandvoss, and C. Lee Harrington (eds.), *Fandom: Identities and Communities in a Mediated World* (New York: NYU Press, 2007), 362.
34 Seiter et al., "Introduction," 6, 8.
35 Ibid., 6.
36 Matt Hills, "Gender and Fan Studies (Round Twelve, Part One): Catherine Driscoll and Matt Hills," *Confessions of an Aca-Fan: The Official Weblog of Henry Jenkins,* August 23, 2007, http://www.henryjenkins.org/2007/08/gender_and_fan _culture_round_t.html.
37 Paul Booth, *Playing Fans: Negotiating Fandom and Media in the Digital Age* (Iowa City: University of Iowa Press, 2015), 120.

38 See, for example: Denise D. Bielby, "Gender Inequality in Culture Industries," in Cynthia Carter, Linda Steiner, Lisa McLaughlin (eds.), *The Routledge Companion to Media and Gender* (New York: Routledge, 2014), 137–46.

39 Heidi M. Schlipphacke, "A Hidden Agenda: Gender in Selected Writings by Theodor Adorno and Max Horkheimer," *Orbis Litterarum* 56 (2001): 300.

40 Catherine Driscoll and Melissa Gregg, "Convergence Culture and the Legacy of Feminist Cultural Studies," *Cultural Studies* 25.4–5 (2011): 573.

41 Ibid., 574.

42 Obsession_inc, "Affirmational Fandom vs. Transformational Fandom," June 1, 2009, http://obsession-inc.dreamwidth.org/82589.html.

43 Ibid.

44 Ibid.

45 Jenkins, *Textual Poachers*, 107–19.

46 Ibid., 107.

47 Bury, *Cyberspaces of Their Own*, 42.

48 Alex, "Why Do the Values and Mission Statements Focus on Female Fans?" *Organization for Transformative Works*, February 8, 2016, http://www.transformativeworks.org.

49 Matt Hills, "From Dalek Half Balls to Daft Punk Helmets: Mimetic Fandom and the Crafting of Replicas," *Transformative Works and Cultures* no. 16 (2014), http://dx.doi.org/10.3983/twc.2014.0531.

50 Booth, *Playing Fans*, 42.

51 Sam Ford, "Fan Studies: Grappling with an 'Undisciplined' Discipline," *Journal of Fandom Studies* 2.1 (2014): 64.

52 Consider, for example, the trend of having celebrities read homoerotic fanfiction featuring their character, or displaying slash fan art, on talk shows as a point of comedy. These incidents, as Bethan Jones describes, help perpetuate and entrench "the idea that slash fiction, and female fan culture, is something to be ashamed of." See: Bethan Jones, "Johnlocked: *Sherlock*, Slash Fiction, and the Shaming of Female Fans," *New Left Project*, February 18, 2014, http://www.newleftproject.org.

53 Sarah Banet-Weiser, "Popular Feminism: #MeToo," *Los Angeles Review of Books*, January 27, 2018, https://lareviewofbooks.org.

54 Ibid.

55 Louisa Stein, "Gender and Fan Studies (Round Two, Part One): Louisa Stein and Robert Jones," *Confessions of an Aca-Fan: The Official Weblog of Henry Jenkins*, June 6, 2007, http://www.henryjenkins.org/2007/06/gender_and_fan_studies_round_t.html.

56 Francesca Coppa and Rebecca Tushnet, "How to Suppress Women's Remix," *Camera Obscura* 26.2 (2011): 131–38.

57 Jason Mittell, "Gender and Fan Studies (Round One, Part One): Karen Hellekson and Jason Mittell," *Confessions of an Aca-Fan: The Official Weblog of Henry Jenkins*, May 31, 2007, http://www.henryjenkins.org/2007/05/gender_and_fan_studies_round_o.html.

58 A brief overview of the debate between Louisa Stein and Robert Jones reveals the gendered stakes of fan scholars potentially revaluing industrial "incorporation" in this period. Stein and Jones's discussion focused on the comparative transformativity of two gendered modes of fan production: fanvids and machinima, which both utilize professionally produced media content (film and television in the case of most vids, video games in the case of machinima) to produce new narratives. The primary distinction is that vidding has historically been ignored or actively attempted to be stifled by industry, whereas video game companies tend to solicit and endorse machinima as a fan practice. Despite Jones's stated desire to not "want to say that machinima is better," his dismissals of vidding as a comparatively "passive" form of textual engagement appeared to do just that. Thus, machinima (and, by extension, its fanboy creators) becomes "evolutionary," "interactive," and "unique," in large part because the medium it derives from is positioned similarly within new media discourse. Vidding, because it is tied to television spectatorship, is comparatively framed as passive and derivative, and its labor, like myriad other forms of women's work, is devalued. See: Louisa Stein and Robert Jones, "Gender and Fan Studies (Round Two, Part One); Louisa Stein and Robert Jones," *Confessions of an Aca-Fan: The Official Weblog of Henry Jenkins,* June 7, 2007, http://henryjenkins.org/2007/06/gender_and_fan_studies_round_t_1.html.

59 Louisa Ellen Stein, "On (Not) Hosting the Session That Killed the Term 'Aca-fan,'" *Antenna,* March 18, 2011, http://blog.commarts.wisc.edu/2011/03/18/on-not-hosting-the-session-that-killed-the-term-acafan.

60 For example, in my own contribution to the aca-fan debates, I took fellow fan scholar Will Brooker, who has an excellent track record of feminist and aca-fannish scholarly output, to task for jokingly equating aca-fandom as a scholarly subject position with "baby talk and sleepover squealing." Though Brooker immediately followed this comment with the disclaimer, "I'm a straight white guy, and as enough of our official vocabulary is decided by straight white guys, I don't want to make any rules for fandom's vocabulary based on my own preferences," his comment struck a nerve precisely because it conflates old fan stereotypes (infantilization and feminization) with a history of feminist writing, devaluing both in the process. See: Will Brooker, "Acafandom and Beyond: Will Brooker, Melissa A. Click, Suzanne Scott, and Sangita Shreshtova (Part Two)," *Confessions of an Aca-Fan: The Official Weblog of Henry Jenkins,* October 22, 2011, http://henryjenkins.org/blog/2011/10/acafandom_and_beyond_will_broo_1.html.

61 Ian Bogost, "Against Aca-Fandom: On Jason Mittell and *Mad Men,*" *Ian Bogost,* July 29, 2010, http://bogost.com/blog/against_aca-fandom/; Jonathan Gray in Louisa Ellen Stein, "SCMS 2011 Workshop: Acafandom and the Future of Fan Studies," *Transform,* March 16, 2011, https://louisaellenstein.com/2011/03/16/scms-2011-workshop-acafandom-and-the-future-of-fan-studies.

62 Catherine Coker and Candace Benefiel, "We Have Met the Fans, and They Are Us: In Defense of Aca-Fans and Scholars," *Flow,* December 17, 2010, http://www.flowjournal.org; Stein, "On (Not) Hosting the Session."

63 Louisa Ellen Stein, "Post-SCMS Musings on the Value of the Word Acafan," *Transform*, March 17, 2011, https://louisaellenstein.com/2011/03/17/why-the-term-acafan-matters-but-maybe-we-could-lose-the-dom-in-acafandom.

64 Ford, "Fan Studies," 53–54.

65 Kristina Busse in Louisa Stein (moderator), "Online Roundtable on *Spreadable Media*," *Cinema Journal* 53.3 (Spring 2014): 153.

66 Ibid.

67 Ibid., 159.

68 Paul Booth in Louisa Stein (moderator), "Online Roundtable on *Spreadable Media*," *Cinema Journal* 53.3 (Spring 2014): 154.

69 Henry Jenkins in ibid., 162.

70 Yvonne Tasker and Diane Negra, "Introduction: Feminist Politics and Postfeminist Culture," in Yvonne Tasker and Diane Negra (eds.), *Interrogating Postfeminism: Gender and the Politics of Popular Culture* (Durham, NC: Duke University Press, 2007), 2; Diane Negra, *What a Girl Wants: Fantasizing the Reclamation of Self in Postfeminism* (New York: Routledge, 2009), 7.

71 Tasker and Negra, "Introduction," 1–3.

72 Ibid., 11.

73 Tasker and Negra, "Introduction"; Angela McRobbie, *The Aftermath of Feminism: Gender, Culture, and Social Change* (London: Sage, 2009), 29.

74 McRobbie, *The Aftermath of Feminism*, 24.

75 Ibid., 26.

76 Marc A. Thiessen, "Yes, Antifa Is the Moral Equivalent of Neo-Nazis," *Washington Post*, August 30, 2017, https://www.washingtonpost.com.

77 Henry Jenkins, "*Star Trek* Rerun, Reread, Rewritten: Fan Writing as Textual Poaching," *Critical Studies in Mass Communication* 5.2 (1988): 87.

78 Gray, Sandvoss, and Harrington, "Introduction: Why Study Fans?" 1–4.

79 Scott Bukatman, "Surveying the World of Contemporary Comics Scholarship: A Conversation," *Cinema Journal* 50.3 (Spring 2011): 138.

80 Francesca Coppa, "Fuck Yeah, Fandom Is Beautiful," *Journal of Fandom Studies* 2.1 (2014): 77. Rebecca Tushnet, "I'm a Lawyer, Not an Ethnographer, Jim: Textual Poachers and Fair Use," *Journal of Fandom Studies* 2.1 (2014): 22.

81 For some examples, see this special issue of *Transformative Works and Cultures* (vol. 10, 2012) on "Transformative Works and Fan Activism," edited by Henry Jenkins and Sangita Shresthova: http://journal.transformativeworks.org.

82 Jenkins, "Afterword," 364.

83 Ibid.

84 Roberta Pearson, "Fandom in the Digital Era," *Popular Communication* 8.1 (January 2010): 86.

85 Sarah Banet-Weiser, *Authentic: The Politics of Ambivalence in a Brand Culture* (New York: NYU Press, 2012), 4–5.

CHAPTER 2. "GET A LIFE, WILL YOU PEOPLE?!"

1　Kristina Busse, "Geek Hierarchies," 73–91; Francesca Coppa, "Writing Bodies in Space: Media Fanfiction as Theatrical Performance," in Karen Hellekson and Kristina Busse (eds.), *Fan Fiction and Fan Communities in the Age of the Internet* (Jefferson, NC: McFarland, 2006), 225–44; Hills, "Negative Fan Stereotypes," 35–47.

2　For further discussion of how Spock's role was originally occupied by a woman, and the structuring absence this creates for female *Star Trek* characters and fans, see: Francesca Coppa, "Women, *Star Trek*, and the Early Development of Fannish Vidding," *Transformative Works and Cultures* 1 (2008), http://journal.transformativeworks.org.

3　Jenkins, *Textual Poachers*, 10.

4　Ibid., 15.

5　Simon Locke, "'Fanboy' as a Revolutionary Category," *Participations* 9.2 (2012): 835–36.

6　Melissa A. Click, "'Rabid,' 'Obsessed,' and 'Frenzied': Understanding *Twilight* Fangirls and the Gendered Politics of Fandom," *Flow*, December 18, 2009, http://www.flowjournal.org.

7　During the 1985 season in which this sketch aired, seventeen of *SNL*'s nineteen staff writers were men. It is also worth noting that this was not the show's first foray into pathologized representations of geek culture. "The Nerds," a recurring sketch that first aired in 1978 and featured Bill Murray and Gilda Radner, may have featured a geeky female character, but it did not frame either as a media fan.

8　Jenkins, *Textual Poachers*, 15.

9　"Dr. Girlfriend" is a reference to a character on the cult Cartoon Network Adult Swim series *The Venture Bros.* (2003–present), a satirical homage to Hanna-Barbera's 1960s animated series *Jonny Quest*. Dr. Girlfriend is costumed in the retro style of Jacqueline Kennedy and voiced by the male cowriter of the show, Doc Hammer, and the clash between her hyperfeminine aesthetic and decidedly masculine aural presence has made her one of the show's most popular characters, and a common character for fangirls to cosplay at SDCC.

10　Hills, "Negative Fan Stereotypes," 40.

11　Ibid., 45.

12　Joli Jensen, "Fandom as Pathology: The Consequences of Characterization," in Lisa A. Lewis (ed.), *The Adoring Audience: Fan Culture and Popular Media* (New York: Routledge, 1992), 21.

13　Ibid., 14.

14　Ibid.

15　Henry Jenkins, Sam Ford, and Joshua Green, *Spreadable Media: Creating Value and Meaning in a Networked Culture* (New York: NYU Press, 2013), 49.

16　Jensen, "Fandom as Pathology," 14.

17 Matt Hills, "'Twilight' Fans Represented in Commercial Paratexts and Inter-Fandoms: Resisting and Repurposing Negative Fan Stereotypes," in Anne Morey (ed.), *Genre, Reception, and Adaptation in the "Twilight" Series* (Burlington, VT: Ashgate, 2012), 120.

18 Jensen, "Fandom as Pathology," 14.

19 Ibid., 13.

20 Gray, Sandvoss, and Harrington et al., "Introduction," 4.

21 Busse, "Geek Hierarchies," 81.

22 Derek Johnson, "Fan-tagonism: Factions, Institutions, and Constitutive Hegemonies of Fandom," in Jonathan Gray, Cornel Sandvoss, and C. Lee Harrington (eds.), *Fandom: Identities and Communities in a Mediated World* (New York: NYU Press, 2007), 294–95.

23 For a small selection of contemporary work on fan representation, see: Lucy Bennett and Paul Booth (eds.), *Seeing Fans: Representations of Fandom in Media and Popular Culture* (New York: Bloomsbury, 2016); Booth, *Playing Fans*, 75–100; Suzanne Scott, "Modeling the Marvel Everyfan: Coulson and/as Transmedia Fan Culture," *Palabra Clave* 24.4 (2017): 1042–72.

24 Christine Quail, "Hip to Be Square: Nerds in Media Culture," *Flow*, February 7, 2009, http://flowtv.org.

25 Lori Kendall, "Nerd Nation: Images of Nerds in US Popular Culture," *International Journal of Cultural Studies* 2.2 (1999): 264.

26 Some examples include Andy in *The 40-Year-Old Virgin* (2005), Seth Cohen on *The O.C.* (Fox, 2003–2007), Ben Wyatt on *Parks and Recreation* (NBC, 2009–2015), Windows in *Fanboys* (2009), and all of the male protagonists on *The Big Bang Theory* (CBS, 2007–present).

27 Some examples include the title characters of NBC's *Chuck* (2007–2012) and Bryan Lee O'Malley's graphic novel series *Scott Pilgrim vs. the World* and its 2010 film adaptation, as well as Josh Futterman in *Future Man* (Hulu, 2017–present).

28 See: Hiro Nakamura of NBC's *Heroes* (2006–2010) or Dave Lizewski in the 2010 film *Kick-Ass*, based on Mark Millar's comic book series. A police procedural variant on this character archetype uses fannish knowledge to solve crimes, which is narratively coded as a "superpower" in its own right. Some examples include "psychic detective" Shaun and his sidekick Gus on *Psych* (USA, 2006–2014), the titular mystery author/detective on *Castle* (ABC, 2009–2016), and Sgt. Terry Jeffords on *Brooklyn 99* (2013–present).

29 Sherrie A. Inness, "Introduction: Who Remembers Sabrina? Intelligence, Gender, and the Media," in Sherrie A. Inness (ed.), *Geek Chic: Smart Women in Popular Culture* (New York: Palgrave Macmillan, 2007), 4.

30 For one example, see: Richard Butsch, "Five Decades and Three Hundred Sitcoms about Class and Gender," in Gary R. Edgerton and Brian G. Rose (eds.), *Thinking outside the Box: A Contemporary Television Genre Reader* (Lexington: University of Kentucky Press, 2005), 111–35.

31 Theresa Jusino, "Denver Comic Con's All-Male 'Women in Comics' Panel Causes Concern among Comics Fans," *Mary Sue*, May 27, 2015, http://www.themarysue .com.

32 Kristina Busse, "Beyond Mary Sue: Fan Representation and the Complex Negotiation of Gendered Identity," in Lucy Bennett and Paul Booth (eds.), *Seeing Fans: Representations of Fandom in Media and Popular Culture* (New York: Bloomsbury, 2016), 159.

33 Ibid., n.p.

34 Liz Lemon on *30 Rock* (NBC, 2006–2013) would be one example of this archetypal depiction of fangirls.

35 See, for example: Tina Belcher on *Bob's Burgers* (2011–present), or the protagonist of Rainbow Rowell's novel *Fangirl* (2013), Cath.

36 For further discussions of Becky and the disciplinary function of gendered fan representations, see: Laura E. Felschow, "'Hey, check it out, there's actually fans': (Dis)empowerment and (Mis)representation of Cult Fandom in *Supernatural*," *Transformative Works and Cultures* 4 (2010), http://journal .transformativeworks.org; Judith May Fathallah, "Becky Is My Hero: The Power of Laughter and Disruption in *Supernatural*," *Transformative Works and Cultures* 5 (2010), http://journal.transformativeworks.org; Melissa Gray, "From Canon to Fanon and Back Again: The Epic Journey of *Supernatural* and Its Fans," *Transformative Works and Cultures* 4 (2010), http://dx.doi.org/10.3983/twc.2010.0146.

37 Catherine Tosenberger, "Love! Valor! *Supernatural*!" *Transformative Works and Cultures* 4 (2010), http://journal.transformativeworks.org.

38 "The Geek Shall Inherit the Earth," *Time.com*, September 25, 2005, http://www .time.com.

39 "Movies: Boys Who Like Toys," *Time.com*, April 19, 2007, http://www.time.com.

40 Adam B. Vary, "The Geek Was King: *Transformers*, Michael Cera, and Comic-Con Are Only Some of the Reasons Why Nerds Ruled This Year," *Entertainment Weekly*, December 21, 2007, http://www.ew.com.

41 "The Geek Shall Inherit the Earth."

42 Chris Nashawaty, "The Dark Knight: *Batman*'s Big Score," *Entertainment Weekly*, July 24, 2008, http://www.ew.com.

43 Ibid.

44 Radway, *Reading the Romance*, 18.

45 Scott Brown, "Scott Brown Rallies America's Nerds to Embrace Their Rise to Power," *Wired*, April 21, 2008, http://www.wired.com.

46 Noam Cohen, "We're All Nerds Now," *New York Times*, September 13, 2014, https://www.nytimes.com.

47 S. T. Vanairsdale, "Beyond Comic-Con: The Rise of the Modern Geek in All of Us," *Esquire*, July 29, 2009, http://www.esquire.com.

48 Patton Oswalt, "Wake Up, Geek Culture: Time to Die," *Wired*, December 27, 2010, http://www.wired.com.

49 Ibid.

50 Scott Mendelson, "Hollywood Doesn't Care about 'Fanboy' Approval," *Forbes*, May 26, 2014, https://www.forbes.com.

51 Alexander Abad-Santos, "How the Nerds Lost Comic-Con," *Atlantic*, July 19, 2013, https://www.theatlantic.com.

52 Joanna Robinson, "Have Fans Finally Won the War for Comic-Con?" *Vanity Fair*, July 20, 2017, https://www.vanityfair.com.

53 For more context on the anti-*Twilight* protests at SDCC 2009, see: Analee Newitz, "Female Fans Prepare to Trample Men at Comic-Con," *io9*, July 10, 2009, https://io9.gizmodo.com.

54 Abad-Santos, "How the Nerds Lost Comic-Con."

55 "The Girl's Guide to Comic-Con 2009," *Los Angeles Times*, http://www.latimes.com.

56 Graeme McMillan, "Introducing the New Face of Fandom: Women," *Time*, 2012, http://entertainment.time.com.

57 Eliana Dockterman, "The Rise of Fangirls at Comic-Con," *Time*, July 25, 2014, http://time.com.

58 Ibid.

59 Jeff Jensen, "TV (Relation)shippers: Just Do It!" *Entertainment Weekly*, February 10, 2012, http://ew.com.

60 Ibid.

61 Ibid.

62 Tom Lowry and Ronald Grover, "Disney's Marvel Deal and the Pursuit of Boys," *Businessweek.com*, September 10, 2009, http://www.businessweek.com.

63 Steven Zeitchik, "Analysis: Disney-Marvel Deal Brings Changes," *Adweek.com*, September 1, 2009, http://www.adweek.com.

64 Jenkins et al., *Spreadable Media*, 129.

65 Teresa Jusino, "Let the World Know #WeWantWidow! Support Today's Black Widow Flash Mob!" *Mary Sue*, June 6, 2015 https://www.themarysue.com.

66 Dani Di Placido, "Nerd Culture Is Fighting a Losing Battle against Reality," *Forbes*, August 3, 2016, https://www.forbes.com.

67 Laurie Penny, "On Nerd Entitlement," *New Statesman*, December 29, 2014, http://www.newstatesman.com.

68 Jesse Hassenger, "*Ghostbusters*, *Frozen*, and the Strange Entitlement of Fan Culture," *A.V. Club*, May 25, 2016, http://www.avclub.com.

69 Devin Faraci, "Fandom Is Broken," *Birth. Movies. Death*, May 30, 2016, http://birthmoviesdeath.com.

70 Adam Epstein, "Internet Fandom Is Running Hollywood," *Quartzy*, April 15, 2018, https://quartzy.qz.com.

71 Brent Lang, "Birth. Movies. Death Editor-in-Chief Devin Faraci Steps Down after Sexual Assault Allegations Surface," *Variety*, October 11, 2016, http://variety.com.

72 For a small selection of the media coverage of the *Rick and Morty* Szechuan sauce debacle as emblematic of "toxic" or "entitled" fan culture, see: Aja Romano, "What *Rick and Morty* Fans' Meltdown over McDonald's Szechuan Sauce Says about

Geek Culture," *Vox,* October 10, 2017, https://www.vox.com; Cameron Williams, "The Rise of Toxic Fandom: Why People Are Ruining the Pop Culture They Love," *Junkee,* October 13, 2017, http://junkee.com.

73 For articles addressing *Rick and Morty* fans' harassment of female writers, and its links to the show's "toxic" fan culture more generally, see: Julia Alexander, "*Rick and Morty*'s Toxicity Is Our Unescapable Story of 2017," *Polygon,* December 26, 2017, https://www.polygon.com; Katie Fustich, "Inside the Toxic, 'Intellectually Superior' World of Facebook's 'Rick and Morty' Fans," *Medium,* January 5, 2018, https://medium.com.

74 Charles Pulliam-Moore, "Fandom Isn't 'Broken'—It's Just Not Only for White Dudes Anymore," *Splinter,* June 3, 2016, http://fusion.net; Sam Barsanti, "Dan Harmon Is Pissed at *Rick and Morty* Fans for Harassing Female Writers," *A.V. Club,* September 21, 2017, https://www.avclub.com.

75 Ibid.

76 Aja Romano, "About Our 'Broken' Fan Culture," June 2, 2016, http://bookshop .tumblr.com/post/145327373853.

77 Ibid.

78 Ibid.

79 Sara Ahmed, *Living a Feminist Life* (Durham, NC: Duke University Press, 2017), 252.

80 Zina Hutton, "Fandom Is Supposed to Be Fun," *Stich's Mix Media,* November 28, 2017, https://stitchmediamix.com.

81 Ahmed, *Living a Feminist Life*, 141.

CHAPTER 3. INTERROGATING THE FAKE GEEK GIRL

1 For some examples, see: Kirk Hamilton, "The Fake Threat of Fake Geek Girls," *Kotaku,* March 27, 2012, http://kotaku.com; Susana Polo, "On the 'Fake Geek Girl,'" *Mary Sue,* March 27, 2012, http://www.themarysue.com.

2 Jesse Emspak, "An Open Letter to Nerd Culture: Wolverine as Toxic Masculinity," *Mary Sue,* May 17, 2016, http://www.themarysue.com.

3 Lori Kendall, *Hanging Out in the Virtual Pub: Masculinities and Relationships Online* (Berkeley: University of California Press, 2002), 100.

4 Ibid., 107.

5 Adrienne Massanari, "#Gamergate and the Fappening: How Reddit's Algorithm, Governance, and Culture Support Toxic Technocultures," *New Media & Society* (2015): 2.

6 Ibid.

7 Ibid., 5.

8 Kendall, *Hanging Out in the Virtual Pub,* 94.

9 Frank S. Pittman, *Man Enough: Fathers, Sons, and the Search for Masculinity* (New York: Perigree, 1993), 106–7.

10 Timothy Nonn, "Renewal as Retreat: The Battle for Men's Souls," in Michael S. Kimmel (ed.), *The Politics of Manhood: Profeminist Men Respond to the*

Mythopoetic Men's Movement (and the Mythopoetic Leaders Answer) (Philadelphia: Temple University Press, 1995), 175.

11 Shepherd Bliss, "Mythopoetic Men's Movements," in Michael S. Kimmel (ed.), *The Politics of Manhood: Profeminist Men Respond to the Mythopoetic Men's Movement (and the Mythopoetic Leaders Answer)* (Philadelphia: Temple University Press, 1995), 302.

12 Alastair Bonnett, "The New Primitives: Identity, Landscape, and Cultural Appropriation in the Mythopoetic Men's Movement," *Antipode* (1996): 277.

13 Kendall, "Nerd Nation," 261.

14 Bonnett, "The New Primitives," 279.

15 Kendall, "Nerd Nation," 265.

16 Michael S. Kimmel, "Afterword," in Michael S. Kimmel (ed.), *The Politics of Manhood: Profeminist Men Respond to the Mythopoetic Men's Movement (and the Mythopoetic Leaders Answer)* (Philadelphia: Temple University Press, 1995), 367.

17 Bonnett "The New Primitives," 277.

18 Terry A. Kupers, "Toxic Masculinity as a Barrier to Mental Health Treatment in Prison," *Journal of Clinical Psychology* 61.6 (2005): 716–17.

19 Massanari, "#Gamergate and the Fappening," 5.

20 Ibid.

21 Jenkins, *Textual Poachers*, 26.

22 Jenkins et al., *Spreadable Media*, 2.

23 Ibid.

24 Jenkins, "*Star Trek* Rerun, Reread, Rewritten," 477.

25 Jenkins et al., *Spreadable Media*, 4.

26 Paul Booth in Louisa Stein (moderator), "Online Roundtable on *Spreadable Media*," 155–56.

27 Henry Jenkins in ibid., 175.

28 Ibid., 165.

29 Jenkins et al., *Spreadable Media*, 21.

30 Ibid., 17.

31 Benjamin Woo, "Nerds, Geeks, Gamers, and Fans: Doing Subculture on the Edge of the Mainstream," in Alexander Dhoest, Steven Malliet, Barbara Segaert, and Jacques Haers (eds.), *The Borders of Subculture: Resistance and the Mainstream* (New York: Routledge, 2015), 18.

32 Ibid. The concept of "winning space" quoted here originated in John Clarke, "The Skinheads and the Magical Recovery of Community," in Stuart Hall and Tony Jefferson (eds.), *Resistance through Rituals: Youth Subcultures in Postwar Britain* (New York: Routledge, 2006), 80–83.

33 Jenkins et al., *Spreadable Media*, 293.

34 It is also entirely possible that some memetic examples of spreadable misogyny are created by subcultural trolls taking delight in sowing discord within geek culture, rather than disgruntled fans.

35 Whitney Phillips, *This Is Why We Can't Have Nice Things: Mapping the Relationship between Online Trolling and Mainstream Culture* (Cambridge: MIT Press, 2015), 29.

36 Ibid., 124.

37 Ibid., 42.

38 Ibid., 145.

39 Ibid., 140.

40 Moya Bailey, "More on the Origin of Misogynoir," *Moyazb*, April 27, 2014, http://moyazb.tumblr.com/post/84048113369/more-on-the-origin-of-misogynoir.

41 For media coverage of these controversies, see: Simi Shakeri, "Television Has a 'Bury Your Gays,' Queerbaiting, and LGBTQ Representation Problem," *Huffington Post*, June 30, 2017, http://www.huffingtonpost.ca; Emma Dibdin, "TV Writers Need to Stop Killing Off Their Gay Characters," *Marie Claire*, August 9, 2017, http://www.marieclaire.com.

42 "The Twitter Rules," https://support.twitter.com/articles/18311.

43 For stories about how police fail to response to digital harassment, see: Adrienne Lafrance, "When Will the Internet Be Safe for Women?" *Atlantic*, May 20, 2016, http://www.theatlantic.com; Anna Merlan, "The Cops Don't Care about Violent Online Threats: What Do We Do Now?" *Jezebel*, January 29, 2015, http://jezebel.com.

44 Amanda Hess, "A Former FBI Agent on Why It's So Hard to Prosecute Gamergate Trolls," *Slate*, October 17, 2014, http://www.slate.com.

45 Jessica Sheffield and Elyse Merlo, "Biting Back: *Twilight* Anti-Fandom and the Rhetoric of Superiority," in Melissa A. Click, Jennifer Stevens Aubrey, and Elizabeth Behm-Morawitz (eds.), *Bitten by Twilight: Youth Culture, Media, and the Vampire Franchise* (New York: Peter Lang, 2010), 207–22.

46 Victoria K. Gosling, "Girls Allowed? The Marginalization of Female Sports Fans," in Jonathan Gray, Cornel Sandvoss, and C. Lee Harrington (eds.), *Fandom: Identities and Communities in a Mediated World* (New York: NYU Press, 2007), 250–60.

47 Suzanne Scott, "Fangirls in Refrigerators: The Politics of (In)visibility in Comic Book Culture," *Transformative Works and Cultures* no. 13 (2013), https://doi.org/10.3983/twc.2013.0460.

48 Jonathan Gray, "New Audiences, New Textualities: Anti-Fans and Non-Fans," *International Journal of Cultural Studies* 6.1 (March 2003): 64–81.

49 Ibid., 74.

50 Joseph Reagle, "Geek Policing: Fake Geek Girls and Contested Attention," *International Journal of Communication* 9 (2015): 2866.

51 Gray, "New Audiences, New Textualities," 65.

52 Vivi Theodoropoulou, "The Anti-Fan within the Fan: Awe and Envy in Sports Fandom," in Jonathan Gray, Cornel Sandvoss, and C. Lee Harrington (eds.), *Fandom: Identities and Communities in a Mediated World* (New York: NYU Press, 2007), 325.

53 Hills, "Negative Fan Stereotypes," 45.

54 Jessica Bagnall, "Nerd Girls Are Real Nerds Too! (and Why This Meme Sucks),"
    Feminspire, January 2, 2014, http://feminspire.com.

55 Angela McRobbie and Jenny Garber, "Girls and Subcultures: An Exploration," in
    Stuart Hall and Tony Jefferson (eds.), *Resistance through Rituals: Youth Subcultures
    in Post-war Britain* (New York: Routledge, 1993), 211.

56 Ibid., 212.

57 Ibid., 211.

58 Ibid.

59 Ibid., 212.

60 Busse, "Geek Hierarchies," 73–74.

61 Ibid., 84.

62 Ibid., 80.

63 Patrick Davison, "The Language of Internet Memes," in Michael Mandiberg (ed.),
    The Social Media Reader (New York: NYU Press, 2012), 122.

64 Limor Shifman, *Memes in Digital Culture* (Cambridge: MIT Press, 2014), 15.

65 Jacqueline Ryan Vickery, "The Curious Case of Confession Bear: The Reappro-
    priation of Online Macro-image Memes," *Information, Communication & Society*
    (2013): 3.

66 Leslie A. Hahner, "The Riot Kiss: Framing Memes as Visual Argument," *Argumen-
    tation and Advocacy* 49 (Winter 2013): 156.

67 Ryan M. Milner, "Hacking the Social: Internet Memes, Identity Antagonism, and
    the Logic of Lulz," *Fibreculture Journal* no. 22 (2013), http://twentytwo.fibrecul
    turejournal.org.

68 Phillips, *This Is Why We Can't Have Nice Things*, 141.

69 Ibid., 143.

70 Jenkins et al., *Spreadable Media*, 251.

71 Gray, "New Audiences, New Textualities," 75.

72 Mel Stanfill, "'They're losers, but I know better': Intra-Fandom Stereotyping and
    the Normalization of the Fan Subject," *Critical Studies in Media Communication*
    (2013): 12.

73 Vickery, "Curious Case," 2.

74 Hills, "*Twilight* Fans," 123.

75 Joanne Hollows, "The Masculinity of Cult," in Mark Jancovich, Antonio Lázaro
    Reboll, Julian Stringer, and Andy Williams (eds.), *Defining Cult Movies: The Cul-
    tural Politics of Oppositional Taste* (Manchester, UK: Manchester University Press,
    2003), 37–38.

76 Benjamin Nugent, *American Nerd: The Story of My People* (New York: Scribner,
    2008), 6.

77 This individual is referred to as Jay Edidin here but professionally published
    under the name Rachel Edidin before coming out as transgender.

78 Rachel Edidin, "Idiot Nerd Girl Has a Posse: Taking Back the Meme," *Feminspire*,
    accessed December 10, 2013, http://feminspire.com.

79 Jenna Salume, "FGG," *Tumblr,* November 20, 2012, http://newageamazon.tumblr
   .com/post/36138776840/oxboxer-i-know-why-everyones-so-scared-of-fake.

80 Sailorswayze, "AM I RIGHT LADIES," *Sailorswayze.tumblr.com,* http://sailor
   swayze.tumblr.com/post/35678126959/am-i-right-ladies.

81 The Doubleclicks, "Be in Our Geek Girl Music Video!" *Doubleclicks,* June 26, 2013,
   http://www.thedoubleclicks.com.

82 *Dear Teen Me* (2012), a book of letters written by notable Young Adult authors
   to their teenage selves, was promoted through a series of book trailers.
   These video trailers, structured around themes like "Be Yourself" and "Love
   Yourself," featured the book's authors holding up handwritten signs of
   encouragement.

83 The institutionalized sexism of fan conventions has been a growing topic of
   debate over the past several years. Events like the 2009 Electronic Arts "Sin to
   Win" contest, which encouraged Comic-Con attendees to "commit acts of lust"
   with the "booth babes"/models working the convention, or the sexual harassment
   of author Genevieve Valentine at Readercon 23 in 2012, have resulted in female
   fans, and cosplayers in particular, mobilizing grassroots campaigns to ensure
   the physical and emotional well-being of female attendees. CONsent, initiated at
   Wondercon in 2013, is one such campaign that attempts to draw attention to the
   ways in which female cosplayers are objectified and harassed.

84 Doreen Massey, *Space, Place, and Gender* (Minneapolis: University of Minnesota
   Press, 1994), 186.

85 Susan Faludi, *Backlash: The Undeclared War against American Women* (New York:
   Crown, 1991), 12.

86 Ibid.

87 Ibid.

88 Ibid.

89 McRobbie and Garber, "Girls and Subcultures," 216.

90 Horkheimer and Adorno, "The Culture Industry," 106.

CHAPTER 4. TERMS AND CONDITIONS

 1 Johnson, "Fan-tagonism," 295.

 2 John Fiske, "The Cultural Economy of Fandom," in Lisa A. Lewis (ed.), *The Adoring Audience: Fan Culture and Popular Media* (New York: Routledge, 1992), 38.

 3 Matt Hills, "*Torchwood*'s Trans-transmedia: Media Tie-ins and Brand 'Fanagement,'" *Participations* 9.2 (2012): 410.

 4 Ibid., 425.

 5 Louisa Ellen Stein, "'Word of Mouth on Steroids': Hailing the Millennial Media
   Fan," in M. Kackman et al. (eds.), *Flow TV: Television in the Age of Media Convergence* (London: Routledge, 2011), 130.

 6 Busse, "Geek Hierarchies," 78.

 7 Fiske, "Cultural Economy of Fandom," 47.

 8 Jenkins, "*Star Trek* Rerun, Reread, Rewritten," 87.

9 Katherine Larsen and Lynn Zubernis, *Fandom at the Crossroads* (Newcastle-upon-Tyne, UK: Cambridge Scholars, 2012), 143–74.

10 Philip M. Napoli, *Audience Evolution: New Technologies and the Transformation of Media Audiences* (New York: Columbia University Press, 2011), 90–100.

11 Jenkins, *Convergence Culture*, 134.

12 Ibid.

13 Ibid.

14 Ibid., 134.

15 Ibid., 169.

16 See: Scott, "Authorized Resistance."

17 Kristina Busse, "Podcasts and the Fan Experience of Disseminated Media Commentary" (paper presented at Flow Conference, Austin, TX, October 2006), http://www.kristinabusse.com.

18 Roberta Pearson, "Participation or Totalization: Fans and Transmedia Storytelling" (paper presented at the DigiCult: Television and the Public Sphere conference, Paris, France, October 23, 2008).

19 Joanna Russ, *How to Suppress Women's Writing* (Austin: University of Texas Press, 1983), 6.

20 Coppa and Tushnet, "How to Suppress Women's Remix," 135.

21 Ibid., 132–43.

22 Ibid., 136.

23 Judith Long Laws, "The Psychology of Tokenism: An Analysis," *Sex Roles* 1.1 (1975): 51.

24 Adorno, "Culture Industry Reconsidered," 98.

25 *Chad Vader* was a fan-produced web series that debuted in 2006. Created by and starring *Star Wars* fans Aaron Yonda and Matt Sloan, the web series' parodic premise focused on Chad Vader's (Darth's underperforming younger brother) daily travails as the manager of a grocery store. "Closer," by contrast, was a Kirk/Spock slash video set to the Nine Inch Nails song, and aesthetically echoing the band's controversial music video.

26 Francesca Coppa, "Gender and Fan Culture (Wrapping Up, Part Four)," *Confessions of an Aca-Fan: The Official Weblog of Henry Jenkins,* November 28, 2007, http://henryjenkins.org/2007/11/gender_and_fan_culture_wrappin_2.html.

27 Tiziana Terranova, "Free Labor: Producing Culture for the Digital Economy," *Social Text* 18.2 (2000): 37.

28 Marc Andrejevic, *iSpy: Surveillance and Power in the Interactive Era* (Lawrence: University of Kansas Press, 2007), 158.

29 Bethan Jones, "Fan Exploitation, Kickstarter, and Veronica Mars," March 15, 2013, http://bethanvjones.wordpress.com/2013/03/15/fan-exploitation-kickstarter-and-veronica-mars.

30 Paul Booth, *Digital Fandom: New Media Studies* (New York: Peter Lang, 2010), 24.

31 Suzanne Scott, "Repackaging Fan Culture: The Regifting Economy of Ancillary Content Models," *Transformative Works and Cultures* no. 3 (2009), http://dx.doi.org/10.3983/twc.2009.0150.

32 Lewis Hyde, *The Gift: Imagination and the Erotic Life of Property* (New York: Vintage, 1983), 57.

33 Ibid., 70.

34 Scott, "Repackaging Fan Culture."

35 Hellekson, "A Fannish Field of Value," 113–18.

36 Ibid., 118.

37 Catherine Tosenberger, "Mature Poets Steal: Children's Literature and the Unpublishability of Fanfiction," *Children's Literature Association Quarterly* 39.1 (2014): 5.

38 For further fan-scholarly analyses of Fanlib, see: Cathy Cupitt, "Nothing but Net: When Cultures Collide," *Transformative Works and Cultures* no. 1 (2008), http://dx.doi.org/10.3983/twc.2008.0055; Henry Jenkins, "Transforming Fan Culture into User-Generated Content: The Case of FanLib," *Confessions of an Aca-Fan: The Official Weblog of Henry Jenkins*, May 22, 2007, http://henryjenkins.org/blog/2007/05/transforming_fan_culture_into.html.

39 "Kindle Worlds," https://www.amazon.com.

40 Gavia Baker-Whitelaw, "The Problem with Amazon's New Fanfiction Platform, Kindle Worlds," *Daily Dot*, May 22, 2013, https://www.dailydot.

41 "G.I. Joe Content Guidelines," *Amazon*, https://kindleworlds.amazon.com.

42 Katherine E. Morrissey, "Fan/dom: People, Practices, and Networks," *Transformative Works and Cultures* no. 14 (2013), http://dx.doi.org/10.3983/twc.2013.0532.

43 Constance Grady, "Why We're Terrified of Fanfiction," *Vox*, June 2, 2016, https://www.vox.com.

44 Mel Stanfill, "The Fan Fiction Gold Rush, Generational Turnover, and the Battle for Fandom's Soul," in Melissa A. Click and Suzanne Scott (eds.), *The Routledge Companion to Media Fandom* (New York: Routledge, 2018), 77.

45 Ibid., 83.

46 Francesca Coppa, "Women, *Star Trek*, and the Early Development of Fannish Vidding," *Transformative Works and Cultures* 1 (2008), http://journal.transformativeworks.org.

47 Alexis Lothian, "Living in a Den of Thieves: Fan Video and Digital Challenges to Ownership," *Cinema Journal* 48.4 (2009): 136.

48 Ibid., 132.

49 "How Content ID Works," *YouTube*, https://support.google.com.

50 Lesley Autumn Willard, "From Co-optation to Commission: A Diachronic Perspective on the Development of Fannish Literacy through Teen Wolf's Tumblr Promotional Campaigns," *Transformative Works and Cultures* 25 (2017), http://dx.doi.org/10.3983/twc.2017.894.

51 Julie Levin Russo, "User-Penetrated Content: Fan Video in the Age of Convergence," *Cinema Journal* 48.4 (2009): 125.

52 Ibid., 127.

53 Ibid., 130.

54 Ibid.

55 Marc Graser, "Disney, Marvel Offer Do-It-Yourself 'Avengers' Vids," *Variety*, April 25, 2012, http://variety.com.

56 Ibid.

57 For a history of fan filmmaking, see: Clive Young, *Homemade Hollywood: Fans behind the Camera* (New York: Bloomsbury, 2008).

58 Eriq Gardner, "CBS, Paramount Settle Lawsuit over 'Star Trek' Fan Film," *Hollywood Reporter*, January 20, 2017, https://www.hollywoodreporter.com.

59 "Fan Films," *Startrek.com*, http://www.startrek.com.

60 CBS and Paramount, "Star Trek Fan Film Guidelines Announced," *Startrek.com*, June 23, 2016, http://www.startrek.com.

61 "Fan Films."

62 Ibid.

63 Gardner, "CBS, Paramount Settle Lawsuit."

64 Eriq Gardner, "'Star Trek' Fan Film Dispute Goes to Jury Trial in Big Ruling," *Hollywood Reporter*, January 4, 2017, https://www.hollywoodreporter.com.

65 Patricia Aufderheide and Peter Jaszi, *Reclaiming Fair Use: How to Put Balance Back in Copyright* (Chicago: University of Chicago Press, 2011), 18.

66 Rebecca Tushnet, "'I'm a lawyer, not an ethnographer, Jim': Textual Poachers and Fair Use," *Journal of Fandom Studies* 2.1 (2014): 24.

67 Horkheimer and Adorno, "The Culture Industry," 56.

68 Fiske, "Cultural Economy of Fandom," 37.

69 Matt Hills, "Fiske's 'Textual Productivity' and Digital Fandom: Web 2.0 Democratization versus Fan Distinction?" *Participations* 10.1 (2013): 136.

70 Fiske, "Cultural Economy of Fandom," 39.

71 Fans and media industries alike have also used Twitter and other predominantly "enunciative" platforms to produce transformative fan texts. This often comes in the form of each "character" having a Twitter account to collectively produce an interactive narrative, or to respond in-character to the events occurring within the media text. For a discussion of these forms of enunciative, interactive world-building, see: Megan M. Wood and Linda Baughman, "*Glee* Fandom and Twitter: Something New, or More of the Same Old Thing?" *Communication Studies* 63.3 (2012): 328–44; Inger–Lise Kalviknes Bore and Jonathan Hickman, "Studying Fan Activities on Twitter: Reflections on Methodological Issues Emerging from a Case Study on *The West Wing* Fandom," *First Monday* 18.9 (2013), https://journals.uic.edu; Julie Levin Russo, "Twansformative? The Future of Fandom on Twitter," August 23, 2010, http://j-l-r.org; Henry Jenkins, "Going 'Mad': Creating Fan Fiction 140 Characters at a Time," *Confessions of an Aca-Fan: The Official Weblog of Henry Jenkins*, January 26, 2009, http://henryjenkins.org/blog/2009/01/mad_men_twitter_and_the_future_1.html.

72 "Nielsen Launches 'Nielsen Twitter TV Ratings," *Nielsen*, October 7, 2013, http://www.nielsen.com.

73 Ian Ang, *Desperately Seeking the Audience* (New York: Routledge, 2016), 15.

74 Ibid.

75 Steven Schirra, Huan Sun, and Frank Bentley, "Together Alone: Motivations for Live-Tweeting a Television Series," *Proceedings of the SIGCHI Conference on Human Factors in Computing Systems (New York: ACM, 2014)*: 2245–46.

76 Stephen Harrington, Tim Highfield, and Axel Bruns, "More Than a Backchannel: Twitter and Television," *Participations* 10.1 (2013): 406–7.

77 Brian Steinberg, "Cable TV Using Latenight Talk Shows to Offset Pricey Hit Series," *Variety*, August 15, 2013, http://variety.com.

78 Ibid.

79 Ruth Deller, "Twittering On: Audience Research and Participation using Twitter," *Participations* 8.1 (2011), http://www.participations.org.

80 Jason Mittell, "Sites of Participation: Wiki Fandom and the Case of Lostpedia," *Transformative Works and Cultures* no. 3 (2009), http://dx.doi.org/10.3983/twc .2009.0118.

81 Ibid.

82 Steven Levy, *Hackers: Heroes of the Computer Revolution*, 25th anniversary ed. (Sebastapol, CA: O'Reilly Media, 2010), 8.

83 Melanie E. S. Kohnen, "Fannish Affect, 'Quality Fandom,' and Transmedia Story-telling Campaigns," in Melissa A. Click and Suzanne Scott (eds.), *The Routledge Companion to Media Fandom* (New York: Routledge, 2018), 337–46.

84 Ibid., 338.

85 Greg Braxton, "Chris Hardwick's 'Talking Dead' Walks off with Zombie Fans," *Los Angeles Times*, March 30, 2013, http://articles.latimes.com.

86 Kristen J. Warner, "ABC's *Scandal* and Black Women's Fandom," in Elana Levine (ed.), *Cupcakes, Pinterest, and Ladyporn: Feminized Popular Culture in the Early Twenty-First Century* (Champaign: University of Illinois Press, 2015), 34.

87 Kristen J. Warner, "If Loving Olitz Is Wrong, I Don't Wanna Be Right," *Black Scholar: Journal of Black Studies and Research* 45.1 (2015): 17.

88 "*Talking Dead*—Yvette Nicole Brown's Reaction to Richonne," *YouTube*, February 22, 2016, https://www.youtube.com.

89 Dayna Chatman, "Black Twitter and the Politics of Viewing *Scandal*," in Jonathan Gray, Cornel Sandvoss, and C. Lee Harrington (eds.), *Fandom: Identities and Communities in a Mediated World*, 2nd ed. (New York: NYU Press, 2017), 300.

90 Dominique Deirdre Johnson, "Misogynoir and Antiblack Racism: What *The Walking Dead* Teaches Us about the Limits of Speculative Fiction Fandom," *Journal of Fandom Studies* 3.3 (2015): 259–75.

91 "*Talking Dead* Ultimate Fan Search: Greg," *AMC.com*, http://www.amc.com.

92 "(Spoilers) *Talking Dead* Highlights: Season 7, Episode 1; Super Fans React to the Season 7 Premiere," *AMC.com*, http://www.amc.com.

93 "*Talking Dead*—Yvette Nicole Brown," *YouTube*, March 28, 2016, https://www .youtube.com.

94 Chloe Dykstra, "Rose-Colored Glasses: A Confession," *Medium*, June 14, 2018, http://medium.com/@skydart/.

95 Dominic Patten, "Yvette Nicole Brown Not 'Jockeying' to Replace 'Friend' Chris Hardwick Permanently after Taking Over 'TWD' SDCC Gig —Update," *Deadline Hollywood*, July 4, 2018, http://deadline.com.

96 Reid Nakamura, "'Talking Dead' Loses Female Executive Producer, 'Handful' of Staffers after Chris Hardwick's Return (Exclusive)," *The Wrap*, August 10, 2018, http://www.thewrap.com/.

97 Annemarie Navar-Gill, "From Strategic Retweets to Group Hangs: Writers' Room Twitter Accounts and the Productive Ecology of TV Social Media Fans," *Television & New Media* 19.5 (2017): 416.

98 Ibid., 3.

99 Fiske, "Cultural Economy of Fandom," 38.

100 Hills, "Fiske's 'Textual Productivity,'" 134.

101 Horkheimer and Adorno, "The Culture Industry," 54.

CHAPTER 5. ONE FANBOY TO RULE THEM ALL

1 Jenkins, *Textual Poachers*, 274–75.

2 Scott, "Repackaging Fan Culture."

3 Bertha Chin, "Sherlockology and Galactica.tv: Fan Sites as Gifts or Exploited Labor?" *Transformative Works and Cultures* 15 (2014), http://dx.doi.org/10.3983/twc.2014.0513.

4 Ibid.

5 Francesca Coppa, "A Brief History of Media Fandom," in Karen Hellekson and Kristina Busse (eds.), *Fan Fiction and Fan Communities in the Age of the Internet* (Jefferson, NC: McFarland, 2006), 43.

6 Karen Hellekson and Kristina Busse, "Introduction: Work in Progress," in Karen Hellekson and Kristina Busse (eds.), *Fan Fiction and Fan Communities in the Age of the Internet* (Jefferson, NC: McFarland, 2006), 11.

7 Catherine Driscoll, "One True Pairing: The Romance of Pornography and the Pornography of Romance," in Karen Hellekson and Kristina Busse (eds.), *Fan Fiction and Fan Communities in the Age of the Internet* (Jefferson, NC: McFarland, 2006), 93.

8 Penley, "Brownian Motion," 144.

9 Ivan Askwith, Britta Lundin, and Aja Romano, "Industry/Fan Relations: A Conversation," in Melissa A. Click and Suzanne Scott (eds.) *The Routledge Companion to Media Fandom* (New York: Routledge, 2018), 373.

10 For more on ecological approaches to the study of fan texts, see: Tisha Turk and Joshua Johnson, "Toward an Ecology of Vidding," *Transformative Works and Cultures* 9 (2012), http://dx.doi.org/10.3983/twc.2012.0326.

11 Constance Penley, *NASA/TREK: Popular Science and Sex in America* (London: Verso, 1997), 113.

12 Suzanne Scott, "'Cosplay is serious business': Gendering Material Fan Labor on Heroes of Cosplay," *Cinema Journal* 54.3 (2015): 149.

13 Ibid., 151.

14 Hellekson, "A Fannish Field of Value," 116.
15 Abigail De Kosnik, "Should Fan Fiction Be Free?" *Cinema Journal* 48.4 (2009): 124.
16 Karen Hellekson, "Making Use Of: The Gift, Commerce, and Fans," *Cinema Journal* 54.3 (2015): 127.
17 Abigail De Kosnik, "*Fifty Shades* and the Archive of Women's Culture," *Cinema Journal* 54.3 (2015): 124–25.
18 Lauren Berlant, *The Female Complaint: The Unfinished Business of Sentimentality in American Culture* (Durham, NC: Duke University Press, 2008), 16.
19 Kristina Busse, "Introduction: Fandom and Feminism," *Cinema Journal* 48.4 (2009): 106.
20 For some discussions of predigital producer/fan interactions, see: Henry Jenkins, "'Infinite Diversity in Infinite Combinations': Genre and Authorship in *Star Trek*," in John Tulloch and Henry Jenkins (eds.), *Science Fiction Audiences: Watching Doctor Who and Star Trek* (New York: Routledge, 1995); Henry Jenkins, "'Do you enjoy making the rest of us feel stupid?': Alt.tv.twinpeaks, the Trickster Author, and Viewer Mastery," in David Lavery (ed.), *Full of Secrets: Critical Approaches to Twin Peaks* (Detroit, MI: Wayne State University Press, 1995); Sam Ford, "Soap Operas and the History of Fan Discussion," *Transformative Works and Cultures* 1 (2008), http://journal.transformativeworks.org; Jonathan Gray, *Show Sold Separately: Promos, Spoilers, and Other Media Paratexts* (New York: NYU Press, 2010), 81–115.
21 Jenkins, *Textual Poachers*, 32.
22 For some discussions of digital producer/fan interactions, see: Larsen and Zubernis, *Fandom at the Crossroads*; Kristina Busse "Return of the Author: Ethos and Identity Politics," in Jonathan Gray and Derek Johnson (eds.), *A Companion to Media Authorship* (Malden, MA: Wiley-Blackwell, 2013), 48–68.
23 Alan Wexelblat, "An Auteur in the Age of the Internet: JMS, Babylon 5, and the Net," in Henry Jenkins, Tara McPherson, and Jane Shattuc (eds.), *Hop on Pop: The Politics and Pleasures of Popular Culture* (Durham, NC: Duke University Press, 2002), 209–26.
24 For discussions of authorial podcasts and textual authority, see: Derek Kompare, "More 'Moments of Television': Online Cult Television Authorship," in Michael Kackman, Marnie Binfield, Matthew Thomas Payne, Allison Perlman, and Bryan Sebok (eds.), *FlowTV: Television in the Age of Media Convergence* (New York: Routledge, 2011); Scott, "Authorized Resistance."
25 Jenkins, *Convergence Culture*, 169.
26 Jenna Kathryn Ballinger, "Fandom and the Fourth Wall," *Transformative Works and Cultures* no. 17 (2014), http://dx.doi.org/10.3983/twc.2014.0569.
27 Elizabeth Ellcessor, "Tweeting @feliciaday: Online Social Media, Convergence, and Subcultural Stardom," *Cinema Journal* 51.2 (2012): 47.
28 Richard Dyer, "*A Star Is Born* and the Construction of Authenticity," in Christine Gledhill (ed.), *Stardom: Industry of Desire* (New York: Routledge, 1991), 133.

29 Ellcessor, "Tweeting @feliciaday," 52.
30 "What Is Geek & Sundry?" *Geek & Sundry*, http://geekandsundry.com.
31 Ellcessor, "Tweeting @feliciaday," 53.
32 Louisa Stein, "#Bowdown to Your New God: Misha Collins and Decentered Authorship in the Digital Age," in Jonathan Gray and Derek Johnson (eds.), *A Companion to Media Authorship* (Malden, MA: Wiley-Blackwell, 2013), 415.
33 Ibid., 413.
34 Ibid.
35 Suzanne Scott, "The Powers That Squee: Orlando Jones and Intersectional Fan Studies," in Jonathan Gray, Cornel Sandvoss, and C. Lee Harrington (eds.), *Fandom: Identities and Communities in a Mediated World*, 2nd ed. (New York: NYU Press, 2017), 387–401.
36 Janet H. Murray, *Hamlet on the Holodeck: The Future of Narrative in Cyberspace* (New York: Free Press, 1997), 98–99.
37 Orlando Jones, "Has Teen Wolf Social Media Lost Its Edge?" *The Tumblr Experiment*, October 2013, http://theorlandojones.tumblr.com/post/64992821505/has-teen-wolf-social-media-lost-its-edge.
38 Orlando Jones, "I Am, Most Respectfully, Orlando Jones," *The Tumblr Experiment*, November 13, 2013, http://theorlandojones.tumblr.com/post/66894876679/i-am-most-respectfully-orlando-jones.
39 Orlando Jones, "The Fandom Menace," *Huffington Post*, November 6, 2013, http://www.huffingtonpost.com.
40 Lucy Bennett and Bertha Chin, "Exploring Fandom, Social Media, and Producer/Fan Interactions: An Interview with *Sleepy Hollow*'s Orlando Jones," *Transformative Works and Cultures* 17 (2014), http://journal.transformativeworks.org.
41 Alice E. Marwick and danah boyd, "I Tweet Honestly, I Tweet Passionately: Twitter Users, Context Collapse, and the Imagined Audience," *New Media & Society* 13.1 (2011): 128.
42 Ibid., 122.
43 Some fan scholars have taken issue with fan studies' embrace of Jones as a keynote speaker at predominantly academic events like Transforming Hollywood 2014 and the 2014 Fan Studies Network conference.
44 Amuseoffyre, *A Muse of Fyre*, September 29, 2013, http://amuseoffyre.tumblr.com/post/62626039410/orlando-jones-is-now-offering-threatening-to-prove.
45 Aja Romano, "Why Fans Are Outraged at Sherlock and Watson Reading Sexy Fanfic," *Daily Dot*, December 16, 2013, http://www.dailydot.com; Pope Alexander, "Graham Norton and Hugh Jackman Read McAvoy/Fassbender Slash," *Jezebel*, May 2, 2014, http://groupthink.jezebel.com.
46 For discussions of these gendered "fan proxy" characters, and fan responses to them, see: Bethan Jones, "Johnlocked: *Sherlock*, Slash Fiction, and the Shaming of Female Fans," *New Left Project*, February 18, 2014, http://www.newleftproject.org; Felschow, "'Hey, check it out.'"

47 The Organization for Transformative Works is a nonprofit that was founded by fans in 2007 to preserve and legally protect fanworks.

48 "Transcript for the Future of Fanworks Entertainment Industry Chat," *The Organization for Transformative Works*, March 29, 2014, http://transformativeworks.org.

49 Orlando Jones, Twitter Post, November 4, 2013, 10:30 p.m., https://twitter.com/theorlandojones/status/397611814520778752.

50 Michel de Certeau, *The Practice of Everyday Life* (Berkeley: University of California Press, 1988), 29–42.

51 Bennett and Chin, "Exploring Fandom."

52 Erving Goffman, *The Presentation of Self in Everyday Life* (Edinburgh: University of Edinburgh Social Sciences Research Centre, 1958), 87.

53 Orlando Jones, "Foreword: Orlando the Fangirl," in Paul Booth and Lucy Bennett (eds.), *Seeing Fans: Representations of Fandom in Media and Popular Culture* (New York: Bloomsbury, 2016), xiv.

54 Matt Ealer, "Comic Hero Fanboys Make Terrible Comic Hero Movies," *Awl*, June 2011, https://www.theawl.com.

55 Scott, "Who's Steering the Mothership?" 44.

56 Roland Barthes, "The Death of the Author," in *Image-Music-Text*, trans. Stephen Heath (New York: Noonday Press, 1978), 148.

57 Jonathan Gray, *Show Sold Separately: Promos, Spoilers, and Other Media Paratexts* (New York: NYU Press, 2010), 112.

58 Michel Foucault, "What Is an Author?" in Paul Rabinow (ed.), *The Foucault Reader* (New York: Random House, 1984), 110.

59 Ibid., 120.

60 Scott, "Who's Steering the Mothership?" 44.

61 Melissa A. Click and Nettie Brock, "Marking the Line between Producers and Fans: Representations of Fannish-ness in *Doctor Who* and *Sherlock*," in Lucy Bennett and Paul Booth (eds.), *Seeing Fans: Representations of Fandom in Media and Popular Culture* (New York: Bloomsbury, 2016), 118.

62 For one example of these incidents, see: Click and Bock, "Marking the Line," 125.

63 Suzanne Scott, "Dawn of the Undead Author: Fanboy Auteurism and Zack Snyder's 'Vision,'" in Jonathan Gray and Derek Johnson (eds.), *A Companion to Media Authorship* (Malden, MA: Wiley-Blackwell, 2013), 442.

64 Ibid.

65 Ibid., 447–52.

66 Alex Pappademas, "Hollywood's Leading Geek," *New York Times*, March 18, 2011, http://www.nytimes.com.

67 Ibid.

68 Will Brooker, *Using the Force: Creativity, Community, and* Star Wars *Fans* (New York: Continuum, 2002), 3.

69 For a discussion of fans' "totemic nostalgia" and how it shaped their responses to the 2016 *Ghostbusters* reboot, see: William Proctor, "'Bitches ain't gonna hunt no

ghosts': Totemic Nostalgia, Toxic Fandom and the *Ghostbusters* Platonic," *Palabra Clave* 20.4 (2017): 1105–41.

70 Ellen Kirkpatrick, "Hero-Fans and Fanboy Auteurs: Reflections and Realities of Superhero Fans," in Lucy Bennett and Paul Booth (eds.), *Seeing Fans: Representations of Fandom in Media and Popular Culture* (New York: Bloomsbury, 2016), 134.

71 Hunter Hargraves, "(TV) Junkies in Need of an Intervention: On Addictive Spectatorship and Recovery Television," *Camera Obscura* 30.1 (2015): 78–79.

72 Matt Hills, "Sherlock's Epistemological Economy and the Value of 'Fan' Knowledge: How Producer-Fans Play the (Great) Game of Fandom," in Louisa Stein and Kristina Busse (eds.), *Sherlock and Transmedia Fandom* (Jefferson, NC: McFarland, 2012), 40.

73 Sophie Charlotte van de Goor, "'You must be new here': Reinforcing the Good Fan," *Participations* 2.2 (2015): 291.

74 Henry Jenkins, "The Guiding Spirit and the Powers That Be: A Response to Suzanne Scott," in Aaron Delwiche and Jennifer Jacobs Henderson (eds.), *The Participatory Cultures Handbook* (New York: Routledge, 2013), 58.

75 For more on how Andras makes space for marginalized fan discourses, see: Jacinta Yanders, "Earpers, Interactions, and Emotions: Wynonna Earp, 'the Best Fandom Ever,'" *Transformative Works and Cultures* 26 (2018), http://dx.doi .org/10.3983/twc.2018.1129.

76 Lynette Rice, "'The Big Bang Theory': Making a Bigger Bang," *Entertainment Weekly*, September 21, 2012, http://ew.com.

77 Ibid.

78 Derek Johnson, "Participation Is Magic: Collaboration, Authorial Legitimacy, and the Audience Function," in Jonathan Gray and Derek Johnson (eds.), *A Companion to Media Authorship* (Malden, MA: Wiley-Blackwell, 2013), 148.

79 Anne Gilbert, "What We Talk about When We Talk about Bronies," *Transformative Works and Cultures* 20 (2015), http://dx.doi.org/10.3983/twc.2015.0666.

80 Johnson, "Participation Is Magic," 147.

81 "Melissa Rosenberg—Jessica Jones," *International Cinematographers Guild Magazine*, January 7, 2016, http://www.icgmagazine.com.

82 Rosenberg, following Ava DuVernay's lead with *Queen Sugar*, committed to exclusively hiring female directors for *Jessica Jones*'s second season in 2018.

83 Borys Kit, "'Wonder Woman' Movie Finds a New Director (Exclusive)," *Hollywood Reporter*, April 15, 2015, http://www.hollywoodreporter.com.

84 Meredith Woerner, "The World Needs Wonder Woman: Director Patty Jenkins Explains Why," *Los Angeles Times*, May 30, 2017, http://www.latimes.com.

85 Charlotte Howell, "'Tricky' Connotations: Wonder Woman as DC's Brand Disruptor," *Cinema Journal* 55.1 (2015): 141–49.

86 Angie Han, "How Director Patty Jenkins Found Her Way to 'Wonder Woman,'" *Mashable*, June 1, 2017, http://mashable.com.

87 If, as I am contending, it might be easier for male creatives to present themselves as "fangirl auteurs," it is also entirely possible that they will be more easily

embraced as feminist fans and be able to capitalize on that identity in ways that female creatives cannot. This has certainly been the case for fanboy auteurs like Joss Whedon, whose work is associated with dynamic and nuanced female characters and whose self-brand is closely aligned with feminist politics and philanthropic endeavors. In August 2017, Whedon's ex-wife, Kai Cole, penned a blog post accusing Whedon of infidelity, suggesting that he had used his marriage as a "shield" to "maintain his superficial presentation [of] him as the lovable geek-feminist." Subsequently, leaked versions of a draft of a *Wonder Woman* film script penned by Whedon sparked further controversy, and he subsequently parted ways from a proposed *Batgirl* film project he was hired to helm in 2018. Whedon's departure was reportedly "a mutual one and reflects the studio's desire to seek more female directors—particularly on projects centered on female characters," and the project has since hired Christina Hodson to write the script. See: Kai Cole, "Joss Whedon Is a 'Hypocrite Preaching Feminist Ideals,' Ex-Wife Kai Cole Says (Guest Blog)," *Wrap*, August 20, 2017, https://www.thewrap.com; Dave McNary, "Joss Whedon Exits as 'Batgirl' Movie Director," *Variety*, February 22, 2018, http://variety.com.

88 Lori Morimoto, "*Hannibal*: Adaptation and Authorship in the Age of Fan Production," in Kavita Mudan Finn and E. J. Nielsen (eds.), *Becoming: Essays on NBC's Hannibal* (Syracuse, NY: Syracuse University Press, forthcoming).

89 Ibid.

90 Scott, "'Cosplay is serious business,'" 148.

91 Melanie Kohnen, 'The Power of Geek': Fandom as Gendered Commodity at Comic-Con," *Creative Industries Journal* 7.1 (2014): 75–78.

92 Benjamin Woo, "Alpha Nerds: Cultural Intermediaries in a Subcultural Scene," *European Journal of Cultural Studies* 15.5 (2012): 660.

93 Marc Graser, "Legendary Buys Felicia Day's Geek & Sundry," *Variety,* August 4, 2014, http://variety.com.

94 "Hot Topic, Inc. Announces Purchase of Assets of Her Universe, Proprietary Fangirl Brand," October 28, 2016, http://www.hottopic.com.

95 Borys Kit, "Legendary Entertainment Acquires Nerdist Industries," *Hollywood Reporter*, July 10, 2012, http://www.hollywoodreporter.com.

96 Suzanne Scott, "The Moral Economy of Crowdfunding and the Transformative Capacity of Fan-ancing," *New Media & Society* 17.2 (2015): 167–82.

97 Jordan Zakarin, "Black Girl Nerds Is Building a Geek Empire from the Outside," *SyfyWire*, September 12, 2017, http://www.syfy.com.

98 Broadnax also offers an intriguing case study of how marginalized fantrepreneurs might be held more accountable than their white and/or male counterparts for perceived transgressions, particularly when their actions most negatively impact the very fans and communities they claim to champion and represent. Broadnax, in partnership with Robert Butler, first presented the idea of Universal FanCon (a fan convention run by and for fans who have felt marginalized or have been actively harassed in mainstream fan convention spaces based on their race,

sexuality, ethnicity, ability, size, or some combination thereof) in 2016. Exactly
one week before the inaugural convention was scheduled to be held in Baltimore
in April 2018, an announcement was made via social media that the con had been
postponed until further notice. Broadnax released a statement distancing herself
from the organizers, but the damage to her reputation within the Universal Fan-
Con community had already been done. Many fans still question whether or how
Broadnax personally profited from the nearly fifty seven thousand dollars raised
via Kickstarter by attendees, and hold her responsible for the loss of personal
investment in travel costs. For an overview of the Universal FanCon debacle,
and Broadnax's role, see Clarkisha Kent, "It Be Your Own People: On Universal
FanCon and the Perversion of Community," *The Root*, April 24, 2018, https://www
.theroot.com.

99 Horace Newcomb and Paul M. Hirsch, "Television as a Cultural Forum," in
Horace Newcomb (ed.), *Television: The Critical View*, 6th ed. (New York: Oxford
University Press, 2000), 563.

100 Amanda Lotz, *The Television Will Be Revolutionized* (New York: NYU Press,
2007), 48.

101 Newcomb and Hirsch, "Television as a Cultural Forum," 564.

102 Kia Kokalitcheva, "How Chris Hardwick Turned His Frustration into a Media
Empire," *Fortune Magazine*, February 18, 2016, http://fortune.com.

103 John Patrick Pullen, "Inside Nerdist's Media Empire for the Internet Age," *Entrepreneur*, August 21, 2013, https://www.entrepreneur.com.

104 Ibid.

105 Michael Ventre, "Chris Hardwick on Becoming TV's Nerd Icon," *Esquire*,
October 22, 2013, http://www.esquire.com.

106 Lorne Manly, "Chris Hardwick, King of the Nerds, Is Expanding His Empire,"
New York Times, April 7, 2016, https://www.nytimes.com.

107 Pullen, "Inside Nerdist's Media Empire."

108 Newcomb and Hirsch, "Television as a Cultural Forum," 571.

109 Dykstra, "Rose-Colored Glasses."

110 Carrie Lynn, "Bring Chris Hardwick Back!" Change.org, June 2018, https://www
.change.org/.

111 The observation that Hardwick's primary demographic support in the wake of
Dykstra's accusation came from white, predominantly middle-aged women was
based on examining thousands of comments on the "Bring Chris Hardwick
Back!" Change.org petition and tweets tagged with #IStandWithChris Hardwick
on Twitter. Because the fallout surrounding Hardwick's suspension was ongoing
as this book was going to press, there was not sufficient time to perform a more
detailed analysis. Accordingly, this evidence may be anecdotal, and usernames
and pictures might be problematically presumed to be representative of the
account owner's lived identity, but the demographic evidence was overwhelming enough that it merited mentioning, particular as it gestures to the failures of
(white) feminism in fan culture.

112 Banet-Weiser, *Authentic*, 4.
113 Chris Hardwick, *The Nerdist Way: How to Reach the Next Level (In Real Life)* (New York: Berkley, 2011), 278.
114 Chris Hardwick, "About," *Id1ot*, 2018, https://id1ot.com/pages/about.
115 Pullen, "Inside Nerdist's Media Empire."
116 "'@midnight with Chris Hardwick' Renewed for Season 3 by Comedy Central," *TV by the Numbers*, July 7, 2015, http://tvbythenumbers.zap2it.com.
117 Sabrina K. Pasztor and Jenny Ungbha Korn, "Zombie Fans, Second Screen, and Television Audiences: Redefining Parasociality as Technoprosociality in AMC's #TalkingDead," in Alison F. Slade, Amber J. Narro, and Dedria Givens-Carroll (eds.), *Television, Social Media, and Fan Culture* (Lanham, MD: Lexington Books, 2015), 186.
118 Ventre, "Chris Hardwick."
119 Allen St. John, "*Talking Dead* Host Chris Hardwick Dishes about Fandom, Spoilers, and *The Walking Dead* Season Finale," *Forbes*, March 29, 2015, http://www.forbes.com.
120 Adorno, "Culture Industry Reconsidered," 105.
121 Ibid., 99.

CHAPTER 6. FROM POACHING TO PINNING

1 Fiske, "Cultural Economy of Fandom," 38.
2 Ibid.
3 Dick Hebdige, *Subculture: The Meaning of Style* (New York: Routledge, 1979), 94, 97.
4 Ibid., 96.
5 Ibid., 97.
6 Avi Santo, "Fans and Merchandise," in Melissa A. Click and Suzanne Scott (eds.), *The Routledge Companion to Media Fandom* (New York: Routledge, 2018), 329.
7 Ibid.
8 One example is the erasure of the only two female characters from the Disney animated superhero team film *Big Hero 6*, prompting the fan activist hashtag #bighero4. For coverage of this, and related merchandising controversies, see: Melissa Atkins Wardy, "Mom Contacts Company over Missing Girl Characters, Company Responds It Is Because Boys Think Girls Are Gross," *Pigtail Pals & Ballcap Buddies*, April 9, 2015, http://pigtailpalsblog.com/2015/04/mom-contacts-company-over-missing-girl-characters-company-responds-it-is-because-boys-think-girls-are-gross/#.WhtEVGQ-cy4.
9 Elizabeth Affuso, "Everyday Costume: Feminized Fandom, Retail, and Beauty Culture," in Melissa A. Click and Suzanne Scott (eds.), *The Routledge Companion to Media Fandom* (New York: Routledge, 2018), 184.
10 Ibid.
11 Maeve Duggan, "The Demographics of Social Media Users," *Pew Research Center*, August 19, 2015, http://www.pewinternet.org.

12 Maeve Duggan and Joanna Brenner, "The Demographics of Social Media Users," *Pew Research Center*, February 4, 2013, http://www.pewinternet.org.

13 Duggan, "The Demographics of Social Media Users."

14 Barbara J. Phillips, Jessica Miller, and Edward F. McQuarrie, "Dreaming Out Loud on Pinterest," *International Journal of Advertising: The Review of Marketing Communications* 33.4 (2014): 649.

15 Lesley Willard, "Tumblr, XKit, and the 'XKit Guy': Towards an Expanded Platform Ecology," in Louisa A. Stein and Allison McCracken, *A Tumblr Book: Platform and Cultures* (forthcoming).

16 Alexander Cho, "Queer Reverb: Tumblr, Affect, Time," in Ken Hillis, Susanna Paasonen, and Michael Petit (eds.), *Networked Affect* (Cambridge, MA: MIT Press, 2015), 47.

17 Mel Stanfill, "The Interface as Discourse: The Production of Norms through Web Design," *New Media & Society* 17.7 (2015): 1060.

18 Usha Zacharias and Jane Arthurs, "Introduction: The New Architectures of Intimacy? Social Networking Sites and Genders," *Feminist Media Studies* 8.2 (2008): 197.

19 Michel de Certeau, *The Practice of Everyday Life* (Berkeley: University of California Press, 1988), 174.

20 Henry Jenkins, "Transmedia Storytelling," *Technology Review*, January 15, 2003, http://www.technologyreview.com.

21 Ellen Gruber Garvey, *Writing with Scissors: American Scrapbooks from the Civil War to the Harlem Renaissance* (Oxford: Oxford University Press, 2012), 175.

22 Ibid., 172.

23 Jenkins, *Textual Poachers*, 26.

24 De Certeau, *The Practice of Everyday Life*, 37.

25 Ibid., 36.

26 For a discussion of how franchise paratexts image their fannish audience, and commonly situate women as invisible or surplus audiences, see: Suzanne Scott, "#Wheresrey?: Toys, Spoilers, and the Gender Politics of Franchise Paratexts," *Critical Studies in Media Communication* 34.2 (2017): 138–47.

27 Mary Celeste Kearney, "Sparkle: Luminosity and Post–Girl Power Media," *Continuum: Journal of Media & Cultural Studies* 29.2 (2015): 270.

28 Julie Wilson and Emily Chivers Yochim, "Pinning Happiness: Affect, Social Media, and the Work of Mothers," in Elana Levine (ed.), *Cupcakes, Pinterest, and Ladyporn: Feminized Popular Culture in the Early Twenty-First Century* (Urbana: University of Illinois Press, 2015), 233.

29 Banet-Weiser, *Authentic*, 8.

30 Ibid., 17.

31 Hebdige, *Subculture*, 94.

32 Ibid.

33 Ibid., 103.

34 McRobbie, *The Aftermath of Feminism*, 115.

35 Wilson and Yochim, "Pinning Happiness," 234.
36 Quoted in Derek Johnson, "May the Force Be with Katie," *Feminist Media Studies* 14.6 (2014): 900.
37 "Hot Topic Acquires Her Universe, Ashley Eckstein Still Overseeing Company," *Comicbook.com*, October 29, 2016, http://comicbook.com.
38 Hills, "From Dalek Half Balls."
39 For more on Disneybounding as a form of everyday cosplay, see: Nettie A. Brock, "The Everyday Disney Side: Disneybounding and Casual Cosplay," *Journal of Fandom Studies* 5.3 (2017): 301–15.
40 Josh Stenger, "The Clothes Make the Fan: Fashion and Online Fandom When 'Buffy the Vampire Slayer' Goes to eBay," *Cinema Journal* 45.4 (2006): 34.
41 Booth, *Playing Fans*, 151.
42 Brad Tuttle, "New Kind of Disney Cosplay Slightly Less Embarrassing Than Original," *Time*, May 19, 2015, http://time.com.
43 For further work on fan crafting, see: Brigid Cherry, *Cult Media, Fandom, and Textiles: Handicrafting as Fan Art* (New York: Bloomsbury, 2016); Dana Sterling Bode, "Beyond Souvenirs: Making Fannish Items by Hand," *Transformative Works and Cultures* no. 16 (2014), http://dx.doi.org/10.3983/twc.2014.0548.
44 Theresa Winge, "Costuming the Imagination: Origins of Anime and Manga Cosplay," *Mechademia* 1 (2006): 71.
45 Tory Hoke, "On Behalf of a Female Boba Fett," *The Campaign for a Female Boba Fett*, https://www.toryhoke.com.
46 Ibid.
47 Ibid.
48 Mary Louise Adams, "The Manly History of a 'Girls' Sport': Gender, Class, and the Development of Nineteenth-Century Figure Skating," *International Journal of the History of Sport* 24.7 (2007): 873.
49 Janet Hethorn, "Skating Dress," *Love to Know,* http://fashion-history.lovetoknow.com.
50 Marjorie Garber, *Vested Interests: Cross-Dressing and Cultural Anxiety* (New York: Routledge, 1992), 1.
51 Ibid., 2.
52 Ibid., 10.
53 J. Jack Halberstam, *Female Masculinity* (Durham, NC: Duke University Press, 1998), 246.
54 Ibid., 249–50.
55 Ibid., 235.
56 Jean Beaudrillard, "The Trompe-l'oeil or the Enchanted Simulation," in Mark Poster (ed.), *Jean Beaudrillard: Selected Writings* (Stanford, CA: Stanford University Press, 1988), 158.
57 Johnson, "May the Force Be with Katie," 899.
58 Ibid., 899.
59 Ibid., 904.

60 For an introductory sampling of scholarly work on fanfiction see: Karen
   Hellekson and Kristina Busse (eds.), *The Fan Fiction Studies Reader* (Iowa City:
   University of Iowa Press, 2014). For scholarly work on fanvids, see (among
   others): Coppa, "Women, *Star Trek*, and the Early Development of Fannish
   Vidding"; Lothian, "Living in a Den of Thieves"; Henry Jenkins, "How to Watch
   a Fan-Vid," *Confessions of an Aca-Fan: The Official Weblog of Henry Jenkins*, September 18, 2006, http://henryjenkins.org/2006/09/how_to_watch_a_fanvid.html.

61 Noelle Stevenson, *How Are You I'm Fine Thanks*, 2012, http://gingerhaze.tumblr
   .com/post/37003301441/how-to-fix-every-strong-female-character-pose-in.

62 "About THI and FAQ," *The Hawkeye Initiative*, http://thehawkeyeinitiative.com.

63 Judith Butler, *Gender Trouble: Feminism and the Subversion of Identity* (New York:
   Routledge, 1990), 174.

64 See: Heidi MacDonald, "*The Hawkeye Initiative* Launches—and Genderswapping
   Will Never Be the Same," *Beat*, December 3, 2012, http://comicsbeat.com; Susana
   Polo, "Introducing *The Hawkeye Initiative*," *Mary Sue*, December 3, 2012, http://
   www.themarysue.com; Laura Hudson, "How to Fix Crazy Superheroine Poses in
   Comics? Swap Them with Hawkeye," *Wired*, December 5, 2012, http://www.wired
   .com.

65 Ann McClellan, "Redefining Genderswap Fan Fiction: A *Sherlock* Case Study,"
   Transformative Works and Cultures no. 17 (2014), http://dx.doi.org/10.3983
   /twc.2014.0553.

66 Kristina Busse and Alexis Lothian, "Bending Gender: Feminist and (Trans)
   Gender Discourses in the Changing Bodies of Slash Fan Fiction," in Ingrid
   Hotz-Davies, Anton Kirchhofer, and Sirpa Leppänen (eds.), *Internet Fiction(s)*
   (Cambridge: Cambridge Scholar's Press, 2009), 105.

67 Winge, "Costuming the Imagination," 71.

68 "About THI and FAQ."

69 Scott, "Fangirls in Refrigerators." For additional examples of memes addressing
   the impossible physicality, contortionist posing, and impractical costuming of
   female superheroes, many deploying transformative fan art as their primary mode
   of critique, see: Kevin Melrose, "When Male Justice Leaguers Strike a (Wonder
   Woman) Pose," *Comic Book Resources*, August 4, 2011, http://robot6.comicbookre
   sources.com; Brian Cronin, "The Line It Is Drawn #79: Male Superheroes See
   How the Other Side Lives," *Comic Book Resources*, March 1, 2012, http://good
   comics.comicbookresources.com; Jill Pantozzi, "What Batman Would Look Like
   Fighting in Stilettos," *Mary Sue*, January 30, 2012, http://www.themarysue.com,
   among others.

70 Courtney, "*The Hawkeye Initiative*: Cosplay Is Political," *Cosplay Feminist*, April 1,
   2013, http://cosplayfeminist.com.

71 Gavia Baker-Whitelaw, "The Costumes and Characters of *The Avengers*," *Hello,
   Tailor*, May 31, 2012, http://hellotailor.blogspot.com.au/2012/05/costumes
   -and-characters-of-avengers_31.html; Noelle Stevenson, "Ghost Protocol
   summary," *How Are You I'm Fine Thanks*, 2012, http://gingerhaze.tumblr.com

/post/21767982288/ghost-protocol-summary-jeremy-renner-is-a; Hoursago, *Needless Procedures,* December 1, 2012, http://hoursago.tumblr.com/post/37002842830/for-real-though-look-me-in-the-eye-and-tell-me.

72 Though Hawkeye (Jeremy Renner) technically makes a brief, and uncredited, appearance in *Thor* (2011), *The Avengers* marked the first time the character was given any notable screen time, and thus "introduced" to fans of the MCU.

73 Trina Robbins, "Gender Difference in Comics," *Image and Narrative* 4 (2002), http://www.imageandnarrative.be.

74 Ibid.

75 Carolyn Cocca, "The 'Broke Back Test': A Quantitative and Qualitative Analysis of Portrayals of Women in Mainstream Superhero Comics, 1993–2013," *Journal of Graphic Novels and Comics* 5.4 (2014): 411.

76 Scott, "Fangirls in Refrigerators."

77 Peter Coogan, "The Definition of the Superhero," in Jeet Heer and Kent Worcester (eds.), *A Comics Studies Reader* (Jackson: University of Mississippi Press, 2009), 86.

78 Ibid., 78–79.

79 Aaron Taylor, "'He's gotta be strong, and he's gotta be fast, and he's gotta be larger than life': Investigating the Engendered Superhero Body," *Journal of Popular Culture* 40.2 (2007): 345.

80 Scott Bukatman, "Secret Identity Politics," in Angela Ndalianis (ed.), *The Contemporary Comic Book Superhero* (New York: Routledge, 2009), 115.

81 Despina Kakoudaki, "Pinup: The American Secret Weapon in World War II," in Linda Williams (ed.), *Porn Studies* (Durham, NC: Duke University Press, 2004), 336.

82 Ibid., 339.

83 Maria Elena Buszek, *Pin-Up Grrrls: Feminism, Sexuality, Popular Culture* (Durham, NC: Duke University Press, 2006).

84 Richard Dyer, "Don't Look Now," *Screen* 23.3–4 (1982): 63.

85 Ibid., 66.

86 Ibid., 67. This also resonates with Laura Mulvey's argument that women are "simultaneously looked at and displayed," and their appearance is thus eroticized and coded to "connote *to-be-looked-at-ness.*" See: Laura Mulvey, "Visual Pleasure and Narrative Cinema," in Leo Braudy and Marshall Cohen (eds.), *Film Theory and Criticism: Introductory Readings* (New York: Oxford University Press, 1999), 837.

87 Ibid., 67–71.

88 Ibid., 66.

89 Thierry Groensteen, *The System of Comics,* trans. Bart Beaty and Nick Nguyen (Jackson: University of Mississippi Press, 2007), 39.

90 Ibid., 45–46.

91 Ibid., 45.

92 This discussion of the "readerly function" of comics evokes Roland Barthes's distinction between readerly and writerly texts. Despite Groensteen's "readerly"

delineation, his conception of comics falls into Barthes's latter category, in which "the reader is no longer a consumer, but a producer of the text." See: Roland Barthes, *S/Z: An Essay*, trans. Richard Miller (New York: Hill and Wang, 1974), 4.

93 Ibid., 54.

94 Ibid., 57.

95 Ibid., 43.

96 Carol A. Stabile, "'Sweetheart, this ain't gender studies': Sexism and Superheroes," *Communication and Critical/Cultural Studies* 6.1 (2009): 90.

97 Michael Doran, "Spider-Woman Gets a New Costume," *Newsarama*, December 18, 2014, http://www.newsarama.com; Rob Bricken, "Batgirl's New Uniform May Be the Best Damn Superheroine Outfit Ever," *io9*, July 10, 2014, http://io9.com.

98 AHolland, "Tumblr DMCA Used to Bully Feminist Comics Blog Eschergirls," *Chilling Effects*, August 4, 2014, https://www.chillingeffects.org/blog_entries/715; Ami Angelwings, *Escher Girls,* August 7, 2014, http://eschergirls.tumblr.com /post/93520850386/so-yesterday-i-found-out-that-randy-queen-artist.

99 It should be noted that, as transformative or parodic fan art has become a common mode of representational and industrial critique, it has also diversified. In addition to sites like *The Hawkeye Initiative* that revel in visually commenting on the anatomical impossibility of superheroine bodies and poses, other fan art movements have emerged to realistically redraw these characters. Drawing on art projects like "If Disney Princesses Had Realistic Waistlines," by Loryn Brantz, the website Bulimia.com adopted this approach for the 2015 "reverse photoshopping" campaign "Comic Book Heroes with Average Body Types."

CONCLUSION

1 "One True Pairing," *Fanlore*, https://fanlore.org.

2 Ibid.

3 John Scalzi, "Straight White Male: The Lowest Difficulty Setting There Is," May 15, 2012, https://whatever.scalzi.com.

4 Ibid.

5 Peggy McIntosh, "White Privilege: Unpacking the Invisible Knapsack," in Paula S. Rothenberg (ed.), *Race, Class, and Gender in the United States: An Integrated Study*, 6th ed. (New York: Worth, 2004), 188.

6 Benjamin Woo, "The Invisible Bag of Holding: Whiteness and Media Fandom," in Melissa A. Click and Suzanne Scott (eds.), *The Routledge Companion to Media Fandom* (New York: Routledge, 2018), 245–52.

7 For more on this topic, see: Anastasia Salter and Bridget Blodgett, *Toxic Geek Masculinity in Media: Sexism, Trolling, and Identity Policing* (New York: Palgrave Macmillan, 2017).

8 Jenkins, "*Star Trek* Rerun, Reread, Rewritten," 87.

9 Richard Dyer, *White: Essays on Race and Culture* (New York: Routledge, 1997), 4.

10 Ibid., 1.

11 Fiske, "Cultural Economy of Fandom," 32.

12 For a discussion of male "geek fragility," see: Salter and Blodgett, *Toxic Geek Masculinity*, 194–96. Because my application is concerned with how the convergence culture industry has facilitated these defensive moves, and how these are deployed by both male and female media fans and fan scholars alike, I pointedly deploy the term "fan fragility" here.

13 Robin DiAngelo, "White Fragility," *International Journal of Critical Pedagogy* 3.3 (2011): 55.

14 Ibid., 55–56.

15 Ibid., 57.

16 Ibid.

17 Ibid., 59.

18 Ibid., 63.

19 Kimberlé Crenshaw, "Mapping the Margins: Intersectionality, Identity Politics, and Violence against Women of Color," *Stanford Law Review* 43 (1993): 1299.

20 Ibid.

21 Patricia Hill Collins, *Black Feminist Thought: Knowledge, Consciousness, and the Politics of Empowerment* (New York: Routledge, 2000).

22 Crenshaw, "Mapping the Margins," 1299.

23 Pande, "Squee from the Margins," 210.

24 Lori Hitchcock Morimoto and Bertha Chin, "Reimagining the Imagined Community: Online Media Fandoms in the Age of Global Convergence," in Jonathan Gray, Cornel Sandvoss, and C. Lee Harrington (eds.), *Fandom: Identities and Communities in a Mediated World*, 2nd ed. (New York: NYU Press, 2017), 174–90.; Lori Morimoto, "Transnational Media Fan Studies," in Melissa A. Click and Suzanne Scott (eds.), *The Routledge Companion to Media Fandom* (New York: Routledge, 2018), 280–88.

25 For some examples, see: Mizuko Ito, Daisuke Okabe, and Izumi Tsuji (eds.), *Fandom Unbound: Otaku Culture in a Connected World* (New Haven, CT: Yale University Press, 2012); Bertha Chin and Lori Morimoto, "Towards a Theory of Transcultural Fandom," *Participations* 10.1 (2013): 92–108.

26 For several exceptions, see: Katie Kapurch, "Rapunzel Loves Merida: Melodramatic Expressions of Lesbian Girlhood and Teen Romance in *Tangled*, *Brave*, and Femslash," *Journal of Lesbian Studies* 19.4 (2015): 436–53; Julie Levin Russo, "The Queer Politics of Femslash," in Melissa A. Click and Suzanne Scott (eds.), *The Routledge Companion to Media Fandom* (New York: Routledge, 2018), 155–64.

27 Eve Ng and Julie Levin Russo, "Envisioning Queer Female Fandom," *Transformative Works and Cultures* no. 24 (2017), http://dx.doi.org/10.3983/twc.2017.1168.

28 Alexis Lothian, Kristina Busse, and Robin Anne Reid, "'Yearning Void and Infinite Potential': Online Slash Fandom as Queer Female Space," *English Language Notes* 45.2 (2007): 103–11.

29 Rukmini Pande and Swati Moitra, "'Yes, the evil queen is Latina!': Racial Dynamics of Online Femslash Fandoms," *Transformative Works and Cultures* no. 24 (2017), http://dx.doi.org/10.3983/twc.2017.908.

30 Mark Duffett, "Beyond Exploitation Cinema: Music Fandom, Disability, and *Mission to Lars*," in Lucy Bennett and Paul Booth (eds.), *Seeing Fans: Representations of Fandom in Media and Popular Culture* (New York: Bloomsbury, 2016), 13–22.

31 David Kociemba, "'This isn't something I can fake': Reactions to *Glee*'s Representations of Disability," *Transformative Works and Cultures* no. 5 (2010), http://dx.doi.org/10.3983/twc.2010.0225.

32 Carolyn Cocca, "Re-booting Barbara Gordon: Oracle, Batgirl, and Feminist Disability Theories," *ImageTexT: Interdisciplinary Comics Studies* 7.4 (2014), http://www.english.ufl.edu.

33 Sasha_feather, "From the Edges to the Center: Disability, *Battlestar Galactica*, and Fan Fiction," *Transformative Works and Cultures* no. 5 (2010), http://dx.doi.org/10.3983/twc.2010.0227.

34 Elizabeth Ellcessor, "Disability, Digital Media, and Dreamwidth," in Melissa A. Click and Suzanne Scott (eds.), *The Routledge Companion to Media Fandom* (New York: Routledge, 2018), 202–11.

35 Mary Ingram-Waters, "When Normal and Deviant Identities Collide: Methodological Considerations of the Pregnant Acafan," *Transformative Works and Cultures* no. 5 (2010), http://dx.doi.org/10.3983/twc.2010.0207.

36 For some examples of work on fans and age/aging, see: C. Lee Harrington and Denise D. Bielby, "A Life Course Perspective on Fandom," *International Journal of Cultural Studies* 13.5 (2010): 429–50; Christine Scodari, *Serial Monogamy: Soap Opera, Lifespan, and the Gendered Politics of Fantasy* (Cresskill, NJ: Hampton Press, 2004); Christine Scodari, "Breaking Dusk: Fandom, Gender/Age Intersectionality, and the 'Twilight Moms,'" in C. L. Harrington, D. D. Bielby, and A. R. Bardo (eds.), *Aging, Media, and Culture* (Lanham, MD: Lexington Books, 2014), 143–54.

37 C. Lee Harrington and Denise D. Bielby, "Aging, Fans, and Fandom," in Melissa A. Click and Suzanne Scott (eds.), *The Routledge Companion to Media Fandom* (New York: Routledge, 2018), 407.

38 Stein, *Millennial Fandom*, 155–70.

39 Hills, "*Twilight* Fans," 123.

40 Sarah N. Gatson and Robin Anne Reid, "Race and Ethnicity in Fandom," *Transformative Works and Cultures* no. 8 (2012), http://dx.doi.org/10.3983/twc.2011.0392.

41 For some examples, see: Johnson, "Misogynoir and Antiblack Racism," 259–75; Christine Scodari, "'Nyota Uhura is not a white girl': Gender, Intersectionality, and *Star Trek* 2009's Alternate Romantic Universes," *Feminist Media Studies* 12.3 (2012): 335–51; Fabienne Darling-Wolf, "Virtually Multicultural: Trans-Asian Identity and Gender in an International Fan Community," *New Media & Society* 6.4: 507–28; Jillian M. Báez, "Charting Latinx Fandom," in Melissa A. Click and Suzanne Scott (eds.), *The Routledge Companion to Media Fandom* (New York: Routledge, 2018), 271–79.

42 See, for example: Stanfill, "Doing Fandom, (Mis)doing Whiteness"; Mel Stanfill, "Straighten Up and Fly White: Whiteness, Heteronormativity, and the

Representation of Happy Endings for Fans," in Lucy Bennett and Paul Booth (eds.), *Seeing Fans: Representations of Fandom in Media and Popular Culture* (New York: Bloomsbury, 2016), 187–96; Woo, "The Invisible Bag of Holding."

43 For discussions of racebending, see: Lori Kido Lopez, "Fan Activists and the Politics of Race in *The Last Airbender*," *International Journal of Cultural Studies* 15.5 (2011): 431–45; Elizabeth Gilliland, "Racebending Fandoms and Digital Futurism," *Transformative Works and Cultures* no. 22 (2016), http://dx.doi.org/10.3983/twc.2016.0702; Henry Jenkins, "Negotiating Fandom: The Politics of Racebending," in Melissa A. Click and Suzanne Scott (eds.), *The Routledge Companion to Media Fandom* (New York: Routledge, 2018), 383–94; Albert S. Fu, "Fear of a Black Spider-Man: Racebending and the Colour-Line in Superhero (Re)casting," *Journal of Graphic Novels and Comics* 6.3 (2015): 269–83.

44 Kristen J. Warner, "(Black Female) Fans Strike Back: The Emergence of the Iris West Defense Squad," in Melissa A. Click and Suzanne Scott (eds.), *The Routledge Companion to Media Fandom* (New York: Routledge, 2018), 253–61.

45 In addition to a forthcoming special issue on queerbaiting from the *Journal of Fandom Studies*, see: Emma Nordin, "From Queer Reading to Queerbaiting: The Battle over the Polysemic Text and the Power of Hermeneutics" (master's thesis, Stockholm University, 2015); Judith Fathallah, "Moriarty's Ghost; or, The Queer Disruption of the BBC's *Sherlock*," *Television & New Media* 16.5 (2015): 490–500; Eve Ng, "Between Text, Paratext, and Context: Queerbaiting and the Contemporary Media Landscape," *Transformative Works and Cultures* no. 24 (2017), http://dx.doi.org/10.3983/twc.2017.917.

46 Ijeoma Oluo, "Admit It: Your Fave Is Problematic," *Matter*, March 31, 2015, https://medium.com.

INDEX

4chan, 20, 89
50 Shades of Grey (novel), 120, 146–147, 149

ableism, 6, 86
Abrams, J. J., 159
acafandom, 41–42, 228, 240
Adorno, Theodor W., 8–13, 16–17; conceptions of audiences, 35, 84, 116. *See also* culture industry, the
advertising, 8, 130, 134, 178
affect: androcentric, 165, 144; "authentic" 134; and excess, 53, 85; as exchange between consumers and corporations, 194; fanboy, 59, 159; fannish, 42, 62 143, 150, 192; feminine 43, 100, 138, 185; as quantifiable, 99, 130; relationship to texts, 90, 111
affirmational fandom: and authenticity, 135, 164; in the convergence culture industry, 112–113, 128, 162; 184, 226; as gendered mode of fan engagement, 13, 36, 38, 45; as industrially sanctioned mode of fan engagement, 37, 48, 148, 225; and male fans, 21, 39, 59, 174; versus transformative fan engagement, 27, 32, 36, 38–39, 47, 62, 134, 198, 233
ageism, 6, 86
alt-right, 4, 17–20, 25, 46
@midnight with Chris Hardwick,176, 179–182
Andras, Emily, 165–166, 264n75
androcentric: comic book culture, 211; conception of fan culture, 4, 12, 88, 121, 142, 182, 186, 188, 207; conception of technological prowess, 41; construction of fan identity, 68, 94, 187, 197, 223; construction of fans as power demographic, 109; fan professionalization, 144; *See also* convergence culture industry; quality
anti-fandom, 90, 92, 98, 130; and gender 90–93, 95, 97–98, 105–108; misogyny in, 102, 104; and race, 105
audiences: agency of, 84; analog, 23; appealing to, 134, 137, 172; conceptions of in the Frankfurt School, 9, 116; as cultural dupes, 116; differences from fans, 57; fan studies, 6; female, 6, 22, 47, 93, 115, 125–126, 268n26; imagined by industry, 154; mass, 11; niche, 182; and passive consumption, 10; queer, 28; tracking by industry, 131
auteur theory, 159–160
authenticity/authenticating, 20, 103, 152, 158, 226; and convergence culture industry, 49; in cosplay, 200–201, 206–207; in fan culture, 75, 108; in fandom, 32, 106, 223; and fan identity, 3–4, 27, 66, 96; fannish, 10–11, 91, 97–99, 134; in fan studies, 32, 203; and gender, 55, 78, 85, 103, 135, 164; and the mainstreaming of fandom, 17; policing of, 107; professional, 124
authorship: and fanboy auteurs, 162–163; in television, 165; transmedia, 159; "undead," 160
Avengers, The (film), 124–125, 193, 212, 271n72

utopianism: fandom and, 93, 104–105, 146; in fan studies, 12, 30, 48, 154, 229

video games, 3, 64, 245n58; and Gamer-Gate, 20, 89; as masculine media, 49, 59–60; women playing, 3, 20, 60, 105
virality, 73, 81, 83–84, 89–90, 115

Walking Dead, The (TV show), 67, 131–134, 138–141, 179
"war on women," 20, 77, 90; in fan culture, 19, 20, 22, 77, 90, 94, 106–108, 229
Warner, Kristen J., 137–138, 233, 236
Whedon, Joss, 212, 264n87

whiteness, 224, 226; fans and, 6, 16; fans of color and, 158; in fan studies, 232; masculinity and, 16, 79. *See also* fanboys; fan culture; fandom; fan identity; fan studies; female fans; geek culture; privilege; race; representation
Women's March on Washington, 25–27
Wonder Woman (film), 69, 167–168, 264n87
Woo, Benjamin, 84–85, 170, 222, 232

xenophobia, 6, 75, 86

YouTube, 114, 121–124

ABOUT THE AUTHOR

Suzanne Scott is Assistant Professor of Media Studies in the Radio-Television-Film Department at the University of Texas at Austin. She is the co-editor of *The Routledge Companion to Media Fandom* (2018).